MW00910594

Jean Niven Lenk

FERTILIZER HAPPENS

A Pastor's Faith, Calling, and Journey with Cancer

WestBow Press books may be ordered through booksellers or by contacting:

WestBow Press
A Division of Thomas Nelson & Zondervan
1663 Liberty Drive
Bloomington, IN 47403
www.westbowpress.com
1 (866) 928-1240

ISBN: 978-1-4908-4723-8 (sc)
ISBN: 978-1-4908-4724-5 (hc)
ISBN: 978-1-4908-4725-2 (e)

Library of Congress Control Number: 2014916080

Printed in the United States of America.

WestBow Press rev. date: 09/23/2014

This book is dedicated, with my love and gratitude, to everyone who has offered prayers, support, and encouragement to me during my journey, especially my dear family.

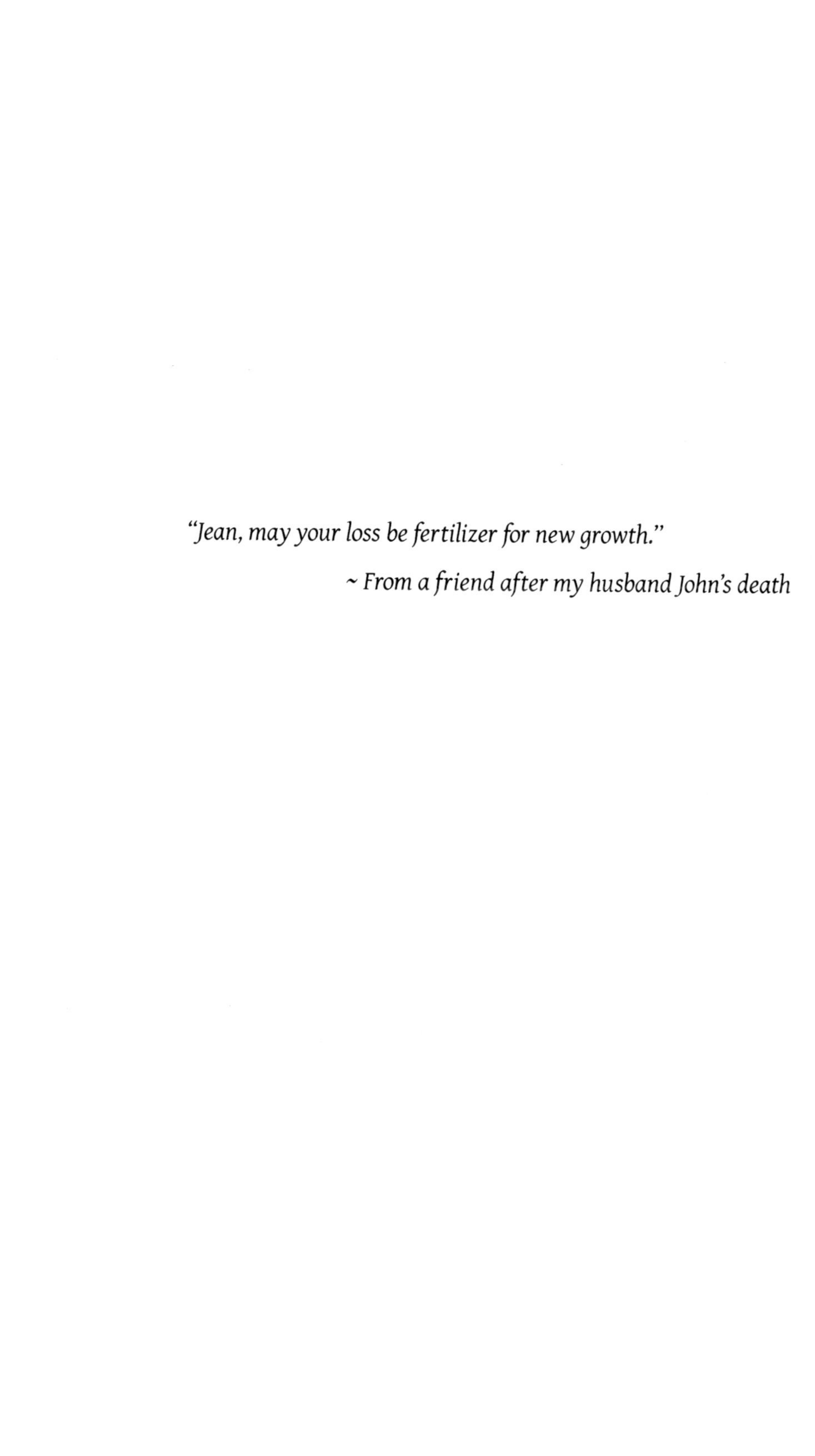

"Jean, may your loss be fertilizer for new growth."

~ From a friend after my husband John's death

CONTENTS

ACKNOWLEDGMENT

I imagine that many people dream of someday writing a book. I know I did. But I lacked two important factors: a compelling topic and the time to write.

When I found myself both a divorcee and a widow at the age of 27, a few friends started to suggest I write about my experiences. But I was not ready. I needed more time to understand and make meaning of my losses.

When I quit my corporate career to enter seminary and then was widowed again, my friends repeated their suggestion. But the timing was not right. I had two young children and was holding down three jobs while attending seminary. The only writing I was doing was term papers.

The years sped by in a whirlwind. As an ordained pastor serving a congregation, my days were devoted to family and church. My writing was confined to sermons.

And then I was diagnosed with cancer, and suddenly I had both a compelling topic and the time, not to mention the need for an emotional outlet. Hence, I started writing a blog, which has become this book.

So I want to thank everyone who ever said to me, "You should write a book!" It took decades, but your prodding finally bore fruit.

I am also indebted to my friend Marcia Olson and my brother Andy Niven, who slogged through my very rough drafts. Their astute editorial suggestions have made this a better, more readable book.

In addition, I am grateful to the staff at WestBow Press, especially Sekou Kante, Miguel Merino, and Donavan Gerken who patiently and responsively guided this newbie author through the unfamiliar publishing process.

My deepest gratitude to all the doctors, nurses, and health care professionals who have literally saved my life multiple times this past year. I am especially indebted to Dr. Sharon Mullane, my primary care physician; Dr. Jonathan Croopnick, my local oncologist; Dr. Abraham Lebenthal, thoracic surgeon at Brigham and Women's Hospital in Boston; Dr. Joseph DiCola, my cardiologist; Dr. Raymond Paul-Blanc, my urologist; all the nurses in the Oncology Suite at Sturdy Memorial Hospital in Attleboro, Massachusetts, as well as the nurses and staff at Sturdy and Brigham and Women's who tended to me during my hospitalizations; and Dr. Monica Bertagnolli, Dr. James Butrynski, and all the staff at Dana-Farber Cancer Institute in Boston.

Finally, my heartfelt thanks to all the members of my beloved family who were so enthusiastic, supportive and patient as I pursued my goal of writing this book. It is my dearest hope that you will pass it along to my future grandchildren so they'll come to know their Grandma Jean.

PROLOGUE

QUESTIONS

The question I have kept asking of myself, and I suspect others have wanted to ask me, is: How could I not know? How could I not know that cancerous tumors were growing in three different areas of my body?

Here's the thing. Cancer is sneaky. It likes to hide and do its dastardly damage incognito. At least that's what happened to me.

I estimate that cancerous cells were growing inside of me for two years before I developed a pain in my back that finally made me take notice. Even then, my response to the pain was to explain it away. After all, I was in my late 50s and figured that any new ache was just a natural aspect of life's progression. A twinge here, a spasm there – hey, nothing to get concerned about; just part of the privilege of growing older.

Indeed, there were any number of perfectly good reasons that my back hurt: I was overweight and out of shape... I was stressed... I needed a new office chair... my mattress needed replacing...

And these explanations made sense – until the pain became too great to dismiss and turned into a diagnosis of Stage IV cancer.

How could this happen? Was this God's doing? Was cancer payback for sinful behavior? A Job-like test of faith? Was it part of some divine plan that my life would be cut short?

I do not believe that the God I worship is punitive or cruel or capriciously mean. I do not believe that the God I have dedicated my life to would deliberately make me suffer and shorten my life.

Rather, I believe simply that stuff happens in life. You can probably guess that "stuff" is not exactly the right word. Manure is closer. But the title of this book is not *Manure Happens* but rather *Fertilizer Happens*. Fertilizer is different than manure. If you look up fertilizer in the dictionary, it means "to enrich" or "to make productive." Fertilizer produces something, often something better. New growth springs from fertilizer.

Yes, stuff happens in life. It's not God. It's not "Satan." It's not punishment. It's just the way life is. Stuff has happened in my life, as it has (or will) in everyone's life. But that stuff can be fertilizer for new growth.

FINDING MY JOY

I grew up in Wellesley, Massachusetts, a suburb twelve miles west of Boston. My father was an advertising executive and my mother a housewife; I have two older brothers.

During my childhood, my mother made sure I received a solid religious education at the local Congregational church (part of the United Church of Christ, a Protestant denomination), which included Sunday school, Junior Choir and Youth Group. I was at the church as many as four times a week for various activities.

But my religious education did not necessarily develop into faith; that was to come much later.

When I was twelve, and with my two brothers grown up and off to college, my parents divorced, and my comfortable and secure childhood gave way to an unsettled adolescence. It was the time of Viet Nam and a growing disillusionment among young people; our buttons read "Don't trust anyone over 30."

In 1968, Bobby Kennedy and Martin Luther King, Jr. were assassinated, and in 1970 four Kent State University students were killed when the Ohio National Guard opened fire during an anti-war protest. The things being taught in church – peace, love, non-violence, and God's abiding presence – seemed incongruent with what was happening in the world. And it was around this time I started to think that there may not be a God after all.

I told my mother I no longer wanted to go to church, but she had a rule: if I did not go to church on Sunday mornings, I could not go out Saturday nights (unthinkable for a teenager!). So I worked out a deal with her: I would go to church on Sunday mornings, but not to attend worship. Instead, I would serve in the nursery taking care of the little kids. This arrangement worked well during my high school years. And then I graduated and went off to college.

I could probably count on one hand the number of times I was in a church during the next 20 years – and then it was only for weddings or funerals. I wanted no relationship with God – but that is not to say I did not need God. Over the ensuing decades, I experienced the challenges and heartaches that are part of life. I sure could have used God's strength to get me through those times – but my heart was closed.

The years passed. I graduated from the University of Massachusetts at Amherst with a major in English. An early first marriage to my college sweetheart ended in divorce after only four years. I married again, to Darcy, and was widowed two and half years later. In my mid-30s, I married yet again, to John, and had my first child, a beautiful little red-haired girl we named Elizabeth. I still did not go to church, but I was beginning to think I might like to. Something was tugging at my heartstrings.

At least twice a day, I would drive by a lovely white church on Main Street in the Boston suburb of Medfield, where we lived at the time.

And I would say, "That's the church I'll go to – when I start going to church." A few more years passed, and I was still just driving by. The thought of walking into a place where everyone knew everyone else was intimidating. I was convinced people would somehow be able to tell I had been away from church for 20 years. I was afraid God might snicker (I guess I believed in God after all).

But I wanted to give Elizabeth the same solid religious foundation my mother had given to me. At least that is what I told myself. Sure, I thought Lizzy should start Sunday school. But I was the one who really needed church.

Tug, tug.

I guess you could say I was having a crisis – a mid-life crisis, to be exact. If you've been through one yourself, then you know it can be a complicated time. I was no longer enjoying the material things that used to make me happy, like a big house and fancy car. The glamour of all-expenses-paid business trips and entertaining on the company's account had long since worn off. I felt trapped by the expensive lifestyle and high-powered career I had so carefully and painstakingly cultivated. I started to look at my life and wonder, what was my purpose? What impact was I leaving on the world? On my last day of earthly life, would I be able to say that I had made a difference, even in some small way?

At the time, I worked for a financial services company, and it seemed that my life's purpose had been reduced to helping people with money make more money. In my 20s and 30s, this may have been enough. But as I approached age 40, I felt increasingly empty. I had been climbing the corporate ladder and had managed to achieve many of the external, material hallmarks of success. From the outside, it looked as if I had "made it." But "success" felt hollow and meaningless. The generous salary, the impressive job title, the well-appointed office – none of them could fill the emptiness in my heart.

Around this time, a neighbor invited me to come with her to church – that beautiful white church I had been passing for years. She loved her church and wanted me to have what she had, to experience what she experienced – a relationship with God nurtured in that community of faith. And so, after a 20-year estrangement from organized religion and with my neighbor's encouragement, one Sunday morning I finally walked through the doors of that church. Even though I was new, people in the congregation gave me a warm and gracious welcome. I entered the sanctuary and took a seat in the back. The first hymn we sang was "Joyful, Joyful, We Adore Thee," one of my favorites from childhood. I was home.

My entire life was forever transformed in the holy moment I walked into that church. The God-shaped hole in my heart was filled. That "something" tugging at my heart turned out to be Jesus.

Before I knew it, I was doing things at church I had never done before. Serving communion... Creating devotional booklets... Putting together worship services... My closed heart was slowly opening to the Divine.

I was amazed to find that the work I did serving God *for no money* was significantly more meaningful and rewarding than anything I had done for a salary. The church gave me a sense of purpose and satisfaction, and feelings of exhilaration and joy, that I had not experienced from any other endeavor, especially my financial services career.

And I was still feeling that tugging at my heart.

Slowly my priorities and values began to change, along with my definition of success. I knew I needed a change in jobs, so I went to a career counselor, thinking she would recommend that I move to a non-profit organization. I met with the counselor several times, and she started off our third meeting by asking me to tell her about my church work. I excitedly explained to her how working for God gave me joy and satisfaction and a sense of purpose. Then she asked me to tell her about my corporate job. I fumbled and stammered, trying to come up with something, when she held up her hand and said, "Stop. I wish I had a mirror. When you talked about your church work, you sat up straight, your eyes brightened, and your face shone. But when you talked about your job, your face went slack, your eyes went dead, and you slumped in your chair."

And then she gave me the best advice I've ever received. "Follow your joy."

God was not just calling me back to church; God was calling me to ministry.

It seemed preposterous. Was I hearing God correctly, or was this just the ego-driven delusions of a self-centered person? After all, I had spent 20 years away from church (and people close to me did not hesitate to point this out). I tried to ignore that tug, but it only grew stronger.

John had been quietly supportive of my faith reawakening, but leaving my career – and the salary – to enter the ministry was going to require major adjustments to our lifestyle. I gathered the courage to sit him down ("Honey, we need to talk") and tell him what was on my heart. I was so relieved when he offered nothing but encouragement. "I want you to do what makes you happy," he responded. Thank heavens. Because when God calls, it's hard to say no.

Sometimes it takes a crisis – mid-life or otherwise – to transform our life. My mid-life crisis was the best thing that ever happened to me because it brought me back to God. It helped me discover my passion, find my joy, and discern God's purpose for my life.

And so, at age 41, I left behind my career and entered seminary to become a pastor. I did not know how my family would be supported while I went back to school, and I did not know where we were going to find the money for tuition, but if I was meant to answer God's call to ministry, I knew God would provide. And God did.

AN EARLY SCARE

I have always taken my health care seriously – annual check-ups and mammograms, periodic colonoscopies, regular BP checks, prudent hand-washing. Never smoked. Never did drugs. A glass of Chardonnay on rare occasions. Other than delivering two beautiful babies after two perfect pregnancies, the only time I spent overnight in a hospital was in my 20s to have my impacted wisdom teeth removed. More recently, I had day surgeries to repair my rotator cuff and have my gall bladder removed.

Then in January, 2011, I had to undergo a hysterectomy. A benign tumor called a fibroid was growing in my uterus. In less than a year it had increased to the size of a grapefruit, and it had to come out. My husband (yes, my fourth) Peter and I met with the gynecologist to learn more about what the surgery would entail. Because of the fibroid's size, I needed major, slice-me-open surgery which involved not just the fibroid, but also the uterus, fallopian tubes, and ovaries. The doctor did not anticipate any complications.

Except... except...

I don't even like to bring this up, she said, but there is the slightest – *the slightest* – chance your tumor is malignant.

Malignant? Cancer? For a couple of seconds, I could not breathe. I glanced at Peter, and he was staring at the floor.

You're past menopause, and fibroids don't usually grow in post-menopausal women, the doctor explained. Yours has grown very large very quickly. I don't want you to be concerned, but I will be having an oncologist assist me in the surgery.

Not be concerned? Even the slightest possibility of cancer was frightening.

What kind of cancer are we talking about? I asked.

She wrote it down for me. Leiomyosarcoma. I could not even pronounce it. Lay-oh-my-oh-sar-KO-ma.

But please don't go looking on the internet, she advised; what you read will only scare you.

Of course, when I got home, I went right onto my computer to look up leiomyosarcoma. Two words kept appearing: "rare" and "aggressive." She was right. I was scared.

A few weeks later, I had my surgery. The fibroid tissue was analyzed by the pathologist while I was still in post-op. The doctor called Peter with the good news: NO cancer.

And I forgot all about leiomyosarcoma.

THE FIRST SIGNS

I have never liked to complain about my physical ills; the last thing I want is for people to roll their eyes and say, "There Jean goes again

– whining about every little ache and pain." And for most of my life "B.C." (before cancer), I did not have many ills to complain about.

But in January 2013, I developed out of the blue that pain in the middle of my back. The location was perplexing. I had occasionally suffered pain at the base of my skull, which was stress-related. Sometimes I developed pain in my lower back, which I blamed on vacuuming! But I had never experienced pain smack dab in the middle of my back.

It will go away in a few days, I told myself. But it didn't. Instead, the pain started disrupting my sleep. Lying on a mattress was excruciating, especially when I tried to turn over (which I tended to do so often, Peter had nicknamed me "Flipper"). The pain became so bad that I sometimes burst into tears.

But I was still sure it was just a temporary situation. My annual physical was scheduled for mid-February. I'd ask my doctor about it then.

And I did – but not until the very end of the appointment ("Oh, by the way..."). Still didn't want to sound like a whiner.

On my physician's recommendation, I went to an orthopedic doctor, who spent two minutes examining me before declaring that I had a muscle pull. Naproxen and physical therapy would do the trick.

A week later, I called the orthopedist's office and explained that my pain was only getting worse. He prescribed a muscle relaxant.

Another week passed, and the pain continued to increase. Another prescription. No relief.

With the pain continuing unabated, I had no choice but to reschedule my follow-up appointment to an earlier date. After hearing my story, the orthopedist said (finally), "Guess it's time for a MRI."

The results of that test changed everything. My work. My plans. My life.

It was cancer. Stage IV. A death sentence.

At first, I did not know what to do with my emotions. Sometimes I would just sit in stunned silence, completely numb. Sometimes, I would sob uncontrollably, feeling I would never be able to stop. And there were times (lots of times) that I was downright angry, particularly at God.

I had to do something constructive, something therapeutic, so these emotions would not get the better of me.

Thus, I started writing a blog about my experience on the Caringbridge website – for anyone who wanted to accompany me on the journey, but mostly for myself. For my sanity. For my healing. For my life.

This is the story of the rest of my life (so far), as it happened.

SUNDAY, MARCH 31, 2013

EASTER

I live by the secular calendar for the hobbies and activities my husband Peter and I enjoy together, for the college and work schedules of my 23-year-old daughter Elizabeth, for the high school and sports activities of my 16-year-old son Ian, and for the doctors' appointments of my 92-year-old father, who lives with us.

I am also an ordained pastor and have served as the spiritual leader of the First Congregational Church (part of the United Church of Christ denomination) in Stoughton, Massachusetts, for the past eight years. As a pastor, I live by the rhythms of the seasons of the liturgical church calendar, such as Advent and Lent.

Holy Week – the most solemn week of the church year – covers the period from Palm Sunday to Holy Saturday, from Jesus' celebratory entry into Jerusalem to his betrayal, arrest, crucifixion, and death. This year, as I was leading our congregation through Holy Week worship services, the journey took on a new and personal dimension for me.

Two days ago, on Good Friday, I learned that I have Stage IV cancer. It evidently started in my pelvic region, and it has spread to my thyroid, both lungs, and the T6 vertebrae in the thoracic region of my spine.

My only symptom – back pain – began in mid-January. When it did not go away, I told my primary care physician at my annual physical in mid-February, and she referred me to an orthopedic doctor. He said it was a muscle strain and put me on pain pills and physical therapy. When that did not work, he ordered a MRI (Magnetic Resonance Imaging test), which I had last Tuesday.

My doctor called me the next day, Wednesday, and said that something "looked funky" with my vertebrae. She ordered me to go immediately to the hospital near my home in Foxboro (which is famous for being the location of Gillette Stadium, home of the New England Patriots). There I was to have blood work and get my prep drink for a CAT (Computerized Axial Tomography) scan, which I had this past Thursday at 6 a.m. I met with the oncologist on Good Friday (the timing is beyond ironic), and he had the unhappy task of telling Peter and me the extent of the cancer. Stage IV – meaning the cancer had spread to organs throughout my body.

My mind raced. I felt like I had been given a death sentence. But through my shock and my tears, I had to keep my wits and make arrangements. Find someone right away to lead that evening's Good Friday youth service. Figure out a sensitive way to relay the crushing news to the congregation. Enlist a person to become Acting Pastor in my absence, since continuing to work was out of the question; all my energy would now be focused on simply staying alive.

And of course, tell my children.

I was immediately started on radiation; my first treatment was on Good Friday afternoon, another took place yesterday, and I will receive it five days a week for three weeks to shrink the tumor in my back. Then it is on to a course of chemotherapy.

This has all happened so fast that it is hard to take in. I managed, through the grace of God, to get through this morning's Easter service at church. I am now on a medical leave of absence for as long as I need.

I have a biopsy scheduled for this coming week so the doctors can determine exactly what kind of cancer I have and then be able to make better decisions regarding my treatment.

This has been an Easter day full of a range of emotions: tears... fear... hope... joy... love...

I am deeply grateful that I will not be making this journey alone. I have my family, my church, and God who will accompany me *through* the valley – not just into it – to healing, hope, and new life on the other side.

"Why Are You Weeping?"
A Sermon Preached by Rev. Jean Niven Lenk
Easter Sunday, March 31, 2013
Text: John 20:1-18

The Easter story begins not with the sunshine and joy of resurrection, but with the tears and despair of loss. It begins not in a sanctuary filled with fragrant flowers and jubilant singing, but in a cemetery with the stench and silence of death.

The Gospel of John tells us that Mary Magdalene goes to the tomb on that first Easter Sunday while it is "still dark..."[1] It is the darkest hour, the one just before the dawn. It is the dark night of Mary's soul; the darkness of her broken heart, her dashed hopes and dreams; the darkness of life without the Light of the World.

When Mary gets to the tomb and sees that the stone has been rolled away and the grave opened, she does not even bother to look inside. Through the blur of her tears and the haze of her exhaustion, Mary can only guess that grave robbers have stolen Jesus' body. Long after the disciples have seen for themselves and returned home, Mary lingers outside the tomb, weeping. We can imagine that she is thinking back on all that has happened, the many lives that Jesus has touched and healed and transformed. And – she is thinking that now it's all over.

As she stands there, remembering and lamenting, two angels appear and ask her, "Woman, why are you weeping?"[2]

Why am I weeping? she must be thinking. How can I not weep? How can you?

Because Jesus is dead, brutally killed by people who felt threatened by him, by people who neither knew nor understood him. From the first day he appeared in Galilee preaching the Good News of the Kingdom of God, he dared them to imagine a different world, a world based on love and generosity in which the last would be first, the hungry fed, the lowly uplifted, the stranger welcomed, and injustice fought. On the final night of his life, the disciples' Master and Teacher washed their feet and broke bread at a Last Supper with them. And then he gave them a new commandment: "Love one another as I have loved you."[3] But before the night was over, Judas betrayed him, Peter denied him, and the rest of his disciples deserted him. And then Jesus was arrested, flogged, crucified, and laid in a tomb.

Why am I weeping? Mary must be asking. *How can I not?*

Mary's weeping is a universal emotion. Crying is the first sound out of our mouths when we are born. And it is often the last sound we hear as we leave this earthly life.

And between birth and death, we weep a lot. How can we not? There is so much to weep about.

Maybe it's financial hardships, health issues, tough times. Maybe it's grief and loss and despair. Maybe it's a broken relationship or persistent loneliness or unrelenting hopelessness. And if we aren't weeping for ourselves, then we need only listen to the news for things to weep about.

A young husband and his pregnant wife are travelling from their home in Brooklyn to a Manhattan hospital in the back of a private taxi when they are struck by a hit-and run-driver. The couple and their unborn baby die.

Why are we weeping? *How can we not?*

A tour bus carrying a college women's lacrosse team goes off the turnpike and crashes into a tree, killing a 30-year-old coach and her unborn baby.

Why are we weeping? *How can we not?*

A 13-month-old boy is shot in the head while in a stroller being pushed by his mother.

Why are we weeping? *How can we not?*

Twenty children and six adult educators are shot dead at Sandy Hook elementary school in Newtown, Connecticut.

Why are we weeping? *How can we not?*

Yes, so many of us are like Mary, walking in the darkness as she did, stumbling in the shadows of separation, sadness, suffering. We, too, carry around grief and regret in our souls; the weight of our own actions and the bad choices we have made; the wounds of pain inflicted by others; the brokenness of illness and loss and devastating diagnoses.

So many of us are stuck in Good Friday. And all too often, we — like Mary — linger at the tombs of our failures and heartaches and disappointments, bewildered and paralyzed, unable to move beyond the fear and despair in our lives.

But as Mary stands at the tomb, tearfully remembering, she sees a man, and he too asks the question: "Why are you weeping?"[4] In the dim light she cannot see his face and thinks he must be the gardener. The Voice speaks again: "Mary!"[5] And suddenly she knows – it is him! In that instant, everything changes. Jesus is *alive* again – the foundation and fulfillment of her hopes, the face of God turned toward her in love. Where there was brokenness, now there is wholeness. Where there was darkness, now there is light. Where there was despair, now there is hope. Where there was death, now there is life.

Good Friday makes us weep. But Easter bids us to dry our tears.

Are you weeping because you have lost hope? Easter says, *Keep on going. There are better days ahead.*

Are you weeping because you are consumed by guilt? Easter says, *You are forgiven. Today you have a fresh start.*

Are you weeping because you feel insignificant and unloved? Easter says, *You are a beloved child of God.*

Are you weeping over a frightening diagnosis? Easter says, *Be not afraid. God is with you every step of the way.*

Are you weeping over the death of a loved one? Easter says, *Death does not have the final word.*

Easter happens every time a glimmer of hope breaks through the darkness of our despair. Easter happens every time the light of God's healing love carries us out of the shadows of loss and grief and disappointment. Easter happens every time we can find the courage to let go, to stop clinging to the past, and turn toward a new beginning and a hope-filled future.

When Mary finally recognizes her beloved teacher, she reaches out to him, wanting to hold on, but he tells her that she must let go of the old life so *new* life can take place. And then he tells her, and all of us, to dry our tears and go – go, to share what we have seen, go to invite others to experience this Easter joy, go and be instruments of Christ's healing grace, go and be conduits of Christ's boundless love.

We're no longer in Good Friday. Today we celebrate *resurrection.*

And so on this beautiful Easter morning, go and spread the news that the tomb is empty, and Jesus lives again! Go, because the world is weeping. The world is waiting. The world is wanting.

Let's dry our eyes and go tell the Good News: *death does not and will not have the final word.*

Christ is risen! Christ is risen indeed! Alleluia and Amen!

MONDAY, APRIL 1, 2013

CALENDARS

My calendar is my second bible, and like I (try to) do with the Good Book itself, I live by my calendar, relying on it to guide me through the day.

I am old-fashioned when it comes to my calendar: I use a good old spiral-bound, heavy-papered, cardboard-covered "analog" version.

And I always do it in pencil.

Good thing – because the appointments and activities that my calendar will be guiding me through in the days, weeks, and months ahead bear no resemblance to the schedule I had been keeping up until the diagnosis that changed everything.

April 1: Eastertide, a new month, the promise of spring in the air, a great Red Sox win over the Yankees – and a completely new life for me. I took out my big chunky gum eraser and eradicated all the old familiar routines of my vocation: not just Sunday worship, but also bible studies, clergy breakfasts, committee meetings, conferences. And that does not even begin to cover the things I cannot plan too far ahead: funerals, pastoral emergencies, and all the comings and goings, joys and heartaches of congregational life.

It was a complete letting go, a giving over (if not up) of the tasks that have long defined my working life and, to a large extent, myself as a person. I had to get my old life out of the way in order to *have* life in the future.

My identity as a pastor has given way to a new role: cancer patient. Biopsies and radiation treatments have taken the place of writing sermons and officiating at weddings. Appointments with doctors, the strangers into whose hands I am placing my life, are now filling my days. Soon chemotherapy will be added to the calendar, perhaps some surgery. I do not know what's in store, but this is my "new normal."

Because if I want life, I must fight for it, every minute, every day. I can no longer assume life is a great – but expected – gift. I must actively pursue it, regardless of the physical, mental, or emotional cost, regardless of how sick I must feel in order to become well.

Prayers, love, great medical care, and a determination to fight for my life – I look forward to turning the pages on many calendars in the years ahead.

TUESDAY, APRIL 2, 2013

UPSIDE DOWN

Day Two of my new life – and it is breathtaking how different it is from the life I was leading just a few days ago.

It used to be that, after sleeping like a log, I would bounce out of bed early in the morning. No need to set an alarm – the pets (Scooter, our Shetland Sheepdog, and Matthew and Itty Bitty, our two cats) would start to get restless and crawl all over me, announcing it was breakfast time. I would go downstairs to feed them and have some time with my son Ian before he left to catch the school bus. I would down a bowl of cereal while reading the *Boston Globe* on my tablet, get dressed, and then it was off to face, with energy and enthusiasm, another day as a church pastor.

Was that really me just a few days ago?

Now, I hardly sleep. The powerful steroids I take to shrink the tumor in my spine keep me buzzed all night long, and pain keeps me awake – physical pain in my back, but also emotional pain in my heart. The radiation treatments sap my energy and make my legs unsteady.

I still go downstairs for a bowl of cereal and then bathe and dress, but it takes everything out of me. By 9:00 a.m., I am exhausted, and I lie down on the parlor couch and try to gather up the strength for the rest of the day's activities: today, a lovely visit from my dear mother-in-law, Connie, and then later, the daily radiation treatment. My 92-year-old Dad sits quietly in his wingback chair near me; my husband Peter is a loving, hovering presence.

A little before 2 p.m., it's off to my radiation treatment, which is just a few miles away in the next town; Peter, my constant companion, takes me. We are so grateful that he is his own boss and that he has the flexibility to temporarily close down his cabinet-making business in order to focus entirely on me.

The treatment takes only a few minutes, but the staff tries to make those moments as comfortable and serene as possible for me. As I lie on the bed under the futuristic machinery, my arms above my head and my hands folded (a perfect praying position), music plays quietly from the sound system. They have put on my favorite station, and I am particularly heartened by the song that greets me today: "L'Chaim!" ("To Life!"), from one of my favorite musicals, "Fiddler on the Roof." It's a sign!

Then, back home to nap fitfully on the parlor couch.

I have been showered with prayers and good wishes these past few days, and if my cancer could be zapped with love alone, I would already be cured. But sadly, that's not the way it works.

WEDNESDAY, APRIL 3, 2013

CHAOS

One look at my offices, both at home and at church, and you would realize that I tolerate chaos well. My desk may look like a bomb hit it, but I can generally locate exactly what I am looking for within seconds. "A clean office is the sign of a sick mind," I have been known to say, quickly adding, "And if you're cleaning your office, you're not working!"

But things are different now, and suddenly I have an overpowering need for streamlined simplicity. So we are now in the process of transforming our front parlor into a place of serenity and healing. Today, we gave away our sleeper sofa to make room for my brand new electronically-controlled power lift recliner, which will be delivered Friday.

I fear I reminded Peter too many times today about exchanging the current side tables with the ones from my late mother's condo (taller, easier to access, and with much better storage); about the power strips I want within easy reach on both of these tables; about the wheels I want added to the coffee table for easier maneuverability.

Suddenly, these details are looming large in my psyche. Perhaps it is because that so much of my life is now beyond my control, I am focusing on the little details where I still have some say.

Tomorrow I undergo a biopsy on the tumor in my spine. I should probably be more concerned about what the results will show and what it will mean for my course of treatment and long-term prognosis. But it is all too much for me to take in right now. Instead, I am worrying about not eating from midnight until after the 11:30 a.m. biopsy. And whether I should go to the nail salon when it opens at 10 a.m. to get my fake gels removed so the oxygen clip will register accurately. Pathetic, I know, but it is about as much as I can handle right now.

THURSDAY, APRIL 4, 2013

DIGGING FOR ANSWERS

Another restless night of virtually no sleep. I had more pain in my back – is the cancer spreading? And now, a new symptom: intractable double vision which negatively impacted my watching of Downton Abbey reruns (one O'Brien is bad enough; two is barely tolerable!).

Had an early radiation treatment today – 5 down, 10 to go. This is the high priority treatment for now. Because my vertebrae tumor is resting so close to my spinal column, there is a very real concern that I could become paralyzed, which would make a lousy situation a whole lot worse. Once the radiation treatments conclude, we will then be able to take full advantage of Boston's outstanding medical establishments, starting with the Dana-Farber Cancer Institute in Boston.

This morning, the radiation doctor decided to cut my steroid dosage in half, which should definitely address my lack of sleep and constant "buzzed" feeling. But at the same time, concerned about my double vision, she has ordered a brain scan for next week (dear God, not in the brain, too!).

Mid-morning, I had enough time to go to the nail salon and have my fake nails removed. I now think my hair coloring is the only artificial thing left about me – everything else is (for better or for worse) genuine. The trip to the salon was deliciously relaxing, and it took my mind off the impending biopsy as well as my forced starvation in preparation.

Peter dropped me off at the local hospital at 11:30 a.m., and I entered the Surgical Day Care suite. I was bumped back on the schedule by 30 minutes due to an emergency but took advantage of the delay to get some desperately-needed shuteye.

For the biopsy, I had to lie on my stomach while the doctor, using a long needle, "dug around" in my T6 vertebrae to get some tissue samples. Mercifully, I was under sedation for most of this time. The whole procedure, including time in post-op, took about five hours. While I was recovering, the staff gave me a painkiller and a little food (I had not eaten in 18 hours), which lifted my spirits and alleviated my discomfort.

Now I am sitting in my living room with my Dad, Ian, and daughter Lizzy, who has resigned her job in Salem to make me her priority (her new job title: "Cheerleader"). It's wonderful having her around, to do extra things like cooking, taking care of Grandpa, and helping my overwhelmed husband Peter.

Right now, I am content. The diagnosis stinks. The circumstances bite. But I feel surrounded by love-drenched prayers, and God's grace abounds – how very, very blessed I am!

FRIDAY, APRIL 5, 2013

NO NEWS

Lizzy, Peter and I met this morning with the oncologist. The results from yesterday's biopsy will not be known until the beginning of next week, so we were talking in generalities about the course of action over the next month. Right now, I am having radiation treatments to reduce the clear and present danger of my T6 vertebrae tumor. Once it shrinks and my type of cancer has been identified, the doctors will be able to suggest the right "cocktail" of chemotherapy.

My new super-duper electric recliner arrived today. It was the first thing we purchased after I received my diagnosis, because my spine tumor makes lying on a flat surface (such as a bed or couch) unbearable. We set the chair up in the parlor, so it looks like that is where I will be sitting during the day and sleeping at night.

I continue to be overwhelmed by and grateful for all the prayer- and love-filled sentiments coming my way; they are lifelines of hope and optimism for me right now.

SATURDAY, APRIL 6, 2013

TRANSITIONS

Somewhere, sometime during this past week, I made the almost imperceptible transition from being a healthy, take-charge, vibrant woman to being a sick, needy cancer patient.

The shift did not happen as soon as I learned I had tumors in multiple parts of my body. No, even with that knowledge, I was able to muster up my strength, think clearly, be decisive, and hold together my family and the church I serve while dealing with my own emotions.

Nor did the transition happen as soon as I started to feel the side effects of treatment – the perpetual buzz from steroids, the fatigue from radiation, and the cumulative effect of emotional and physical strain.

But last Sunday, when I was back home after leading Easter worship and changing into more comfortable clothes, I recognized in the moment that as I was shedding the "uniform" of my vocation, I was dispensing with so much more than heels, stockings, and professional garb. I was peeling off a way of living – in which my heart and mind was focused toward others; casting off what I saw as my role in the world – as a conduit for God's grace and a connector of people to Christ.

As the week unfolded, I stepped forward through a portal, drawing back the curtain separating me from *then* and *now.*

The efforts of daily life now loom large for me; showering, dressing, going to a radiation treatment or doctor's appointment have become major undertakings. And I now need to lean on others, lest I stumble and stagger under the weight of my new life – and my weakness in trying to navigate it.

My world has become, quite simply, all about me and my fight for life. I am sorry I cannot take care of others anymore. All pastoral care is now incoming. I have finally made it to the top of my own priority list. Funny how it took Stage IV cancer for me to finally be okay with that.

This new person who has emerged on the other side seeks simplicity, quiet, peace. Small and comfortable spaces which will cradle rather than overwhelm, chambers of tranquility where everything is gentle, calm, tender.

Are healthy people just naturally louder? When I was well, did my penetrating voice and clicking steps irritate and offend the frail and weak? How could I have missed this? Because now I want no fast moves or rushing around or hurrying up. No loud noises, no chatter, no extraneous sounds seeking to fill up the empty space of quiet.

Peace – that's what I need, what I crave.

SUNDAY, APRIL 7, 2013

LOVE

Sunday morning. The non-negotiable "main event" of my week. The focus of a week's worth of planning and preparation – and also of my painfully misguided thinking that one of my human constructs might lead the souls present in those worshipful moments to a holy encounter with God.

But not today. Sundays will no longer bind me as before to a vocation, a church, a people. Sundays will no longer intrude as a counter-cultural alternative to having weekends off.

Sunday has now become just one more day in the battle.

But today there was some unfinished business to take care of. I attended coffee hour (but not worship – I did not have the energy to be out for two hours) at church so the people in the congregation could say good-bye to me. They showered me with love, gifts, and good wishes.

I have spent the last eight years trying to save the church – both this small, beloved local church and the church universal. I have just enough ego to think I can do it; just enough desperation to think if I do not try, it will not happen; just enough distrust not to put it totally in the hands of God.

And then what happens? Without my doing anything at all, God shows me the church at its best, shows why this precious human-and-divine institution has endured for so long (and will long after I depart).

We equate the term "organized religion" with dogma, rules, and systems of belief. But "religion" comes from the Latin *religare*, meaning to reconnect, and it originally meant faith, devotion, love, awe, transcendence, and living life in awareness of the holy.[6]

It is not about do's and don'ts, right and wrong, true and false, them and us. This purer, truer kind of "religion" – of reconnecting – is all about binding ourselves to God and to each other. It is all about getting down to the essence of Christ's message: love. It's all about love. That is the only thing that matters. Loving unconditionally, loving generously, loving others as God has loved us.

That's what I felt today. In my admittedly imperfect, frail, and fragile human way, I have loved these dear people in the congregation. I hope they know how serving as their pastor has been one of the greatest joys of my life; I hope they know how much they have meant to me, how I have seen Christ in their faces and in their hearts and in every little act of devotion and service they have offered. And I hope they feel I have served them well.

And now they are giving it all back to me. That is the church. That's why the world needs the church. Why I need it.

I am grateful that now I can simply rest in this love. Nothing to prove. No new tricks to pull out of my hat. No silver bullets to address the challenges.

Just feeling the love.

MONDAY, APRIL 8, 2013

CANCER – WE'VE MET BEFORE

I will admit that over the decades, I have copped a wee bit of an attitude toward cancer. Did not run in our family. No genetic markers. No predisposition. No history. Nope, not us.

My Dad will turn 93 in May. His main health issue is COPD – Chronic Obstructive Pulmonary Disease, which makes breathing difficult (40 years of untamed smoking will do that). But no cancer.

My beloved mom died last October, taking full control of her departure from this earthly life with the conscious decision to pull herself off the beta blockers that were keeping her congestive heart failure in check (but making her feel wretched). But no cancer.

My great grandfather on my mother's side did have a bout with prostate cancer. Surgery at age 92. He recovered and lived to be 97, for heaven's sake! My aunt (who shared a mother but not a father with my mom) died of colon cancer in her early 80s. My cousin (who shared a grandmother but not a grandfather with me) died in her mid-50s of a brain tumor. But those were mere anomalies, I told myself.

My brothers have duodenal ulcers, coronary artery disease, but not cancer. "Sorry, Big C, you have no stake here in this family," I used to think. "You don't scare me. I do not live in fear of your invading my world." And I didn't.

The thing is – I have faced this demon cancer before, in a most personal and heartbreaking way.

Rewind to spring, 1980. Eight months before, the local Town Clerk had taken time from her lunch hour to marry Darcy and me in her apartment. Her downstairs neighbor served as the witness. We were deliriously happy. I adored Darcy's scrappy irreverence and street-wise demeanor; he loved me back.

This should have been my first, real, true marriage. Unfortunately, it wasn't. In an effort to find security and realize my completely unrealistic fairytale dreams, I had already managed to squeeze in an awful, abusive post-college starter marriage right after graduating. The only good that came out of that union was a realization that I was a Christian. He was of a non-Christian faith, and when I tried to worship in his tradition, I realized that I needed Jesus to make God real to me.

Over Memorial Day weekend, 1980, I was recovering from a week-long bout with bronchitis. Darcy and I were watching Friday night TV. He got up during the commercial to use the bathroom. When he came back, I mentally noted that I had not heard the toilet flush. I looked up, and his face was ashen. "I just peed a whole lot of blood." Funny how life can turn on vivid images and simple sentences – and how our (at least my) instinct is to smooth over, calm down, find the reasonable explanation. "I'm sure it's nothing," I said. I did not know that, of course, but hoped just saying the words out loud would make it so. "Call your doctor in the morning."

Even the doctor had a reasonable explanation – those frisky newlyweds! But he pursued other possibilities, too. Darcy spent the first week of June in the hospital undergoing increasingly sophisticated testing. Scans and x-rays and intravenous pyelograms. And by the end of the week, we had a diagnosis: renal cell carcinoma. A great big malignant tumor had invaded his left kidney. He underwent surgery on Monday, June 9, 1980; out came the kidney, the rib on which it rested, and lymph nodes.

While Darcy was recovering in the hospital, the urologist who had performed the surgery summoned me to his office. He was brief and to the point. The cancer had already spread to the lymph nodes. "Seeds" of cancer had probably been "planted" throughout his body and would "bloom" in the coming months. "Your husband has less than two years to live," he stated flatly. My 31-year-old husband was dying.

And that was about it. Radiation was the only treatment protocol, but it did nothing to stem the growth of the tumors. Every new scan revealed that the cancer had spread to additional organs. By Christmas, it was in his left lung. Out came the lung; a long bout of pneumonia in his right lung followed. Then a tumor showed up in his right lung and eventually his brain. He died on March 12, 1982, in the Palliative Care Unit on the eighth floor at UMass Medical Center in Worcester, Massachusetts. One year, nine months from diagnosis to death.

I spent years trying to make meaning of Darcy's death and eventually found a place of peace. This is how I explained it in a sermon:

> Many years ago, I watched my young husband Darcy suffer for 21 months with terminal cancer. We had been

married only eight months when he was diagnosed and given less than two years to live. And I asked why – why God had doomed Darcy to an early death, why God would allow Darcy to suffer so, and why God would leave me a widow at age 27. But there were no answers to my questions – at least not then.

But fourteen years later, in 1996, while serving as a student chaplain during seminary, I started to get some answers. An interesting thing happened when I would arrive at the hospital: I found myself time and again going to the oncology unit. None of my fellow students wanted to go near the place, but I felt comfortable there, sitting with patients as they underwent their chemotherapy treatments and talking with family members about the heartbreak of seeing their loved ones struggle with the disease. It did not take me long to understand why I was drawn to the oncology unit. Through my experience with Darcy's illness, cancer – and cancer patients – did not faze me, and I wanted to minister in the service to which Christ calls all of us, just as we had been ministered to during Darcy's illness.

Thus, fourteen years after Darcy's death, I was finally able to make meaning of it by taking the experience of his illness and turning it into something positive, by giving back to the patients and families in the oncology unit. Although I still do not understand why Darcy had to die, I do know that as a result of his death, my ministry is more purposeful and profound. I do not believe for one second that it was "God's plan" for my husband to die of cancer so I would be a better

> minister. I could not worship, much less devote my life to, a God like that. But the fact of the matter is I *am* a better minister because of this experience, for it has helped me to understand suffering and offer compassion from a deeper place in my heart.

TUESDAY, APRIL 9, 2013

NEWS!

Finally, some definitive news on what kind of cancer I am dealing with. And although it has been a long day, I am now oddly energized, which just goes to show that being able to name what we are dealing with is preferable and less exhausting than living in the shadow of unknowing.

So, I have a sarcoma. Sarcoma can start in any part of the body, such as the bone or soft tissue. About 60% of soft tissue sarcomas begin in an arm or leg, 30% start in the trunk (torso) or abdomen, and 10% occur in the head or neck. Sarcoma is rare, accounting for about 1% of all adult cancers.

Or, as my oncologist put it, it's a "freaky thing." Yup, that's me – don't get carcinoma or leukemia or lymphoma, Jean. Get an uncommon cancer, a cancer difficult to treat. Be unique! Be different!

It looks like the sarcoma started in my pelvis, but it does *not* appear to have had anything to do with my January 2011 hysterectomy. We do not know exactly what kind of sarcoma it is, but this leads to the next piece of good news: there is a Sarcoma Clinic *right in our own back yard,* at Dana-Farber Cancer Institute in Boston.

Dana-Farber is a world-renowned cancer research center. It treats 300,000 patients annually and works in affiliation with Brigham and Women's Hospital, which is a block away. What a blessing that it is only a 45-minute drive (if there's no traffic) from our home in Foxboro!

My oncologist is getting me hooked up immediately with the Sarcoma Clinic, and hopefully within the next week, I will be evaluated there and my particular kind of sarcoma further defined so that chemotherapy can begin.

In the meantime, it's good to know that things will be moving forward without delay and a path toward healing will soon be revealed.

WEDNESDAY, APRIL 10, 2013

COMIC RELIEF

This would have been a great day to be videotaped. Any pretensions of dignity, fortitude, and grace in the face of overwhelming obstacles would have melted in the reality that I am a complete slob, I enjoy food way too much, and I am dealing with my new diagnosis and the sudden reality of my life now on my own terms. In other words: I don't care one bit what I look like; I don't care if my fat white belly is hanging out under my shirt; I don't care if my hair looks like a rat's nest. And I don't care if anyone *does* care!

First on the docket today was a MRI brain scan, to see if there is a biological reason why I am experiencing double vision (which makes TV watching difficult and reading impossible).

The scan requires getting into one of those long awful tubes for an interminable about of time, and I will admit – I am a complete claustrophobe. With the scan scheduled for 8 a.m., I had to take my first tranquilizer at 7 a.m. so I would not have a panic attack. That meant I had no sooner awoken from another bad night's sleep than I was taking drugs to send me to oblivion. On our way to the hospital, I took a second trank (just to be safe), which meant that by the time I arrived at the entrance, I needed a wheelchair.

I only vaguely remember being wheeled in to the scan room and placed on the table. I have no memory of going inside the tube or being there for any length of time. I think I remember being put into a wheelchair afterwards and that people were giggling at me – that's fine, I love finding the humor in *anything*, and I have no problem being the punch line myself.

And let me say right here – I have no fear about what the scan will show. If it's clean, great – one less place from which to eradicate the cancer. If there's cancer – no sweat, we'll deal with it. Maybe it's just that I am now living my life with the conviction that the veil between life here and life there is much more fluid than we make it out to be.

My favorite scriptural passage – the one that has always spoken deep to my core – is 1 Corinthians 13:12: "For now we see in a mirror dimly, but then we will see face to face. Now I know only in part; then I will know fully, even as I have been fully known."[7] We'll know someday. *We'll know someday.* And I've got to tell you – I find that just a wee bit exciting; not quite ready to find out now, but when the time is right – what a great adventure it will be!

So – continuing on my day today. After the scan, there's a blank in time, and the next thing I know, I am sitting back in my living room on my recliner (dubbed the "Queen Jean throne"), eating a Big & Toasted from Dunkin' Donuts. Only, rather than going down my gullet, most of it tumbled down the front of my shirt and right down onto the floor for the dog to eat.

I spent the next couple of hours in some sort of altered state – call it rest, call it peace, call it getting over my drug-addled condition. But I started to come back into the world in the first part of the afternoon, just in time to have a lovely, prayerful, powerful visit from Diane, our Student Pastor. Wow, has she been exposed to unexpected lessons of pastoral ministry recently – but again, that's the grace of God. And God has graced her with what she needs during this time, so she can write these lessons upon her heart for her future ministry and also share them with the people in the congregation who need her pastoral guidance right now.

Friends have been sending me boxes filled with healing (hand lotion), pampering (scented soaps) and fun (red sparkly "Wizard of Oz" slippers). I particularly like the maracas that arrived in the mail, courtesy of my friend Paula!

It is certainly possible to find laughs and joy in the midst of a cancer diagnosis – you just have to go looking for them.

THURSDAY, APRIL 11, 2013

BLESSINGS

So many blessings to share with you today!

Brain scan *clear!* (Okay, start all those jokes about how the docs found *nothing* between my ears.)

The back pain has disappeared for now, and I have taken myself off painkillers.

With the steroid prescription reduced, I am actually getting a little sleep at night.

Had a lovely visit from former Student Pastor Mary, who is taking over as Acting Pastor at UCC Stoughton.

Most exciting – I have my first appointment at the Dana-Farber Sarcoma Center next Tuesday!

And – lest any of you think that I am sitting on my recliner all day long feeling sorry for myself, ruing my rotten luck, beseeching God with "why me's?" and consumed with thoughts of illness and dying – stop, stop, you just don't know me!

In fact, in these past weeks, perhaps more than any time in my life, I have been acutely aware of the absolute joy and beauty of this precious gift of life with which God blesses us. It reminds me of something I wrote in a sermon years ago. Back then, I was just riffing off the wisdom of noted theologian, writer and pastor William Sloan Coffin, but I think I can now claim some of this wisdom as my own.

I have written about my husband Darcy, who died of cancer in 1982. Sadly, I was widowed again 15 years later. John died when our daughter Elizabeth was eight years old, and our son Ian was only eight months. In the ensuing years, as Ian grew old enough to understand that his Daddy was in heaven, we talked about death, and he asked the question that perhaps we all ponder sometime in our life: "Mummy, why did God make it that people have to die?"

I mumbled something about life being more precious when you know it will not last forever. Indeed, we live most fully and poignantly in the awareness of our own mortality.

In his book *Credo*, the late Coffin states unequivocally that "Death is more friend than foe," and he challenges us to consider the alternative. "Life without death would be interminable – literally, figuratively." Coffin points out, "We'd take days just to get out of bed, weeks to decide 'what's next?' Students would never graduate, faculty meetings and all kinds of other gatherings would go on for months."

Coffin then makes this statement: "Death cannot be the enemy if it is death that brings us to life. For just as without leave-taking there can be no arrival; without growing old there can be no growing up; without tears, no laughter; so without death there can be no living."[8]

My prayer for each of you is that you live fully and joyfully into each moment of your life. Please do not wait for a tragedy or grim diagnosis. Start now. Life is too beautiful to squander one single moment!

SUNDAY, APRIL 14, 2013

EVEN THE WORST DAYS CAN BE FILLED WITH GRACE

It occurs to me that I have had a rather impressive list of "Worst-Day-Ever" contenders in my life.

For instance, this past March 29 (Good Friday) was devastating – that's when I received, out of the blue, my diagnosis of Stage IV cancer. And yet... and yet... the day was also imbued with love, prayers, and dear people simply being there for me. One of my first phone calls was to church member Marcia; I had no choice but to ask her to take over that evening's Youth Good Friday Service, and I knew she would be there for me ("anything I can do... whatever you need...."). I told her my diagnosis over the phone (she started bawling among the vegetables at the supermarket), and when we met at the church a little while later, we just held each other and wailed. Sometimes that's all you can do – just hold on dearly to people you love and let the tears flow.

Another candidate for "Worst Day Ever" was the night, when I was 12, that my parents told me they were getting a divorce. They had come home early from a party, and there was no warning – they just came into my room where I was playing records and told me. Of course, I cried and was angry and confused and frightened about how my life was going to change. But it was also a relief. My whole life, I knew my parents' marriage was unhappy; our household was not peaceful. It felt as if the Sword of Damocles was hanging over our family, just waiting to fall. The thing is, once a decision is made, the healing can begin; the future can start afresh. I was much happier once my parents separated and found peace and contentment apart, because I too could then be peaceful and content. (Note: Kids are not stupid – because of my own experience, I do not advocate that parents stay together "for the sake of the children.")

There are still other "Worst Day Ever" contenders. Was my Worst Day Ever the night my first husband (for the last time, I promised myself) slapped me around, and I knew I had to get out of the marriage, once and for all?

Or was the Worst Day when Darcy got his terminal diagnosis? Or was it the day he died? Or was it one of the many days in between, as his life slipped away and all we could do was watch helplessly?

Was the Worst Day Ever when I learned of John's drug addiction? Or was it the day I had to bring a restraining order against him? Or the day I found out our house was being auctioned for mortgage non-payment? Worst Days are not limited just to situations involving illness, life and death. Worst Days can be filled with the human emotions of shame, betrayal, and bitter disappointment.

And none of these Worst Day candidates were actually made up of 24 hours of straight heartbreak. I cannot write these words without thinking of the parents who lost their beautiful children at Sandy Hook on December 14.

But there is one day I want to share with you, for even though I think it tops my Worst Day Ever (because it was the Worst Day Ever for my kids, too), it was so filled with the grace of God that even sixteen years later, my heart is moved in remembering it.

May 25, 1997 – Sunday of Memorial Day Weekend

By now, I was half way through seminary, and we were living in Quincy, just south of Boston, in John's childhood home. I went to church in the morning (I was not yet a pastor, and sat in the congregation) and then came back home to spend a quiet afternoon with him and our two children. John said he was going in to the Boston Globe (located in the Dorchester section of Boston and where he had worked since his 16th birthday) to make sure the Robotics System he ran in the Press Room was ready for the incoming second shift. It was not necessary for him to go in to work. While I wanted to be supportive of his conscientiousness, I was just a tad suspicious that he was concocting a reason to leave so he could get high. I peered into his deep blue eyes, as I had so many times before, and asked: "Are you using?" Looking straight back at me, he said, "No." Sad, but not angry, I said, "Honey, if I find out you're lying to me, I am going to have to leave you. I just can't live like this anymore."

And out the door he went, taking the one car that ran. I needed to go shopping later – we were out of formula for Ian – but there was time. It was about 1 o'clock.

Three o'clock. Four o'clock. Five o'clock. This was before cell phones, and there was no way I could get in touch with him to tell him to get his butt home. And then, in one clear-headed moment, I suddenly knew in my heart of hearts that John was never coming home again.

And so what did I do? I started to clean the house. I had bundles of nervous energy to expend, and I knew that the next couple of days would be a blur of visitors and arrangements. So I cleaned the house.

By early evening, the kids were getting hungry and antsy. I sat on the living room couch with baby Ian in my arms and Lizzy next to me. "Mommy, when's Daddy coming home?" she asked. "Soon.... Soon..."

And we just waited. Then a car pulled up in front of our house. "It's Daddy!" cried Lizzy. But then she looked out the window. "No, wait, mommy it looks like a police car."

"Stay here," I told her, and with Ian in my arms, I went out to greet the two Boston cops who were coming up the walk to give me the worst news possible.

"It's my husband isn't it." It was not really a question.

"Yes – Mrs. Sangster, we're sorry to tell you ..."

"... he died today," I finished their sentence. "Was it a heroin overdose?"

"It looks like a heart attack." I was doubtful. I knew it was drugs. We later learned that John OD'd in the men's room at the Globe, probably soon after he arrived early in the afternoon. His body was not discovered until the second shift came in around six.

"Is there anything we can do for you?" one of these brave, dear policemen asked.

"Yes – could you hold my son? I have to go back inside and tell my little girl."

The cop gently took Ian in his arms and held him lovingly.

And in that moment, I felt God giving me the strength and the words to go back into that house and give my beautiful Lizzy the worst news possible. Wise words from a seminary professor[9] entered my head: "with children, don't use euphemisms." State the truth in clear, simple terms.

So I turned and went back inside, and there was my little red-headed girl sitting on the couch. I wrapped myself around her and said, "Honey, Daddy died today." I took a deep breath and continued. "And we're going to be okay." And we have been.

When the cops asked again how they could help, I mentioned the formula. While one went to get it, the other sat in our living room and asked if he could pray with us. Here I was the seminary student (he did not know), and this policeman is holding our hands, leading us in the Lord's Prayer. Grace abounds!

I do not remember their names, but I remember their kindness on the Worst Day of my life – when light and love and goodness could still penetrate the shadows of sorrow and heartbreak.

It took me years to make meaning of John's death. It was a complicated bereavement – grief and sadness mixed with anger and bitterness. I was heartbroken and bereft. And I was upset at what he had done to his beautiful family, how feeding his addiction had become his #1 priority (not to mention, he left me in complete financial ruin). For years, I was too ashamed to even acknowledge that he had died by OD – I used the "heart attack" theory first offered by the cops as a cover story.

But slowly, over the years, I was able to find my peace. Here are excerpts from a sermon I wrote about it a few years ago.

"Making Meaning – Part II"
A Sermon Preached by Rev. Jean Niven Lenk
March 14, 2010
Text: Luke 13:1-9

Over the past five years that I have been your pastor, I have occasionally shared with you the story of how I have been widowed twice: my husband Darcy died in 1982, and my husband John – the father of my two children – died in 1997. I hesitate to mention this part of my life too often, because serving as your Pastor is not about me; it's about our relationship with God through Christ and with each other.

But every three years, the parable of the fig tree shows up in the schedule of scripture lessons, and I think this passage – and the season of Lent in general – is an opportunity to share with you a little of my story, especially in light of Easter, and the new life with which God has so graciously blessed me. So even though there is no "I" in the word sermon, there is an "I" in the word testimony. I ask for a little grace this morning, and I thank you for allowing me to give my testimony.

... Jesus tells a parable about fertilizing a fig tree. Fertilizer. That's a nice term for manure. And manure is a nice term for well, you know....

You may have heard the story about President Harry Truman. Always an earthy talker, Truman once offended a friend of his wife's by referring repeatedly to "the good manure" that must have been used to nurture the fine blossoms at a Washington horticulture show. "Bess, couldn't you get the President to say 'fertilizer'?" the woman complained. Replied Mrs. Truman: "Heavens, no. It took me 25 years to get him to say 'manure.'"[10]

Whatever you call it, it happens in life. In the news recently, the fertilizer has been January's earthquake in Haiti and the one in Chile two weeks ago. And I know most of you have your own stories of fertilizer, of heartache and suffering. It may be financial worries, a failed relationship, a chronic illness, a grim diagnosis.

The circumstances of our fertilizer may be different but I think there is one universal: the question why? Now, as I have often said, there is no easy answer to that question, and I am not going to offer up some saccharin platitude as explanation.

The fact of life is – fertilizer happens. If we're fully alive, we are going to experience pain and suffering, but suffering can be transformative. New growth can spring from the fertilizer of our lives. Our broken hearts can be renewed by God, and our broken lives can be revitalized. But it will happen on God's time, not according to our own schedule.

Three years ago, the last time I preached on the parable of the fig tree, I talked about my husband Darcy's death from cancer and how it took me 14 years before I was finally able to make meaning of it.

But I have never shared with you about John's death. The reason is that for many years, I could not make meaning of it. And for many years, I was too ashamed to talk about the circumstances.

My husband John was a smart, sensitive, witty, lovely guy. One of the nicest fellows you could ever meet. He was also addicted to heroin. It has taken me a long time to be able to say those words. Because people look at you funny. "You married a heroin addict? What's wrong with you that you would be willing to have drugs part of your life?" And if I said, "Well I had no idea when I married him," people would look at me as if asking, "What's wrong with you that you didn't know?"

And so, I did not talk about it; I kept the truth of my life hidden, even after an overdose took John's life. That was in 1997, when our beautiful daughter Elizabeth was eight years old, and our precious son Ian was only eight months old. And for years, I tried to find some way to make his death, and the cause of his death, meaningful. But for years, it all just seemed like just a meaningless waste.

Until recently. Because in the past couple of years, I have been called to minister to people with drug addictions. And what I found was that I was not repulsed or scared or turned off by them or their circumstances. Now make no mistake – drugs are a scourge which ruins finances, families, futures, and lives. I also know that addiction is a disease, not a moral weakness, and it permeates every level of society, every kind of family, every socio-economic status. Because of my experience with John's illness, I could pastor without judgment or pre-conceived notions of what kind of people use drugs. And I knew that as much as I cared about and wanted to help people with this illness, they were the only ones who could kick their addictions. No one else could do it for them.

All of these things I had learned from John and his illness. Almost eleven years after his death, I was able to put to positive use those heartbreaking lessons. And as a result, I have been able to make meaning of this devastating loss.

In the days and weeks following John's death, I received an outpouring of love and support in the forms of visits, phone calls, prayers, and condolence cards. It was on one of these cards that a friend wrote these helpful words: "Jean, may your loss be fertilizer for new growth."

It may take us years, even decades, to see new growth spring from the fertilizer of our lives. For some, the new growth may never come, because not all suffering is redemptive. Suffering is redemptive only if it transforms and brings new life – which is what Jesus came to offer. My life, and the lives of my children, have indeed been renewed and transformed in the years since John's death, and the greatest blessing God has given us is their new Dad and my husband Peter, with whom I celebrated five years of marriage this past week.

Suffering is human; it is a part of life. God does not instigate our suffering as punishment for sin; rather, God holds us in our suffering, uplifting and strengthening us. Jesus calls us to repent, to turn toward God, in both the good and bad times of our lives. And God will help us find new meaning and growth springing from the fertilizer of our lives.

Christ shows us the way through suffering and offers us something beyond – hope, meaning, and new life. That is the journey to the cross. And that is the promise of Easter. Amen.

MONDAY APRIL 15, 2013

I'VE ALREADY GOT MY HAPPY ENDING!

One of the great blessings of being so wiped out from radiation these past few weeks is that I have had absolutely no energy to overthink my diagnosis and prognosis. Not thinking about survival rates, how much time I might have left, or how grueling the next few months of treatment might be. Just relishing having my family gathered around me (waiting on me hand and foot!); loving all the touching notes I have been receiving filled with love and prayers and unexpected blessings; and enjoying visits from special people in my life.

It's funny, but my life is so much better now than it was before my cancer diagnosis, because now it is focused on what is most important; every moment bursts with the fullness of life lived centered in love, family, and relationships.

Once I start as a patient at the Dana-Farber Sarcoma Clinic tomorrow, I will have to overcome my lethargy and deal with the realities of my cancer diagnosis. Do I have a snowball's chance of having my cancer vanquished? Is my cancer something that can be "beaten back" for months, or years, or decades? Is this going to be a steady decline, or will I be able to regain some level of health and resume some kind of "normal" life?

We do not have answers to these questions right now. Indeed, they may not be revealed for months or years. And let me also say – just because I can write with seeming dispassion about my situation, *I want to live!* I am going to fight, believe me, and do whatever I have to do to eke out as much of this earthly life as I can.

But here's the thing I want to emphasize: no matter how things turn out, whether I die at 59 or 89, I've already got my happy ending!

And here it is:

When I was in high school, the boy assigned to the seat next to me in tenth grade Algebra was tall and gangly, with long red hair (like snowboarder Shaun White before he chopped off his locks). His name was Peter, and his arms and legs were so long, he had difficulty fitting into the desk-chair. He was also a "hippie," which meant that he had little in common with my All-American girl image; we never saw each other as dating material. But he was sweet and funny, and we enjoyed spending the year together suffering through math.

And that was that.

I skipped my senior year of high school, heading off to UMass Amherst at the tender age of 17. And I did not think of that skinny redhead again until 1985.

It was between my second and third marriages, and I was living in Hopkinton (only a few blocks from the start of the annual Boston Marathon) and focusing on my career. I had just received a promotion at my company to the new ops center we were opening in Dedham, and I had decided to put my house on the market to move closer to my new job.

One evening, I received a phone call from my real estate agent; he had an offer to present to me. "Great – come on over!" He arrived and handed me the paperwork. I looked through the offer and then at the bottom saw the name of the person who wanted to buy my house: Peter Lenk.

"Wait," I said to the agent, "Is this guy tall, skinny with red hair?"

"Yes," he responded, surprised. "He's sitting out in my car."

"Well for crying out loud, bring him in! I know him – we went to high school together!"

A minute later, Peter – followed by his new bride Michele – were walking into my living room. Because I was now using my married name, I said, "Pete, take a look at me. Do you recognize me?"

"Jean?!"

Peter and Michele bought my house in Hopkinton. And that was that.

Until October 2003. The Wellesley High School Class of 1972's 30th reunion (one year late). Across the room at the Wellesley College Club, I saw that tall, skinny redhead. His hair was shorter, but other than that, he had not changed all that much.

"Hey, Peter! You still living in my old house?"

"No, but my ex-wife is."

And that was that. We were married eighteen months later. A wonderful father for my children. A life partner for me. My *petros* – my rock – my Peter.

One day as we were taking a drive down "memory lane" in Wellesley, he pointed to a large brown shingled house on Glen Road. "I went to nursery school there – Brookgarden." "So did I!" So it turns out that we first met when we were three years old – but it took another 47 for us to realize we were soul mates.

I cannot imagine going – and I would not want to go – through my current situation without him. A magnificent man of honor, integrity, and decency. He is my strength, my heart, my best friend, my partner, the love of my life.

Regardless of how things turn out, I feel so deeply blessed; God is so good. What a crazy, wild, wonderful life I am having – and no matter what happens, I've already got my happy ending.

TUESDAY, APRIL 16, 2013

THE NEWEST PATIENT AT DANA-FARBER

So, I am an official cancer patient at Dana-Farber.

I am upset. I don't want this. But it's my life now. Okay.

Do not get me wrong; Dana-Farber goes out of its way to make its patients comfortable. The Yawkey Building, where the Sarcoma Center is located, offers an interfaith chapel, a two-story healing garden, and a great cafeteria. These architectural components are designed to maximize patient comfort. But all the features cannot erase the fact that the people who come here have cancer. And that now includes me.

We found a subdued Boston this morning. Traffic was down and police cars were a common sight because of yesterday's Marathon Bombing tragedy. Inside, however, the building was bustling with staff and patients.

My heart aches for the loved ones of the three bombing victims who died too young, and I pray for the people who were injured. I know it is selfish of me to say, in the tragedy's aftermath, that I am preoccupied with myself right now. I know that the three who died will not see age 30, while I am feeling cheated that I may not see 60.

But maybe I am feeling something else, too – proud? Because every patient who comes to Dana-Farber has made the decision to battle cancer rather than give up. And that now includes me, because I am a fighter!

I've never been afraid of anything in my life (okay, maybe rats and flying), and I am not starting now. My whole life has been a testament to resilience, endurance, faith, new hope, new life, and resurrection. And this is only the latest chapter. And every scar – emotional or physical – that I incur in this battle, I will wear as silent witness to this fight for my life.

And that, quite frankly, is what this is, my beloved friends – I am in the fight of my life for my life. My new Dana-Farber sarcoma specialist made that clear. My head spun with his talk of response rates, survival rates, and quality of life. I only remember one thing he said: "Do you have months or do you have a couple of years? I'd say somewhere in between." Oh, there are treatments and protocols and trials, but it will be a battle. However, I will not go down easily.

I have my last radiation treatment – #15 – tomorrow morning. My Dana-Farber doctor wants me to have about three weeks off to recover from its debilitating effects, and then we can start on an aggressive chemotherapy regimen. I go back to Dana-Farber next Wednesday for an echocardiogram, to ensure that my heart is strong enough for the chemo (I have the heart of a lion!). Then back to Dana-Farber to see the doctor a week from Friday, by which time pathologists hopefully will have identified exactly what kind of sarcoma I have.

I expect to begin chemo the first part of May, and the next phase of battle begins.

WEDNESDAY, APRIL 17, 2013

LOVE MAKES A FAMILY

When I was young, I used to imagine what my life would be like when I grew up – what kind of career I would have, whom I would marry, how many children I would have. I cannot tell you how many hours I spent as a girl daydreaming about the future and my fairytale wedding, handsome husband, and beautiful babies. I have read that this is all perfectly normal – it is a universal human instinct when we are young to envision what we will become and how our lives will unfold.

It is not a surprise that we humans also want to have say over the things that happen in our lives. And it can take quite a few years – perhaps a whole lifetime – for us to realize just how little control we have over our circumstances. How many of us, now older and wiser, can look back and see how our journeys of life have taken twists and turns we never could have anticipated? I could never have imagined the path my life would take – and how circumstances would lead me to have *several* fairytale weddings and *several* handsome husbands!

The focus of my hopes and dreams centered on the concept family. My husband and I would have children. Our children would then have children. And we would be one big, happy family bound together by love, certainly, but perhaps as significantly, by blood and genetics.

Except... that is not how things have worked out for my children and me. We have a different kind of family – one that binds a number of people together by love, honor, integrity, trust, and human goodness.

And of course, family has been particularly on my mind these past few weeks since my diagnosis. I want the peace of mind that my children will have a family to support them and be there for them long after I am gone. And they will. But it is not based on blood relations.

First, of course, is Peter. When he came (back) into my life nine years ago, he immediately became a wonderful "Dad" to my son Ian and a trusted adult presence to my daughter Lizzy. And he has promised to always be there for my children.

Then there are Peter's children, Tim and Beryl. Ian was thrilled to get an older brother; Lizzy loves having a sister; and I do believe Tim and Beryl enjoy having Lizzy and Ian (as well as me) in their lives.

Then there is Michele, the mother of my stepchildren (I never call her "Peter's ex"). She has always been wonderful to my children, accepting them right into the family, and I know she will be there for them no matter what.

I had the honor of officiating at Michele's wedding to Greg three months after Peter and I got married. (Do you ever hear stories like this?) And right after my diagnosis, she wrote me this note: "To the lady with whom I share so much (children, houses, *husbands*) ... If we could share the cancer, I would gladly do so." The words of a most generous, good-hearted woman; I am proud to call her friend, and grateful to call her family.

There are many others in this great extended family – Peter's mom, Connie; sister Susan; brother-in-law Charley; niece Marisa. My brothers and sisters-in-law and cousins and nieces and nephews. People from our church.

And it is the love that binds us that makes us a family.

THURSDAY, APRIL 18, 2013

HAIR

I have always had good hair.

Of course, I was not convinced back in the mid-60s, when all I wanted was the long, straight hair that was all the rage. Marianne Faithfull hair. Patti Boyd Harrison Clapton hair. Cher hair.

Instead, my hair came with an annoying wave. My mom was envious, telling me I would always have "bounce" to my hairstyles. But I wanted straight, long hair. So I wrapped my hair around my head at night using four inch bobby pins, and then in the morning I ironed it – yup, right on the ironing board, just like a shirt sleeve.

But despite my efforts, my hair always seemed to have a mind of its own. I would wake up in the morning, and the left side would be going this way, and the right side would be going that way, and the bangs would be sticking straight out.

When I went off to college, I got a shag cut. And then, over the years, I went through every possible kind of style – short; shoulder-length; bob; even a dreadful mid-80s permanent (Lord help me, what was I thinking?).

But, just as my mom had predicted, over the years, I began to appreciate my hair – thick, fast-growing, and yes, with that wave that gave every hairstyle extra body and fullness.

But these past few weeks, my hair has started to become more than I can handle. The need to wash and dry and style it has become overwhelming. Something that I did without thinking for so many years is now bringing me to my knees. And of course, all that hair is going to fall out in a few weeks when I begin chemo.

So today, I went and got it chopped off. It is liberating! It is also shocking to me.

My husband looks at me, and he says, “You’re beautiful.”

But I look in the mirror, and I do not recognize the person I see. I am still Jean – with the same spirit and heart I’ve always had. But who is this bloated face under the short-cropped hair staring back at me? It is humbling. I will stop short of saying humiliating. I realize that I have to let go of my pride. My beauty must now come not from my face nor my hair (if it ever did), but from a deeper, stronger, more profound and enduring place.

And I think maybe that is a lesson we could all use.

FRIDAY, APRIL 19, 2013

MEASURING A LIFE

How is a life measured?

It is easy to see from public death notices that our culture measures a life in longevity, in the number of years lived.

These came from today’s newspaper:

George Beverly Shea, 104.

Pat Summerall, 82.

Frank "Lumpy" Bank, 71.

I cannot help but thinking that perhaps we are missing something important here. Certainly, for people facing a serious illness as I am, the traditional dimensions of time and space start to become irrelevant. I do not have 30 years left, so the "measurement" of my life is going to be in shortened terms. But surely that does not make my life any less important, or significant, or meaningful.

So, at the next level, a person's life may be measured in accomplishments and achievements.

"Francis Lawrence, 75; raised profile of Rutgers as president"

"Nathan Azrin, 82; applied theory to help people change"

"Colin Davis, 85; conductor formed special ties to BSO" [Boston Symphony Orchestra]

I have a few "accomplishments" for my obituary – degrees earned, positions held – but the significance has not been in the achievements themselves. Rather, their significance has come from the people I have served, the relationships I have made, and the work I have done *because and through* them.

As I have been especially pondering the meaning of life and death over these past couple of weeks, I am more and more convinced that the true measurement of one's life must focus on love. Love shown. Love freely given and graciously received. Lives touched with love. Hearts motivated by love.

Everything else pales in comparison. Nothing can create, heal, restore, repair or cure like love. This, I believe from the bottom of my heart, is the best – perhaps the only – true, honest, and meaningful way to measure a life.

"Legacy of Love"
A Sermon Preached by Rev. Jean Niven Lenk
Sunday, April 29, 2007
Text: Acts 9:36-42

One day a couple of years ago, my father said to me, "Jeanie, I need to talk with you." By the tone of his voice, I knew it had to be something important, and indeed it was – he wanted to go over his funeral arrangements with me.

Now, let me say that my Dad is in great health for someone who is turning 87 in a few weeks. But he likes to have everything in order, and that includes the details of his funeral. So we sat down, and he went over all the arrangements he had made. And then he handed me a piece of paper, on which he had scribbled some points to be included in his obituary.

There were the facts and figures: that he was born in Rochester, NY; that he graduated from Dartmouth College; that he has three children, nine grandchildren, and one [now four] great grandchild(ren).

And there were the interesting aspects of his life: that he was a dive bomber in the Navy during World War II and went down in the Pacific; that he spent most of his career in advertising; that he played drums in different jazz bands over a span of 70 years; and that he had a passion for golf.

But as I looked over the draft of his obituary, I could not help thinking how inadequate it was; was this all there was to show of Dad's life? Because my father is so much more than just his education, his survivors, and some hobbies. There was nothing in that obituary to convey how great a guy he is, or how wonderful a father, or how generous a man.

What about the hours he spent rooting me on as I struggled to learn how to ride a two-wheel bicycle? What about the time he was away on a business trip but over the phone encouraged me as I toiled to learn my multiplication tables? What about the times, long before the women's movement, that he urged me to have a career? What about all the times he inspired me to take chances, to stick my neck out, because falling short was always better than not trying at all? What about the times, after I was all grown up, that he was there when I had to tell him, more than once, "Daddy, my husband is very sick"? Where, in between the lines of that obituary, was all the love that he has shown?

An obituary can never sum up the total of a person's life, because there is so much left unsaid, so much still hovering between the lines. And in this morning's scripture lesson, we are left with the same feeling that there is so much more to the story than what is written.

The main character has two names; in Greek, her native language, she is Dorcas, and in Aramaic, Tabitha; both mean "gazelle," which speaks of a gracefulness and gentleness of spirit.

There are only seven verses in Tabitha's story, but what a story it is. Tabitha is insignificant by worldly standards because she is a woman when it is men who are in power, and her talents are restricted to using her hands rather than her voice. But however insignificant she may be by the standards of the world, she is mighty by God's, for she uses her gifts to help the disenfranchised and marginalized of society.

We read in our passage that Tabitha is "devoted to good works and acts of charity."[11] Through the ministry of the apostle Philip, she has become a follower of Christ, and she openly gives of herself by serving the poor through her gifts at sewing. She has a particular ministry of making robes and other articles of clothing and giving them to poor widows, who love her for her many acts of kindness. We can imagine, between the lines of her short story, that as she helps clothe these women in fabric, she is also clothing them with dignity; through her gifts, she builds up and encourages her less fortunate sisters. And in the process, she becomes beloved in her community.

One day Tabitha gets sick and dies, and those she leaves behind are bereft. In tribute to their friend, the widows take out the robes and other articles of clothing that Tabitha has made and show them to one another as they mourn her death. We can picture the tear-stained faces of these women as they share their memories of all the kindnesses Tabitha has shown them. And that community is left to wondering – how are we going to replace Tabitha? Who can give and show love in the special way that Tabitha did?

Her friends learn that the disciple Peter is visiting a neighboring town, and they send him a message: "Please come to us without delay."[12] Peter goes to Joppa and prays over Tabitha's body, commanding her to get up. And Tabitha lives again, to carry on her good works and acts of charity. Her sewing – and her outpouring of love – continues, and the community survives intact. They don't even have to try to replace her; but they never could have, anyway – because there is no one else like her.

Tabitha, like each one of us, is irreplaceable. We are each special creations of God with our own unique gifts. And no one can give and show love in the same unique way that each of you do – or that any of us does.

Think about it – who could replace the love and caring of your mother? Your father? Your daughter? Your son? And who could replace *you*?

The early church could have survived without Tabitha. But that doesn't mean her death would not have made a difference. The church would have been weaker, and no one could have been able to do exactly what she did in the unique way she did it. The world would have been diminished by her loss.

We see in Tabitha's story that one person's gifts and love can change a church, a community, perhaps even the world. We never read of Tabitha again in scripture. But Joppa was an important city in the spread of Christianity, and no doubt word of Tabitha's wonderful ministry and miraculous resurrection was spread to other ports by people on the trading vessels that were launched from Joppa.

She "became a symbol of resurrection life in the Joppa church because her simple acts of compassion and caring expressed, in a visible and tangible way, something of the incarnation and resurrection of Jesus Christ."[13]

Tabitha's community had much to show of her love. And so, think about it – what will you be remembered for?

Alfred Nobel had not given that question much thought until one day, he awoke to read his own obituary in the paper. It was his brother Ludvig who had died, but an overzealous newspaper had published the death notice of the wrong Nobel. It described him as "the dynamite king, the industrialist who became rich from explosives." It made Alfred Nobel sound like nothing more than a merchant of death. Nobel was upset by what he read, upset that his legacy would be one of destruction. And so, he resolved that day to change the course of his life and do something positive for society. He left his entire fortune to be awarded to individuals who have done the most to benefit humanity, and the result is the five Nobel Prizes that are awarded each year. Now, Alfred Nobel's name is associated with winners of this prize, such as Martin Luther King, Jr. and Albert Schweitzer. Nobel transformed his life from one of *success* to one of *significance.*

When you die, what will you be remembered for? What will be your legacy? Tabitha, who was insignificant by worldly standards, is known to us today, almost 2000 years after she lived, because of her good works and acts of charity.

As her spiritual descendants, may we all follow in her footsteps by living lives that are focused not on success, but on significance. May we, like Tabitha, leave a legacy of Christian love. Amen.

SATURDAY, APRIL 20, 2013

59

Up until three weeks ago, I was ready to completely skip this birthday. Fifty nine – what's so special about that? Almost the end of one decade; not quite the beginning of the next. A sort of age netherworld.

Sixty – now 60 I was looking forward to! I had already checked the calendar (yes, I am a planner) and found that I would be turning 60 on (wait for it) Easter Sunday – perfection for a pastor. A beautiful morning celebrating the Resurrection, and the rest of the day celebrating – well – *me!*

And I had already announced to my family: I am not cooking on Easter Sunday, 2014; instead, I expect to be treated to Easter dinner.

Now, I look back a bit ruefully on my rather cavalier attitude toward my 59th birthday. First, life is God's greatest gift, and every birthday is worth savoring and celebrating.

But also, today – the birthday I was ready to skip – has been such a sweet day. Many people I love were here: Peter, Lizzy, Ian, Dad; my brother Andy; my stepson Tim; his mom Michele; my mother-in-law Connie; my sister-in-law Susu; her husband and daughter Charley and Marisa.

I even got to pick the menu: Greek salad and pizza, along with – of course – birthday cake.

While we had said "no presents," they brought gifts: comfy nightgowns, candy, flowers (lots of flowers!) and from my kids a special scrapbook which we will put together, the three of us. I think the most special present came from my sister-in-law Susu, who has fought her own battle with cancer, myeloma, over the past dozen years. She gave me the same kind of special angel pendant she wore during all of her treatments at Dana-Farber, with prayers that mine will be just as effective.

Today, like every day, we are on an emotional roller coaster. Fatigued, I find it hard to control my emotions. One minute I can be laughing and finding humor in the craziest things, or reveling in another great Red Sox win.

And the next, the tears are streaming down my face. (This happens especially when my husband and I look at each other – we just dissolve.) They don't last long, but the tears do come. I don't care. They are cleansing. They are healing. And they are honest. I just don't have the energy to be anything but completely authentic right now. I can't shield others from the pain my diagnosis is causing.

I am so sorry. I am so sorry. I am so sorry. I wish it were not so. But there is nothing I can do about it. I am just grateful it is me who is sick and not my children – that would truly bring me to my knees.

Others have to deal with my illness in their own way; everyone who is being affected by my cancer is coming from a different perspective.

And I have to deal with it in my own way.

So, while I would never have predicted it four weeks ago, my 59th birthday has been delightful, for the right reasons under the wrong circumstances. And having cancer has indeed reminded me, in the starkest terms, how beautiful is this, my "one wild and precious life" (poet Mary Oliver).

SUNDAY, APRIL 21, 2013

TOP TEN GOOD THINGS ABOUT HAVING STAGE IV CANCER

10) I am in complete charge of the remote controls and what's on TV. If I want to veg out on HGTV all day, that's exactly what I am going to do – no guilt, no apologies.
9) If I start to get tired, I just close my eyes. Oh, were we in the middle of a conversation? Sorry!
8) I can contentedly spend my entire day and night in my recliner without feeling like a sloth.
7) People wait on me hand and foot without thinking that I am (too much of) a selfish diva.
6) The way I look has become less and less important, and I have begun to realize that in the whole scheme of life, such

superficialities are just (or should be) way down on the priority list.

5) My kids won't leave my side.
4) I am no longer worrying about my weight; in fact, thanks to steroids, I have become "Jean, Jean, the Eating Machine." Hey, my oncologist told me to "stay well nourished," and I am doing my best to follow his orders. My kids gave me an 18 oz. Russell Stover gift box for my birthday – thank you very much (oh, I am supposed to share?)!
3) There is no room in my life for negativity or anger or pessimism or animosity; I want only love, peace, healing, and joy to prevail in my little world. Wouldn't it be nice if we all came to a similar place of being?
2) I have finally realized that no, I am not in control. Oh how we humans deceive ourselves into thinking that we rule the world – or at least our own lives. I had my life all planned out (like I've said before, I am a planner), and it is humbling to find out how deluded I have been all this time. As John Lennon famously said, "Life is what happens when you're making other plans." Or, as we like to say in the church biz, "Wanna hear God laugh? Make plans." Now, I don't take a moment for granted; every minute is precious. I focus on the here and now, not on what I will be doing in five or ten or twenty years.
1) I have been the overwhelmed recipient of an outpouring of love, prayers, and good wishes. So many people I knew in school, in my corporate life, at church camp, in the churches I have served, jobs I have held, from all of the many places I have been, have reconnected with me and been so generous with their care and compassion and loving words. It is kind of like being at your own wake – but in a very good way! Wouldn't it be lovely if we did not wait for a Stage IV cancer diagnosis or other kind of misfortune before showering the people we

love with love? As for me, I will never again let pass by an opportunity to tell someone I love them.

MONDAY, APRIL 22, 2013

I KNOW IT'S A CLICHE....

...But when you have your health, you *do* have just about everything!

My health decline has been breathtaking (not in a good way) in its swiftness.

I still cannot get over that less than a month ago, I was my energetic, focused self – facing each day with enthusiasm and vigor. That nagging back pain was disconcerting, but I was determined not to let it get me down.

And now, I look at my calves – they have atrophied in the past few weeks, taking on a different shape from the old, sturdy, stubby, familiar legs that have served me so well all these years. Those legs barely hold me up these days; I am weak and wobbly. And when I do get out of my chair, I shuffle around, holding onto the furniture like an aged shut-in.

But the hardest part of the day is getting dressed. It takes me hours to build up the motivation. Once I do, I then stand at the bottom of the stairs. As I look up, I feel like I am facing Mt. Olympus, so overwhelming they appear to me. Peter or Lizzy takes my arm, and up we go, one step at a time. Once upstairs, I need to rest and gather strength for the shower. Afterwards, I have to sit again before putting on fresh clothes. I never realized the hand/eye coordination required for putting my feet into socks and pants!

And then, back downstairs I go, with someone spotting me so I don't totally collapse on the trip down. Once I am back in my chair, clean and fresh, I can relax a little.

But as swift as my physical decline has been, perhaps even more disconcerting to me is the non-functioning of my brain. I have always prided myself on having a sharp, inquisitive, and creative mind. And it has abandoned me. Yesterday, I fumbled for way too long trying to change a Facebook setting. The task was just too much for me, and I gave up.

In the early hours of this morning, I decided I wanted to watch that wonderful musical with Liza Minelli and Joel Grey set in Berlin – but all I could think of was "Willkommen." I sat very still for about 15 minutes trying to come up with the title. And this was not just a "senior moment" – I had *nothing*! Finally, I went through the "On Demand" movie alphabet – thank heavens, there it was under "C" – "Cabaret."

Last week, it took me ten minutes to come up with the term "Pharisee" – unheard of for a pastor.

So what I am wondering is – am I destined for the rest of my life to be a not-so-sharp sick person? Will I ever regain the health to walk with strength and purpose? Will I once again hop out of the car (not to mention *drive* a car) and run into CVS to pick up some things? Will I again have the wherewithal to be a contributing member of society – or at least my household?

I would like to think that my current situation is more a result of radiation and steroids rather than the cancer itself. But... I've heard about "chemo brain," and that's still yet to come. What does my future hold?

I look at the world in a simple, bifurcated way now: healthy people and sick people. The healthy people move with grace and strength and purpose. They seem to be on their way to something – the future? They make walking and moving and living look so... easy. And they do not have wretched cancer invading their organs.

Then there are sick people – like me. We struggle with even the simplest aspects of living – showering, getting dressed, mobility. And every day, we are fighting the good fight against that which threatens to shorten our life.

Are you a healthy person? All I can say is – never take it for granted! Treasure your health, prize it, appreciate it, and do whatever you can to hold onto it!

Because – I know it's a cliché, but when you have your health, you do have just about everything.

TUESDAY, APRIL 23, 2013

THINKING OF MY MOM

This past Sunday was the six-month anniversary of my mother's death. I am big on dates and anniversaries, and under "normal" circumstances, I would have had April 21 written on my heart, and it would have been a day of extra special remembering of this most beautiful of women.

But "normal" is a thing of the past, and I guess I was not all that surprised when I realized this morning that I had completely missed the date. So today, I am doing the remembering.

Olive Clark Niven was all about family. The only "job" she ever wanted was to be a mom; it was her calling and life's work. When her children grew up, she reveled in being a grandmother. She practically raised my two children, and her mark upon them and me will endure forever.

My mom was brilliant, bookish, and petite. But she was no pushover! I think in many ways, she was the first feminist I knew. After she and my father divorced, someone asked her if she ever wanted to remarry. "Are you kidding? And have some man tell me whether or not I can buy a pair of shoes? No way!"

It was a beautiful thing for me to watch her develop a sense of independence. I grew up in a pre-feminist world and then suddenly emerged as a young adult into a post-feminist world; that was a challenge in itself. But for mom's generation, she was expected to provide the perfect home, marriage, and family. And then when it all fell apart, she had to move beyond the limitations that had defined a "woman's place" and make a new life for herself. I was so proud of her.

Throughout my life, my mom was always there for me. Through good times and bad, she was just a phone call away – whether I was 18 or 58. And knowing the importance of her presence in my life throughout the years, I cannot help but think how I want my children to have their mother there for them. (It's bad enough they lost their Daddy when they were so young; can't I be spared?) I have wisdom to dispense, hugs to give, support to offer, and unconditional acceptance and love to lavish on them (and their children!). Every child needs that, no matter how old.

My mom was independent in controlling her own departure from this earthly world. A few years ago, she was diagnosed with congestive heart failure and put on beta blockers. She absolutely hated their side effects: "I feel like I'm dying, and I want to." So she just stopped taking them. Everything went along okay until last June, when she started gasping for breath in the middle of the night and her energy began to diminish. Her cardiologist wanted to put her back on the beta blockers; she needed to think about it. And then after a week she said to us, "Okay, I'll go back on, even if it's just to eke out a little more time with all of you." It took about a month for her to feel the side effects, and that was that. She took herself off. It was hard to watch her writing her own death certificate, but she was clear-headed, practical, and absolutely resolute in her decision. I supported her totally, although my heart was breaking.

Last fall was a sad time for all of us. Mom was failing day by day, and the inevitable was in sight. When she died, I was bereft. The tears came easily – morning, noon and night. I cried when I looked at the picture of her on my bureau, cried just to wake up into a world where my mother was no longer physically present.

My mom lived around the corner from us in Foxboro, and when we put her condo on the market in January, it was hard to drive by and see the "For Sale" sign. When the condo sold, it was hard to clean it out one last time.

The sale of the condo occurred on Tuesday, March 26 – the same day I had my MRI which revealed my T6 vertebrae tumor. By Friday, I had my Stage IV cancer diagnosis. And suddenly, in a moment, the acute sadness of losing my mom lifted. She's okay. She's at peace. And for that I am grateful.

In fact, if my mom were still here, my diagnosis would have devastated her. I think telling my children was easier than telling her would have been. I can imagine how she would be, were she still here – worried, helpless, concerned. In the quiet of her home, she would be praying and weeping. And I would be trying to help her cope, when it's hard enough to cope myself. While I miss her presence, I am so very very glad she is being spared all this.

My beautiful mom's spirit is with me. I hope it isn't anytime soon, but I know that hers will be the first face I see when I enter heaven. And that both makes me weep and brings me great comfort.

"The Smallest Coin ~ The Biggest Heart"

A Eulogy for My Mom
Olive Jane Clark Niven
by Jean Niven Lenk
October 28, 2012

On behalf of Olive's family, I want to thank all of you for being here today and for all the love and support you have shown us over the past difficult weeks.

The whole time I was growing up, my mother would give her height as 5'2" and ¾. Every quarter of an inch counts when you're that short! In her later years, she barely hit the 5 foot mark as she "settled like a box of cornflakes," to use her words.

But in all the ways that counted – her inner strength, her enduring faith, her resilient spirit, and her capacity to love, mom was a giant.

If there is one tangible image that I carry with me of her love, it is a dime. A dime is the smallest coin. But to me it represents my mom's unconditional love and care. From the time I was a little girl, long before there were cell phones, my mom would make sure I had a dime in my pocket every time I left the house.

Having that dime meant I could call home on a pay phone and get in touch with her no matter what. Whether I was lost, or had gotten in some sort of predicament, or simply needed a ride home, I knew I could call my mom whenever, wherever and she would be there for me. The smallest coin represented the biggest heart in the world.

And throughout my life, my mom was always there for me, my children, and all of us; generously and unhesitatingly, she always put her family first.

When I was a teenager, after my parents divorced, she worked extra hard so that I could stay in my hometown of Wellesley. It was very important to her that my life and my schooling not be disrupted by a move to a different town, because as a young girl growing up in the Depression, she moved around a lot as her father followed available jobs. Sometimes she was in a school for only two weeks before moving on to another state, and she made sure that I had the stability she herself had not experienced growing up.

Yes, my mom was always there for me. I remember once, when I was in my late 20s all grown up and living on my own, I struggled home from work one day feeling rotten. I called mom and could only croak out two words, "Mommy, sick." And on the other end of the line was her soothing voice saying the only words necessary, "I'm on my way." It turned out I had a case of Legionnaire's pneumonia, and for two weeks, my mom stayed with me and nursed me back to health.

And it wasn't just when I was sick that my mom was there; it was also in the most heartbreaking times of my life that she offered her unconditional love and support. When my husband Darcy was dying of cancer and had only a few months to live, mom quit her job to come and stay with us to take care of him. She set her alarm to get up at 2 o'clock every morning and give him his pain medication, so I could sleep through the night to have the energy to get up and go to work the next morning.

Fifteen years later, when my husband John died suddenly, mom immediately moved in with me to take care of Lizzy, who was 8 years old at the time, and baby Ian, who was 8 months old, so I could finish seminary. My mom was their second mother, and they shared a very special relationship.

We all lived together – mom, my kids, and me – for eight years. And then when Lizzy was a sophomore at Ipswich High School, and I reconnected with Peter and then got called to this church, mom made a most generous and selfless offer: she would stay in Ipswich with Lizzy so she could graduate with her class.

Once Lizzy was out of high school, there was only one place my mom wanted to live: in Foxboro, near us. And she was able to live independently and very happily in her own condo for the last five years of her life.

Mom may have been small in stature and quiet in demeanor, but she was a strong, not to mention brilliant, woman. When she graduated from Attleboro High School in 1940, among seven superlatives she was voted by her classmates were cutest, most ambitious, and most sophisticated girl – and she was also the Salutatorian, graduating second in her class.

Mom went off to Skidmore College in upstate New York, but World War II intervened, and she left in her junior year to get married to my Dad. For the next three decades, she raised her three children. She always said that her true calling in life was being a mom and later a grandmother. That was her life's work, and the most important thing in the world to her.

But it was always her goal to someday finish her degree, and when she was in her fifties, after she had raised her family, she went back to Wheaton College in Norton. At the age of 58, she got that degree, graduating magna cum laude and being elected to the Phi Beta Kappa honor society. We were all so proud of her.

Mom was a woman of great faith, and she instilled that in me. Every Sunday as I was growing up we went to church, and she ensured I received the foundation of a strong Christian upbringing, which helped me through the ups and downs of life. And I have tried to pass the Christian faith along to my own children.

Mom had a special prayer[14] that she said over me every night as I was growing up. "May the Lord bless you and keep you. May the Lord make his face to shine upon you and be gracious unto you. May you have sweet dreams, a pleasant night's sleep, and wake refreshed in the morning, dear little girl." I know she said that prayer every night over my children too, and I am sure she said it every night of her life for all of her children and grandchildren and great grandchildren, no matter how far away they were.

Until the end of her life, mom kept her mind sharp by reading books, doing *New York Times* crosswords and the daily Jumble in the newspaper, and enthusiastically watching tennis on TV, especially her very favorite player, Roger Federer.

Mom gave my brothers and me a great gift by being pragmatic, realistic, and prepared about the end of her life. She put her affairs in order years ago and showed us exactly where everything was so we would know where to go and what to do when the time came. And she wanted to go her way, on her terms.

Last summer, when the side effects of her heart medication made her feel miserable, she took herself off of them and declared "I'm done. I've had a lovely time, and I've enjoyed every minute." She did not want any invasive procedures or extraordinary measures. "Let me go," she said.

In her last days, the few words she was able to say were full of gratitude and love. "I've been so blessed. I've been so blessed. I love you all so much, darling people."

And last Sunday, that heart that loved so unconditionally and so generously and so devotedly for almost 90 years finally gave out.

Mom, I am so grateful to you, for it is because of you that I have become the woman I am, the mother I am, the pastor I am, because you showed me how to be strong and courageous and independent, you showed me how to love totally and unconditionally, and you showed me how to put my faith in God.

Beloved and beautiful mom, you will never be far from my thoughts or my heart, and you will live on in the lives of your children and grandchildren and great grandchildren, a wonderful legacy of the most wonderful mom in the world. Miss you and love you forever and ever.

WEDNESDAY, APRIL 24, 2013

24 YEARS

It was a sunny, cool, beautiful spring day twenty-four years ago today – April 24, 1989 – when I walked into the bustling lobby of Brigham and Women's Hospital in Boston for the very first time. I was one day overdue with my first baby, and the events that had occurred over the course of the morning indicated that before the day was over, I would be a new mom.

I had recently gone out on maternity leave, and my Dad was staying at our house in case John had to be at work when the time came. Dad drove me into my morning appointment with my doctor in Brookline, and in the midst of my exam, my water broke. The office staff found this very exciting, but for me it was a mess – I was completely drenched. They told me to go straight to Brigham and Women's – this baby was on his/her (we didn't know) way!

Ever the planner, I had weeks before packed an overnight bag and put it in my car. I now held that bag close to me in an effort to cover my wet spots as we were processed through admitting and brought up to a room on the maternity floor. I made contact with John and then, because my water had already broken, I was started immediately on Pitocin to induce labor.

My poor Dad! Back when his kids were born, he simply got a call at the office: "Congratulations, Mr. Niven, you have a bouncing baby boy (or girl)!" Things had certainly changed. He stood by my bed holding my hand as I writhed with labor pains. He was a dear, but he was clearly uncomfortable seeing his baby girl in such discomfort and for such a delicate reason. In fact, he was so relieved and in such a hurry to leave when John walked into the room that Dad stepped on his foot as he beat it out the door!

Even with the Pitocin, my labor slowed down, especially after I received the blessed epidural. In fact, the rest of the afternoon and the evening passed uneventfully. Finally, as we were moving toward midnight, the doctor and nurses wanted to get things moving ("I've already filled in April 24 as the birth date!"). With the help of some major league pushing on my part (those childbirth classes did prove helpful after all), along with forceps deftly handled by the obstetrician, the most beautiful baby in the world arrived at 11:47 p.m.

"She's got red hair!" exclaimed John, who cut the umbilical cord. A redhead! I was totally besotted. Although I had had reddish-brown hair as a youngster, and both my Dad and John's father had red hair as boys, my baby girl's red hair was an unexpected delight; the genetics had aligned beautifully. The head nurse was so taken with this newborn that she whisked her down the hall to show off to her colleagues.

And as lovely as my Elizabeth was then and continues to be, her inner spirit and giving heart are her most beautiful aspects. There are so many reasons why I am proud of her; here is just one. While working as a counselor at church camp a number of summers ago, she heard a call to care for special needs adults, and until recently she managed a group home of five residents. You have to have a special heart for that kind of work – and she has it. (She has since left the job so she can concentrate on just one adult – me!)

So, 24 years ago today, I went to Brigham and Women's for the first time. I returned in 1996 to give birth to Ian. Both of these times, I was bursting with new life.

As a pastor, I have made many visits to parishioners there over the years – the healthy minister trying to bring assurance of God's healing presence to an ill patient.

And today, I returned to that bustling lobby, this time in a wheelchair. I was there for my echocardiogram, to ensure that my heart is up for the intensive chemotherapy that is in my future. Needless to say, it feels so different being at the hospital as a sick patient. Rather than bursting with new life, I am trying to eradicate that which threatens my life.

Twenty-four years ago today. One of the best days of my life.

Today. One of the best days of my life – because I am here and alive and enjoying every moment, especially the birthday of my beautiful daughter.

THURSDAY, APRIL 25, 2013

SMALL STEPS AND SHRIMP SCAMPI

Finally!

Now that I am a week out from my last radiation treatment and tapering off of the steroids, I am actually seeing small but steady progress toward regaining my strength.

The following may not sound very significant, but for me they are strong indicators that things are going in the right direction.

I have slept very well the past couple of nights – so well, in fact, that the pets have woken me up looking for their breakfast! Feeding them is one little bit of my "B.C." routine I have tried to continue, but in my sleeplessness over these past few weeks, I have put out their food before they even came looking for it – anytime between 4:00 and 5:00 a.m. Both yesterday and today, however, I was sound asleep when they came down hungry at 5:45!

The last few days, I have enjoyed visits from family, church folk and clergy colleagues and have actually had the emotional bandwidth to ask how they were doing and to really care about their answers! A week ago, I could not handle anything but my own stuff.

I think my synapses are snapping with greater acuity.

Rather than have somebody wait on me, I have been getting my own food and beverages, to everyone's relief.

I have been spotted emptying wastebaskets, clearing away dirty dishes, polishing my side tables, and even putting a load of laundry in the washer.

While I am still having trouble negotiating stairs, I am not as completely wiped out by the task of showering and dressing.

Yesterday, Peter and I went food shopping on our way back from Boston – and as long as I was hanging onto the cart, I was able to maneuver around the store fairly well.

The most telling: I was motivated to make my Shrimp Scampi this afternoon. And it was delicious!

Regaining my physical and emotional strength is so important to my being able to face the next phase of my treatment: chemotherapy. Physical strength helps me emotionally, and vice versa. With my recent progress, I know I will be able to rally my resources and focus everything I've got on simply staying alive.

Since my diagnosis, I am so much more aware of the simple beauty of this world. Yesterday was such a glorious spring day that even the traffic delays in and out of Boston did not bother me. After my echocardiogram at Brigham and Women's, Peter parked me on the second floor balcony in the lobby while he delivered some records to my Dana-Farber doctor a block away. From my perch, I watched people come and go and listened to some beautiful music that was rising up from somewhere below me. As a healthy person, I would never have had the patience to sit there for 20 minutes, but for me yesterday, it was a slice of heaven.

When Peter returned, we took the elevator downstairs, and I saw the source of the beautiful strains that had lifted my spirits: a musician and her rustic harp. I had Peter wheel me over to her so I could tell her what a gift her music was to me – and she said she and her music needed me, who had the ears to listen.

Are patients more... patient? The origin of the word "patient" – both an ill person and "one who bears delay with calm" – is the Latin *patiens:* to undergo, suffer, bear.

I hope that my illness will change me so that I always have the ears to listen, the eyes to see, and the heart to love this beautiful world, in all its simplicity and splendor; that I will have the patience to just sit and take it all in. Wouldn't it be wonderful not to first have to be a patient in order to have that kind of patience?

FRIDAY, APRIL 26, 2013

ANOTHER VISIT TO DANA-FARBER

Today Peter and I made another trip in to Dana-Farber to meet again with my sarcoma specialist. We had hoped to have more answers – what kind of sarcoma I have, what the chemo protocol and schedule would be, when it would begin, and so on.

Unfortunately, he did not have as much information as we had hoped -- but he had other possibilities we welcomed.

The fact of the matter is, sarcomas are rare. Only 1% of adult cancers are sarcomas, and some are never clearly identified as to specific kind. The pathologists at Dana-Farber are still looking at my tissue samples from my April 5 biopsy to determine more specifically what I have, but the doctor said there is a chance that it may never be clearly identified beyond, simply, "sarcoma."

The interesting news is that he seems to think there is a chance that the tumor in my T6 vertebrae is slow-growing. I am going in for another CAT scan next Tuesday, and then by comparing it to my March 28 scan, he will be better able to determine how the tumor has reacted to the heavy-duty radiation I received earlier this month. A comparison of my lung tumors to a month ago will also be made. He seems less concerned at this point about the tumor in my thyroid.

In the meantime, I am just taking one day at a time. Not stressing about what may be or not be in my future. Just living into the beauty of every minute.

Peter says that now he knows why he has been so drawn to the story of Job, which he has been reading at church in the quiet moments before worship begins. He thinks Job's conversation with God is the most profound piece of literature in human history. Peter says he would gladly give up all his possessions and sit naked and penniless in the street, like Job, if he could just have me healthy again.

"Job's Questions – And Ours"
A Sermon Preached by Rev. Jean Niven Lenk
Sunday, October 8, 2006
Text: Job: 1:1, 2:1-10; Matthew 5:1-11

The following are true stories.

An elderly woman lives out her last days in a nursing home, struggling against a body which is slowly shutting down. And her daughter turns to me and says, "I don't understand why God is putting my mother through this."

A young woman, having already suffered a miscarriage, carries a baby to full term, only to have her beautiful daughter die within an hour of being born. And the mother cries to me, "I *do not* understand why God did this to me."

A teenager writes, wondering why our "loving God" isn't around when marriages break up, or when a friend considers suicide, or when children must live – and die – in poverty.

Because of true stories like these, Job is our contemporary in a way few other biblical characters can be. He is one of the most compelling figures in the Old Testament, and it is his unexplainable, unjustified, innocent suffering that does it.[15]

This morning's lesson tells us that Job "was blameless and upright, one who feared God and turned away from evil."[16] He was a good and faithful man with a loving wife, ten children, and much property. But then, Job's world collapses.

It happens because one day, God and Satan start chatting about Job. This Satan is not the devil we usually think of. The idea of a devil that operates as a separate and opposing force to God did not develop until hundreds of years after the Book of Job was written. In Job's time, Satan served as a respected member of God's "council," a heavenly being who operated as a kind of divine prosecutor. His name is translated as "The Accuser" or "The Adversary," and he had no power to do anything except the power God gave him. His job was to bring people to trial when God said so – and only if God said so.

So one day, up in heaven, God says to Satan, "What have you been up to?"[17] And The Accuser tells God that he has been, "Going here and there, checking things out on earth."[18] God asks, "Have you noticed my friend Job? There's no one quite like him – totally devoted to God and hating evil."[19] We can imagine The Accuser putting his arm around God's shoulder, shaking his head, and saying, "So do you think Job does all that out of the sheer goodness of his heart? Why, no one ever had it so good! You pamper him like a pet, make sure nothing bad ever happens to him or his family or his possessions, bless everything he does – he can't lose! But what do you think would happen if you reached down and took away everything that is his? He'd curse you right to your face, that's what."[20]

And wanting to get to the real motivation behind Job's piety, God says, "We'll see. Go ahead – do what you want with all that is his. Just don't hurt *him*."[21] And God permits The Accuser to begin testing Job.

In a matter of just a few verses, Job's idyllic life falls apart. First, God allows Satan to take Job's property and family. All of Job's servants are slaughtered by enemies; all his camels are stolen, and lightning kills his sheep. Then, a desert wind comes along, knocking down his house and killing all his children as they are eating dinner together around the table. Yet, even with all of these devastating calamities, Job falls upon the ground and worships God, crying, "The Lord gave, and the Lord has taken away. Blessed be the name of the Lord."[22]

But in this morning's Scripture lesson, Satan the Accuser is not impressed by Job's continued devotion, and he asks God, "What do you think would happen if you reached down and took away his health? He'd curse you to your face, that's what."[23] And God responds, "All right. Go ahead – you can do what you like with him. But mind you, don't kill him."[24] So, with God's permission, Satan makes itching sores erupt all over Job's body, from the soles of his feet to the top of his head. And finally, left to scratching himself with broken pieces of pottery, Job erupts, cursing the day he was born. *Why didn't I die at birth!* he laments. *Why am I suffering? I am innocent!*

In Job's world, it is believed the good get rewarded and the bad get punished. And he has been a good person. He has done nothing wrong. He has been faithful. And yet, God is punishing him. "God has no right to treat me like this – it isn't fair!"[25] he cries, and with his words, Job raises perhaps the biggest, deepest questions any of us ask. If God is good, and loving, and all-powerful, why is there innocent suffering? Why do bad things happen to good people?

Job asks these questions, and so do we. When things go well with us and in the world around us, it is not hard to believe in a loving, just and powerful God. But when we experience tragic suffering in our own lives and see it in the world, we begin to have doubts and question our beliefs. We want a world that is orderly and balanced and fair, a world that has a kind of moral arithmetic in which the guilty are punished and the good are spared. But life does not work that way. And when, like Job, the bottom falls out of our world – torn apart by pain or illness or death, we – like Job – cry out to God, "Why?"

Later on in the book, three friends try to comfort Job, but they cannot accept that Job's suffering can coexist with Job's innocence and God's justice. And so they defend God, arguing that Job must have done something to deserve his suffering. After listening for 35 chapters to uncomforting words that only add to his pain, Job finally tells his friends to be quiet. The only one he wants to hear from is God; he wants an explanation for his suffering straight from the Source. And at last God speaks.

"Where were you when I laid the foundation of the earth?"[26] God asks Job. "Have you commanded the morning since your days began?"[27] "Do you give the horse its might?"[28] "Is it by your wisdom that the hawk soars?"[29] God goes on for four chapters with a voice rising in a magnificent symphony of questions. But God's response does not answer Job's questions, nor ours.

Why do some people suffer more than others? Why do some have more tragedy in their lives than anyone should have to bear? Why the debilitating disease, the tragic accident, the death of a young person whose life is just beginning? Why is there suffering? Why you, your child, your spouse? Why mine? The questions are endless.

And the answer? I could stand here and talk about the frailty of our mortal lives, or the fragility of the order of creation, or the consequences of human irresponsibility – and perhaps we would be able to come up with some partial explanations. But in the final analysis, the answer is: we just do not know.

I think, in the end, if there is any response to the problem of unjustified suffering, then it is this: for most of us, the worst thing that can happen is not to suffer without reason, but to suffer without God, to suffer without the hope or consolation or promise of new life that God offers.[30]

In his Sermon on the Mount, in the poetic verses called the Beatitudes, Jesus says, "Blessed are those who mourn, for they will be comforted."[31] The literal meaning of the Greek word translated into English as "comforted" [*parakalao*] is "to be called to the side of." When we are in mourning and in pain, we are called to the side of God. It is not just in our times of unwavering faith or spiritual devotion, but perhaps even more in our times of doubt and questioning, our times of confusion and suffering, that God is at our side. Blessed are those who mourn, for in our sorrow, sadness, and grief, God is right there next to us.

In Job's story, after hearing God's poetic response to his cries and questions, Job's vision is transformed. He begins to see the universe not through human eyes, but through God's eyes. And through God's eyes, Job sees a mixture of birth and death, of creation and destruction, of suffering and joy. Job begins to comprehend God's divine magnificence and his own earthly insignificance, and he says, "I had heard of you by the hearing of the ear, but now my eyes see you."[32]

What Job wants us to know is that God does not abandon us. Even though we may want answers to our questions, what we really need is God. And God will respond. When we have nothing left but a piece of broken pottery with which to scratch our sores, we still have the God of all creation, the God who laid the foundation of the earth, who commands the morning, who gives might to the horse and flight to the hawk and has made everything that breathes.[33] That God will never abandon us, for God will always be where God has always been – loving, sustaining, and caring for God's own. Amen.

SATURDAY, APRIL 27, 2013

TIME

Time is a funny thing.

I used to have *no* time. I know I prided myself on how busy I was; it made me look important, purposeful, committed, successful. Between work (and a pastor's job is really 24/7), elderly parents, and young children, there was just not enough time in the week – or energy at the end of the day – to curl up with a good book, or enjoy an evening in Boston with Peter, or spend some time on a hobby. My poor collection of stamps, depicting figures and scenes from the Old and New Testaments, needs about a year's worth of work to get it into some order.

And yet, when I had no time, I thought I had all the time in the world – thirty more years.

Now that those thirty years are looking unlikely, I have plenty of time. Not being able to work certainly helps. But perhaps I simply did not pay enough attention to the time I had, when I thought I had time.

Since my diagnosis, my children have spent a lot more time with me; sometimes they have slept all night in chairs next to me, just to be close. What we do while we are together is unimportant; it is simply being with each other that means everything. In fact, in response to my illness, they have cleared their calendars to spend more time with me.

Peter and I are together constantly as he cares for me and serves as my chauffeur, cook, manager, and nurse.

And my Dad and I watch every Red Sox game together (and they're off to a great start!).

Yesterday, I was so physically and emotionally spent after our trip to Dana-Farber that once we got home, I could barely talk or do anything but lie in my chair. Today, however, was a new day, and I geared myself up for one of Peter's and my favorite little trips: to the Lobster Hut in Plymouth. We took the long, scenic route down, and at every turn we saw forsythias and cherry trees and flowers in bloom set against the blue sky – magnificent! And being near the water both energizes me and calms my soul. Peter had a scallop plate, I had scrod, rice, and fish chowder, and most of all, we had time together in a setting that could not be beat. It was chilly out on the deck, and we were the only ones out there, but we had dressed for the weather – no way was I going to go all the way to Plymouth just to sit indoors! This is living; these are the precious moments in life.

But it was not what I expected to be doing today. For over a year, I have wanted to see "The Book of Mormon," which won the 2011 Tony Award for Best Musical. It looked like a fun show with a lot of heart, humor, and great music, and it would be coming to Boston this spring. So, last December, I was able to get tickets to the Saturday, April 27th 2 p.m. performance and gave them to Peter for Christmas. Today was going to be a wonderful day for us in Boston.

But... illness intervened. I was not up to such a busy afternoon. But I could not have been happier that Lizzy and Ian gladly took the tickets and had some special sibling time together. And they loved the show!

I could sit here and rue all the time I used to waste on misplaced priorities. But I am not going to beat myself up. That's the way I used to live my life. But it's not the way I live my life now, nor will it be in the future.

Cancer is such a reality check and a life-changer. I cannot imagine right now going back to the lifestyle I maintained up until just a month ago.

Out of this, I have every hope that I will emerge a person more focused on the important things in life – love, family, relationships, beauty, treasuring every moment and enjoying every minute. I think it has already begun.

"Spending Our Lives"
A Sermon Preached by Rev. Jean Niven Lenk
Sunday, March 7, 2010
Text: Isaiah 55:1-3a

In our scripture lesson this morning, the prophet Isaiah asks a question, a question as relevant in our the 21st century as it was some 2,600 years ago: "Why do you spend your money for that which is not bread, and your labor for that which does not satisfy?"[34]

It is an especially pertinent question during the season of Lent, when we are called to look deep into our hearts, to reassess our lives, and to be honest with ourselves about how we have separated from God, God's people, and God's purpose for our lives.

Part of that introspection is to look honestly at where we are focusing our attention and how we are spending our time – or more, to the point, how we are spending our lives.

"Spending our lives" – it is an interesting phrase when you think about it. When we spend money, we exchange it for something we consider to be of equal value. Can we say the same thing about what we get in return for the precious moments of our lives – moments we will never get back?

Consider the following:

A government report finds that Americans spend more time watching TV, listening to the radio, surfing the Internet and reading the newspaper than anything else except breathing.[35] Most of that time is spent watching an average of 4 1/2 hours of television a day, far more time than we spend on any other medium.[36] About 13 hours each week is spent surfing the Web, and that does not include e-mailing.[37]

Watching TV and surfing the web – is that how we want to be spending our lives?

Another study has shown that, between grocery store television screens, digitally delivered movie libraries and cell phone video clips, the average American is exposed to 61 minutes of TV ads and promotions a day.[38]

Watching ads – is that how we want to be spending our lives?

So... if you kept track of the way you spend every minute of your day, every day of your week, every week of the year – what would you come up with? Would you be satisfied with the way you are spending your life?

Through the prophet Isaiah, God challenges us: "Why do you spend your money for that which is not bread, and your labor for that which does not satisfy?"

God's challenge is also accompanied by a gracious summons to a different way of being, what your pew bible[39] describes as "an invitation to abundant life." God says, "Listen and come to me. Hear, so that you may live."[40]

God is calling us to refocus our priorities, to redirect our precious resource of time, to change the way we are spending our lives. But it's not so easy to do, is it? Most of the time, we are focused on our daily needs. We are busy, involved, often unaware of our spiritual life as we go about our jobs, the demands of life, and our various interests. There are so many other invitations out there – things shouting for our attention, imploring us to spend our lives on them, promising us satisfaction and fulfillment and a better life. And so, we continue on our life-spending sprees, not even realizing that we are running on empty, thirsting for the Spirit and hungering for something greater.

A pastor[41] tells the story of one woman who did not realize how she was spending her life until a medical crisis all but took it. After suffering a stroke accompanied by a heart attack, she lay in the hospital in a comatose state for almost a week before giving any sign of recovery. Several weeks later, when she was finally able to speak, she told a story so astonishing her son[42] had trouble believing it.

The woman said Jesus had come to her as she lay in her hospital bed, unable to move or speak, and told her it was time for her to take an assessment of her life. He asked her to place everything she had ever done in her life in one of two piles. The first pile was for those things that she now could see had real meaning, and a second pile for those things she now could see had been a waste of her time and life.

Though she was a person of enormous skill and accomplishment, the woman was astonished to discover that her pile of meaningfully-spent time was quite small while her pile of wastefully-spent time was huge. Once her inventory was complete, Jesus came again and swept both piles away. Then he said to her, "I am giving you more life. How will you spend it?"

When the woman told her son about the dream, he rationalized it away as simply the effects of the massive doses of drugs his mother had been given during her comatose state. Jesus coming to her in a coma? He was dubious; his mother had a nominal faith at best and went to church only on holidays or when her grandchildren sang in the choir.

But as the weeks turned to months and his mother returned to health, the son began to reconsider his swift conclusion. She was no longer the frenetic woman she had once been, distracted by a thousand different things. Rather, she was focused only on a few things that were truly important to her, including worship, Bible study, prayer, and a ministry of visitation to the sick – activities she would not have spent her time on in her previous life.

When asked about the change, the woman would openly talk about Jesus' visit while she was in that hospital bed. Transformed, she was no longer nominally religious but truly committed to Christ, and she spent the rest of her days embracing the gift of new life she knew Jesus had given her.

If Jesus asked you to place the moments of your life into two piles, would your wasteful pile be bigger than your meaningful one? What might you need to sweep away in order to embrace God's love and invitation to abundant life? Where does your commitment to Christ need to be made or renewed, so that you can know the new life that comes through him?

"Why do you spend your money for that which is not bread and your labor for that which does not satisfy?" Lent is a good time to look at how we are spending our lives, on what activities we are exchanging the precious moments God has given to us. And it is a perfect time to respond to Jesus' gracious and love-filled invitation: "I am the bread of life. Whoever comes to me will never be hungry, and whoever believes in me will never be thirsty."[43] Amen.

MONDAY, APRIL 29, 2013

WHAT A MONTH!

It was just one month ago, on March 29, that I learned I have Stage IV cancer. What a month this has been!

First, the shock of the diagnosis from seemingly out of nowhere. And then, the whirlwind of doctors, radiation treatments, biopsies, CAT scans and trips to Dana-Farber. But as I sit here thinking of what an emotional (and physical) roller coaster the past month has been, I can also see that it has been a precious time of re-evaluating, re-focusing, and re-connecting.

I think the first two weeks, I was just getting used to going from a healthy (or so I thought), energetic "in charge" individual to a sick, exhausted cancer patient. I will admit that those first couple of weeks, I was thinking a lot about my own mortality. How long did I have? Would I still be here in a year? Would I get to see my son graduate from high school in 2015? Would I ever hold a grandchild? It's not that I am afraid of dying; I just don't want to leave this earthly life yet.

But thinking about dying is no way to live. And as the days of this past month have gone by, I have discovered how the dimensions of time and space do not serve seriously ill people well; rather, entire lifetimes can be packed into moments – it is a matter of attitude.

I never used to have the time to entertain, and now almost every day I welcome into my home people who offer love, compassion, and support. I feel blessed by the opportunity to re-connect with my family members and other important people in my life.

I used to see time as both a limited resource (not enough time in each day to accomplish what I needed to do), and also a barrier to the future (still a number of years to get through before I could enjoy retirement). Now that my time appears limited (at least from what I had expected), it has become priceless. And so I make sure that every moment I am fully aware and enjoying God's gift of life.

I am now refocusing on the basics, which for me is all about love. There is no space for anything but love, peace, forgiveness, and joy. Everything else is secondary.

So as I enter my second month living with cancer, I am seeing how the gloom and shadows of the first couple of weeks are giving way to more hopeful prospects. With the effect of steroids and radiation receding into the past, I am getting stronger and better able to function, to include climbing upstairs and doing other things for myself.

Of course, we still have many questions – what kind of sarcoma do I have? Has the T6 vertebrae tumor responded to radiation treatments? Have my lung tumors grown? What will be my chemo protocol?

So... we continue to wait, but with patience and an awareness that even when there are more questions than answers, there are also many things that bring joy to my life rather than deplete it. And I am just fine with that!

TUESDAY, APRIL 30, 2013

IS THIS MY RETIREMENT?

For the last couple of years, a subject that has increasingly occupied Peter's and my conversations has been retirement. It has long been our plan that once Ian graduated from high school in 2015, we would assess where we were financially and determine whether we were ready to take the big step toward this next phase of our lives. We have both worked hard for almost 40 years, and the prospect of spending leisurely time together sounded wonderful.

One of the on-going discussions we would have is: to where would we retire? This would involve both a practical response and one straight from the heart. Peter – ever the financial pragmatist – would focus first on tax-free New Hampshire. Yes, but it is cold in New Hampshire, I would counter – figure on at least 10 degrees less than Massachusetts.

Okay, then – if it's warm we want, what about Florida? With the housing bust down there, we could pick up a condo right now for a really good price. But... we're just not that crazy about Florida.

What about North or South Carolina instead? We had fun on our trips to the Outer Banks, Myrtle Beach, and Charleston – but they were not where we wanted to settle down.

And so, Peter and I would always circle back to the place where we knew in our hearts we would end up: Cape Cod. We both spent every summer of our childhood there (he in Chatham, I in Harwich Port), and it *was* like home to us, a special place where we knew we would be happy. And we had it all figured out: once Ian was off at college and the time was right for us to sell our Foxboro home, we would buy a Cape house that we could rent out during the summer (and bring in some extra cash). We would spend the summer in our camper, either traveling or parked in a campsite.

It sounded like a plan.

But of course, all plans are off these days. And I am wondering if what I am experiencing right now is, in fact, my "retirement."

I had envisioned walks on the beach, exploring the nooks and crannies of the coast in a little motor boat, and evenings spent on a screened porch with a good book and cool ocean breezes. And while these are all things I still hope to experience, suddenly they are not nearly as important to me as they once were.

I will be happy no matter where I am – as long as I am *alive.*

WEDNESDAY, MAY 1, 2013

STILL NO ANSWERS

Unique. Distinctive. Matchless. Rare.

Under different circumstances, I suppose I would be happy – perhaps even honored – if any of these words were attached to me.

But not now, as the doctors still try to figure out what kind of cancer I have and how to treat it.

Today began inauspiciously at 2:30 a.m.; while making a visit to the bathroom, I heard my cat Matthew meowing from behind the door to the basement. Somehow, he had snuck down there during the day and had been trapped after we unwittingly closed the door. As I made my way over to the cellar door, one foot slid this way, and the other slid that way, and I found myself in a heap on the floor. I hadn't just fallen – I had badly twisted my left knee. Yeeeoooow! I called and called for Peter, and when he finally heard me, he came bolting downstairs to rescue me. Thank heaven there is no video of my skinny Peter trying to lift my ample girth off the floor – but he did it, bless his heart!

The knee injury has at least temporarily put the kibosh on my daily trip upstairs to bathe. Fortunately, my Dad's suite on the first floor comes complete with a handicap-accessible shower, which he is graciously letting me use.

I am, however, going to start using a walker; I just cannot have any more falls.

Then this afternoon, we went back to Dana-Farber. First on the schedule: an x-ray of my knee. Fortunately, nothing is broken; it is just badly twisted. Then blood work and another visit to my sarcoma specialist.

He wants a completely new biopsy of my vertebrae. The one from early April did not yield a lot of information, certainly not enough to determine the kind of sarcoma I have. In fact, it showed "no overt features of malignancy," although he still believes that there is cancer in my spine.

So... I will be going to Brigham and Women's next week for the entire day to have some of my multiple bilateral pulmonary lesions biopsied. They are unchanged from a month ago, so they are not – as my doctor puts it – "galloping away," which of course is good news. My Dana-Farber doctor believes the lung tumors will give better answers regarding my kind of cancer than did the vertebrae tumor. He says mine is not a "typical presentation" of cancer (there's my uniqueness again). I must say, I am getting a little anxious that it is taking so long to identify the kind of sarcoma I have. My feeling is once it can be named, then it can be dealt with, because it's hard to visualize an enemy that cannot be defined.

THURSDAY, MAY 2, 2013

CHOOSE JOY!

You may have heard about the couple in Florida who are building a 90,000 square foot house – yes, *90,000* square feet.

I try not to judge people whose lifestyles and decisions are different than my own, but when I see people putting an overly high priority on things like money, possessions, power, and looks, I do ask this question: they may think they're happy, but do they have joy?

Joy and happiness are completely different things, and I believe most of us think happiness is what we should strive for. After all, "the pursuit of happiness" is one of our inalienable American rights.

But happiness is also fleeting, because it is a temporary reaction to immediate circumstances.

Joy, on the other hand, is having our deepest needs met. Joy is not dependent on external circumstances, but is grounded in the eternal. Joy is deeper and richer than happiness, and it can endure both the triumphs and sorrows of life. It is joy, not happiness, that will fulfill our longings, and joy – true joy – comes from God.

Here's an example.

Back in 1982, when my husband Darcy died of cancer, I was bereft. The center of my universe was gone. My life seemed to have no purpose or direction; I was at emotional loose ends. And I was desperately lonely and unhappy. More accurately, I was clinically depressed, and when I thought of my future, all I saw was a black abyss. At that point in my life, I had no relationship with God – I did not even know what "joy" was – and my own internal resources were not enough to pull me out of the pits. Fortunately, with the help of therapy, anti-depressants, and the grace of God, I was able to work through my grief and move forward with my life.

By 1997, when my husband John died, I *did* have a relationship with God. Moreover, I was in seminary and on my way to becoming an ordained pastor. It was heartbreaking and devastating to lose John. I was desperately unhappy. But I had joy – a joy that came from my relationship with God, a joy that filled my heart despite my circumstances, a joy that made me hopeful and excited about my future and put me on the path toward building a new life.

So, what about now? Am I happy?

Actually, I am not unhappy at all. All the things that used to seem important have quickly fallen away.

I could be upset at the shocking change in my looks, but I'm not; it's still me inside, despite the bloated face that stares back at me in the mirror.

I could focus only on how my life expectancy has suddenly been cut by decades. But who wants to focus on death when there's so much living to do?

I could bemoan the fact that I am just a shadow of the person I was a month ago – my mobility, brain function, and energy have all been compromised. But I can still walk, and get around, and visit with people, and go places, and do a lot of the things that make life worthwhile.

I could feel sorry for myself. But that is the last thing I am doing. I do not know why I had to get cancer, but it just gives me an opportunity to show cancer it chose the wrong person to mess with!

But more important than being happy, I am filled with joy – a joy that comes straight from God, who has planted it in my soul and will never take it from me, no matter what.

"From Happiness to Joy"
A Sermon Preached by Rev. Jean Niven Lenk
Sunday, September 20, 2009
Text: Habakkuk 3:17-19; John 15:9-11; 16:2-22

I received in my email this past week an invitation from the UMass Amherst Alumni Association to attend a breakfast to meet the authors of the book *Happy at Work, Happy at Home*, which is described as a step-by-step guidebook for working mothers on how to "have it all."

This new book is one of thousands on the market giving us advice on how to be happy. Here is a sampling of what is available on Amazon.com. There's *You Can Be Happy No Matter What*, and *Be Happy Without Being Perfect: How to Worry Less and Enjoy Life More*, and *The 100 Simple Secrets of Happy People: What Scientists Have Learned and What You Can Use*, and also *Be Happy: Release the Power of Happiness in YOU!* In fact, there are almost 700,000 books listed on Amazon with the word "happy" in the title. Selling happiness is clearly big business.

So I invite you to consider for moment... what do you need to be happy? What is the one thing you lack that if you had just a little more of it, your life would be a whole lot happier? Maybe it's money... or friends... or time.

Our nation's forefathers guaranteed in our Constitution the inalienable right to pursue happiness, and advertisers remind us every day of all the things we lack and still need to purchase in that pursuit. They want us to think that we can satisfy the yearning in our hearts with a fancier car or a bigger house or the latest hi-tech gizmo. And we have been conditioned by our culture to believe that possessions, beauty, success, power, and money will bring us the happiness we crave.

But the painful truth of experience is that happiness is fleeting. It is a temporary reaction to immediate circumstances. The word "happiness" comes from the Middle English word for luck or chance – as in *hap*hazard or *hap*penstance. Happiness comes from external circumstances, coming and going with whatever is happening in our environment. Yes, it can be exciting to bring home something new and put it on or try it out or chow it down. Something new, something fun, something delicious may make us happy for a while, but that happiness will not last, because happiness is about meeting our surface needs, not our yearnings inside; happiness will not fill the God-shaped hole in our hearts.

What I believe we really crave is not happiness, but joy. Joy is having our deepest needs met. Joy is not dependent on external circumstances but is grounded in the eternal. Joy is deeper and richer than happiness, and it can endure both the triumphs and sorrows of life. It is joy, not happiness, that will fulfill our longings. And joy, true joy, comes from God and from being in right relationship with God, who plants it deep within our innermost beings.

Unfortunately, the word "joy" has been misused and its meaning distorted over the years. It may have begun with *The Joy of Cooking*, a wonderful cookbook I have had on my kitchen shelf for decades. Then came *The Joy of Sex* (which, by the way, I don't have), followed by *The Joy of Vegan Baking* and (I'm not making this up!) *The Joy of Pickling: 250 Flavor-Packed Recipes for Vegetables and More from Garden or Market.*

With the word "joy" being used in so many different ways, the meaning of the word has been twisted into a synonym for "happiness." But

Jesus did not come to make us happy. He came to fill our lives with real and lasting joy.

In this morning's Gospel reading, Jesus tells his disciples, "I have said these things, that my joy may be in you, and that your joy may be complete."[44]

Jesus spoke those words to his disciples on their last night together. While they were gathered in an upper room in Jerusalem celebrating the Passover feast, just before he was betrayed and arrested, just before he was condemned to die and nailed to a cross, Jesus talked with his disciples about joy. He knew that their time together was almost over, and he knew that they would feel lost without him. So in his farewell speech, Jesus said to his disciples, "So you have pain now; but I will see you again and your hearts will rejoice, and no one will take your joy from you."[45]

Jesus did not tell his disciples that they would have joy in their lives because everything was going to fall into place for them. He did not promise them that joy would come with prosperity or health or popularity or success. He did not say that joy would ward off pain, suffering, loss, or death.

Jesus said, "If you keep my commandments, you will abide in my love, just as I have kept my Father's commandments and abide in his love. I have said these things to you so that my joy may be in you, and that your joy may be complete."[46]

Joy does not come when all the circumstances in our lives work out in our favor. Joy comes when the love of God dwells at the center of our lives.

In the book *The Disciple's Joy* by Michael Foss, there is a beautiful story about a couple named Walt and Marsha.[47] Marsha had once been actively involved in her church but was now disabled and bedridden. As she lay asleep on the couch, her husband said to his pastor, "Isn't she beautiful?... When I look at her, I see the young woman I married." When Marsha awoke from her nap, her eyes turned to the pastor, who could see, too, that Marsha was indeed beautiful. "Joy is a deep well that can refresh us in the driest desert," writes Foss. "Walt and Marsha shared that joy. Even as they shared in her pain, their joy was transparent." Foss goes on to write that when Marsha died shortly thereafter, Walt's heart was broken. He was not happy. But he had joy. He and Marsha had shared a deep joy in spite of their circumstances. "Their joy transformed their suffering into moments that transcended the pain and affirmed all the pleasure, happiness and achievements they had experienced and shared for years." And that kind of joy can only come from having a relationship with God.

That is why Jesus promises his disciples – and us – joy, even in the midst of loss, sorrow, and death. And that is why Habakkuk, in this morning's Old Testament lesson, speaks of joy in this paradoxical manner: "Though the fig tree does not blossom and no fruit is on the vines; though the produce of the olive fails and the fields yield no food; though the flock is cut off from the fold, and there is no herd in the stalls, yet I will rejoice in the Lord."[48]

Joy does not rely on good times or the absence of sorrow and pain; it is not dependent on health, wealth, comfort, or general well-being. Joy is a divine gift which endures in the face of adverse circumstances. Joy persists in spite of the negative happenstances of daily living. Joy is rooted, grounded, and cemented in our unmovable, unshakeable, and constant God, and joy comes from having faith in and being in right relationship with God.

And how can we develop that faith and nurture our relationship with God? By doing the same things that have shaped the lives of faithful people since the day Jesus called the first disciples. Joy comes by being attentive to God every day in prayer; by keeping Sabbath time and re-orienting our lives to God every week in worship; by growing in our knowledge of God's purposes by reading and reflecting on scripture every day. Joy comes by using our God-given gifts and talents to serve the needs of others, by nurturing one another in caring relationships that build authentic Christian community, and by living generous lives of regular, intentional, substantial and committed giving.

Jesus did not come to make us happy. He came to fill our lives with real and lasting joy, and he promises that our joy will be complete whenever we allow the love of God to dwell at the center of our lives. May we open our hearts, let the love of God in, and live in joy. Amen.

FRIDAY, MAY 3, 2013

GRACIOUS RECEIVING

My next biopsy has been scheduled for Monday, May 13 at 7 a.m. at Brigham and Women's. The doctors will get tissue samples from my lung tumors, which we hope will hold enough information to determine exactly what kind of sarcoma I have.

I have mentioned several times in my postings how humbled I have been by the outpouring of love that has come my way since my diagnosis. Not just humbled but completely overwhelmed, too. I had no idea how many people I had connected with over my 59 years on earth, and they have reached out to me over the past month with not only love, but also prayers, support, visits, and tangible gifts. I have also heard from parents, siblings, cousins, neighbors, and friends of friends who have shared my situation. I have an incredible web of prayerful support encircling Planet Earth!

It is indeed humbling and overwhelming. I have never been comfortable being on the receiving end of such thoughtfulness. On my birthday and at Christmas, I blush and squirm with discomfort when opening my presents. I hate the attention.

But I love giving to others – whether it is a present, or a card, or a prayer shawl, or just my time. Being a pastor is a giving vocation, and it's what I do. Likewise being a mother, and a caregiver for elderly parents, and a wife – it's about serving and giving to others.

During my years as a pastor, there have been people who have willingly received my outreach and support with serenity, grace and gratitude. But there have also been people who were reluctant to do so – who became sheepish, uncomfortable, embarrassed, sometimes even indignant to be put into a "receiver" role.

Perhaps that's because a receiver is in a position of vulnerability and weakness. Being a receiver requires acknowledging to the giver, "You have something that I need."[49] The giver, on the other hand, stays in control and may even feel a little superior – stronger, healthier, more capable.

These days, rather than being a giver, I am the receiver. Because I *am* vulnerable and weak and needy now. I am in a position of needing assistance from others, whether it is a hand to get me up on my feet, a wheelchair to get around Dana-Farber, or the medical expertise of a whole host of health care professionals to prolong my life.

And rather than fight that reality, I have no choice but to give in to it. This is my life now. And the best thing I can do is to accept all the help, all the love, all the prayers, all the support with a gracious and receiving spirit, and with gratitude from the bottom of my heart.

SATURDAY, MAY 4, 2013

INVALID

Yesterday, Peter was gone all day working with his friend Tom on a cabinet installation. After taking a month off from his business, it is important that he get back into some kind of work routine. Not only is it good for his psyche to be actively engaged in something other than my illness, but we also need the income. Medical bills have started to come in, and the cost of treating cancer is shocking, even with good insurance; each of my 15 radiation treatments cost $400, and we're on the hook for 20%.

So, yesterday it was just my Dad and me at home. We really make quite a pair. He's almost 93 and while remarkably healthy for his age, he needs a walker to navigate safely around the house. Then there's me, who is not healthy, and since twisting my knee the other night, I've started using a walker, too.

After enjoying the visits of several friends, I made myself a little salad mid-afternoon. I was walking slowly back toward the living room with the bowl in my hand, and before I knew what was happening, it had slipped out of my clutch and landed on the dining room floor. The bowl smashed into pieces, and the lettuce, vegetables, and Bleu Cheese dressing were in a pile on the rug. I looked down at the mess and felt like crying – not just because I would not be enjoying my beautiful salad, but even more so because now I had to figure out how to clean it up before our Sheltie Scooter discovered it.

My Dad, ever gallant, said, "Let me clean it up. You go sit down." There was no way I was going to let my Dad get down on all fours, but we worked together. I eased myself down onto the floor while Dad got the wastebasket and paper towels. My knee throbbed, but I had no choice. It took a while, but I managed to get everything cleaned up off the floor.

And then it was time to get myself back on my feet. The task felt impossible. The radiation treatments and steroids have left my legs very weak, especially the muscles which enable me to stand up. Dad held his walker steady, and I tried to pull myself up, but I could not get a purchase. Then Dad braced his arm against the counter so I could grab on and pull myself up. Fifty plus years ago, there were plenty of times that my Dad put out his strong and loving arms to hold his little girl, to carry me, guide me, lift me up. And while he no longer has that kind of strength, somehow his arm held while I arduously pulled myself up and got back on my feet.

Under different circumstances, I might have been able to find some humor in this whole situation. But this time I couldn't; it just seemed all so pathetic. And when I was finally standing upright, I began to weep – both with relief and also at my diminished capabilities.

There is a politically incorrect word to describe me: invalid (from the Latin word *invalidus*, meaning "weak"). An invalid is a person who is too sick or weak to care for himself or herself. And that's me. I feel especially vulnerable when it is just Dad and me, because the fact of the matter is, together we really do not add up to one person capable of functioning on our own. Anything can happen – a fall, a spill, whatever – that is beyond our ability to cope.

And that word invalid – it also means not valid. Not having force or authority. I feel like that, too. And I think it is an unfortunate fact of life that the sick and weak of society are often seen as less than full human beings – it is easy to dismiss or overlook us. I can understand how sick people are seen as a drag; it is so much more pleasant to avoid us and stick with the strong, healthy, and capable.

That is my pathetic tale from yesterday. But now I am ready to wrap up this pity party and move into this beautiful new day.

Lizzy is hosting a cookout here at the house later this afternoon; it will be great having young people around and seeing some of her friends from elementary school. My stepdaughter Beryl is back from six months in Steamboat Springs, CO; she visited last evening and will be coming back for the party. Peter is puttering around the house. Ian is off at a track meet. Ever faithful Dad is in the parlor with me, sitting in his wingback chair reading the paper. And with all these people around, I am feeling less the vulnerable, inVALid INvalid and more the full and worthy human being I am, despite my illness.

SUNDAY, MAY 5, 2013

DO-IT-YOURSELF CHURCH

It is Sunday again. And today marks my fifth consecutive Sunday of *not* being the pastor, the worship leader, the preacher. My fifth consecutive Sunday of not going to worship.

This after 14 years, two months of being a pastor and of Sunday worship being the focal point of my week. I counted it up – that is over 700 Sundays. Add in another eight years of faithful worship-going as a lay person, and we are talking about more than 1,000 Sundays of worship over the past twenty-plus years.

The past four Sundays I was pretty much down and out due to radiation and steroids, but today I wanted church. I am not nearly ready to venture out to attend worship yet. But now that I am finally off those 'roids and regaining more energy every day, I felt up to a little "do-it-yourself" church.

So at 10 a.m., when worship began at the First Congregational Church of Stoughton, I pulled up the worship bulletin (which I put together months ago) on my computer. I imagined people arriving at the church and greeting one another. I envisioned the sanctuary, Christopher at the organ, the choir up on the chancel, Student Pastor Diane (on her last day) leading worship.

I went on YouTube.com and found the Taize chant "Glory to God," and played it, imagining the congregation singing it as the introit.

I said a prayer of invocation, and then played a YouTube version of "Glorious Things of Thee Are Spoken" for my opening hymn, the same as at church.

Then a prayer of confession, and into a YouTube "One Bread, One Body" as the prelude to communion. Even without partaking of communion itself, I felt transported (as always) by "One Bread, One Body" to what the Celts call a "thin place" – where the veil that separates heaven and earth is lifted and one is able to receive a glimpse of the glory of God.

I said a prayer of thanksgiving and the Lord's Prayer, and then YouTube again for "Give Thanks," which the congregation would be singing at the conclusion of communion.

I prayed to receive the message God wanted me to learn from today's scripture lesson, which was the story of Jonah and the Big Fish. (This year we introduced "Bible Top 40," and between Homecoming

Sunday last September and Father's Day next month, we are looking at the 40 most well-known Bible stories.) I read the book of Jonah in the bible, and then I pulled up one of my old Jonah sermons and re-read it.

YouTube serenaded me with the Hymn of Reflection "Come Down, O Love Divine," and then for the prayer time, I used prayer beads to help center me. My prayer today on each of the 33 beads: "Heal me, Lord."

I even played a YouTube "Three Fold Amen," to conclude the prayer time. Then "Open My Eyes That I May See," for a closing hymn, and "God Be with You Till We Meet Again" for the benediction response.

I added two more hymns: "Lord Have Mercy" by Michael W. Smith (which also gets me to that "thin place") as well as "He Leadeth Me," which my Wellesley High School classmate Bob (also a UCC Pastor) told me last night he would be using in the worship service he was leading this morning and thought was especially appropriate for me.

So, how was my "do-it-yourself" church? Did I feel a connection to God? To the congregation ten miles away? Was I just going through the motions, or was I able to feel the Holy Spirit's presence? While Jesus promised to be present whenever "two or three" were gathered in his name, would just little old me be sufficient?

I was completely unprepared for my reaction to my little worship service: I wept throughout. Really wept. Wept through the prayers, through the hymns, through it all. Wept in a disintegrate-the-kleenex, in an obliterate-the-mascara kind of way.

It was so healing, so cleansing. And my weeping meant that I was really opening myself up to God. I have often found my eyes welling up with tears during worship, especially when I pray. These tears result from the very intimate connection I feel with God, and such emotional closeness can occur only when we open ourselves up and allow ourselves to be vulnerable. I have found myself at times wanting to avoid deep prayer, because I know where the journey will lead – down through the protective layers of time and denial and rationalization, to the place where my deepest pains and losses and brokenness dwell, uncovered and raw. I am renewed and comforted and energized by prayer – but it can be frightening to open up and become so exposed.

I think this is a struggle that many of us go through: deeply desiring connectedness, whether with God or another individual or with a community, and yet simultaneously fearing it – fearing the vulnerability necessary for such intimacy to occur. Such intimacy requires trust; we must be willing to lower our defenses – enough to open ourselves to being touched by a Power greater than ourselves.

As a cancer patient, I am indeed vulnerable in so many ways – physically, emotionally, mentally, certainly – but spiritually, too. Even as a pastor, I have wondered over these past five weeks if my diagnosis would change my relationship with God, would cause me to question God's goodness and love, would cause me to become angry at God.

But today, I was reassured that my faith holds strong, despite everything, and God continues to hold me tenderly, providing strength in my weakness, and lifting my spirits in the face of my illness.

It was a good day to "go" to church, even in my little congregation of one. Because the God who loves all of us unconditionally and eternally, the God who will never forsake us, was with me, as God always is and will continue to be.

"Life's Not Fair – and Neither Is God"
A Sermon Preached by Rev. Jean Niven Lenk
Sunday, September 18, 2011
Texts: Jonah 4:6-11; Matthew 20:1-16

By now, most young people have begun another school year in which they will be learning all the things they need to know about life. Well, maybe not *all* the things. According to one education reformer,[50] there are lots of important aspects of life that kids do not learn in school but should, and not all of them have to do with academics. Here is a sampling of some rules about life that kids won't learn school; maybe some of us parents have actually said these things to our children.

Rule #14: Enjoy this [time of your life] while you can. Sure parents are a pain, school's a bother, and life is depressing. But someday you'll realize how wonderful it was to be a kid.

Rule #4: If you think your teacher is tough, wait 'til you get a boss.

Rule #1: Life is not fair. Get used to it.

I am sure that at some point in our lives, we have all cried, "It's not fair!" And while we may think of those words as a child's lament, fairness – or lack of it – remains a critical issue for adults, too. In fact, studies[51] show that it is human nature for us to bristle when we think we have gotten the short end of the stick, especially when it happens in the workplace.

If you have ever had a boss who was less capable than you were, or discovered that a person with less experience was making more money, or if you have ever been passed over for promotion in favor of someone who was less qualified, then you know the feeling. It just isn't fair.

And that is the reaction of the laborers in the vineyards in Jesus' parable. The landowner promises the workers who go out early in the morning a day's pay. To those who go out later in the morning, the landowner promises to pay "whatever is right."[52] There are also laborers who go out at noon and work half the day, and some who go out at three and work the half the afternoon. And then there are laborers who go out at 5:00, and they only work an hour.

Now, our sense of fairness would say that the ones who worked the most hours would earn the most money. But in the parable, at the end of the day, each of the laborers is given a full day's pay, even the ones who started working at five o'clock. The first ones hired protest when they receive the agreed-upon wage, complaining not because they have been cheated – they haven't; rather, they grumble because of the landowner's generosity towards the late-comers, who worked a mere hour. The late-comers have hardly broken a sweat, but they too receive a full day's wage. And the landowner does not improve matters when he responds, "Don't I have the right to do what I want with my own money? Or are you envious because I am generous?"[53]

We can certainly understand why those first-hired workers protest, because this parable challenges our sense of justice and turns upside down the notions of fairness and reward we have learned from childhood – that we are to work for what we get and get what we work for. But this is not a parable about fair wages or a lesson on workplace relationships. This parable is about God's grace, and the landowner, representing God, pays the laborers based not on *their* efforts but rather on *his* generosity.

In our Old Testament lesson this morning, Jonah is also angered by God's generosity. Following God's orders, Jonah has gone to the sinful people of Nineveh and told them God wants them to repent of their sins.

Jonah is actually looking forward to God giving the Ninevites what – in Jonah's mind – they deserve for their sinful actions. But instead, God forgives them and gives them a fresh start. Jonah is jealous that God has forgiven the Ninevites; it offends his sense of fairness, so he yells at God and stomps off in a tizzy, planting himself out in the middle of nowhere to pout. But even though Jonah is disappointed and jealous and angry at God, does God turn away from him? No, God provides a bush to shelter Jonah from the sun; but then Jonah takes the great sheltering bush for granted. And when God takes the bush away, Jonah starts complaining again.

Finally God tells him, in effect, *Jonah, you only knew the shelter of the bush for a day and a night. I have known the people of Nineveh since I created them. You didn't create the bush. But I created the people. I choose to love all people.*

This is our God, who lavishes upon us grace – the unmerited, utterly unconditional, completely free, no-strings-attached, cannot-be-earned gift of God's love and favor.

In so many other faith traditions, people have to do something to earn God's approval. Whether it is using a prayer wheel, or going on pilgrimages, or giving alms to the poor, or avoiding certain foods, or performing a certain number of good deeds, or praying at a certain time in a certain position each day, or going through a cycle of reincarnations – follow this way of life, these traditions say, and you stand a good chance of gaining favor with God and eventually achieving salvation.

But this morning's scripture lessons show us that God's love is for everyone; we cannot earn it, and we do not deserve it. We can spurn it; we can try to run from it; we can hold it at arm's length; we can even try to kill it. But God loves us, no matter what.

And that makes grace a concept that is radical, counter-cultural, and for some even offensive. Because grace throws out our measurements of fairness, our understanding of a meritocracy where we earn things – including God's favor – based on our achievements. Our world might be pretty clear on who's deserving and who isn't, who belongs and who doesn't, who's up and who's down, who's our equal and who isn't. But that's not the way it is in God's world.

God loves all people – the good ones, the bad ones, even the ones who don't love God back. It just doesn't seem fair. And you know what? It isn't.

God isn't fair, because God is a God of grace.

God loves the happy and the angry; the generous and the jealous; the do-gooders and the no-gooders. God loves those we love, and God loves those we have a hard time loving. God forgives and frees us from our mistakes of the past, enabling us to start over and over and over again. There is no sinner, no outcast, no unworthy person, *no one* who falls beyond the reach of God's gracious love. There is nothing we can do to make God love us more, and there is nothing we can do that will make God love us less.

In spite of our anger, jealousy, or disappointment with the way life may treat us and those we love; in spite of our blunderings, our many frailties, flaws and faults; in spite of what we do or fail to do to deserve it; *in spite of everything*, God continues to bless us with infinite, unconditional, and boundless love.

The fact of the matter is: God is not fair! Rather, God is generous and gracious. From the most enterprising to the least motivated; from the saint to the scoundrel; from the one who has worked long and hard in the vineyard of the Lord to the one who shows up just in time to help put the tools away – we are all offered the same grace-filled compassion and generosity.

Is life fair? No, it isn't, and in response we may protest, grumble and complain.

Is God fair? No again, and in response, may we simply say, "Thanks be to God!" Amen.

TUESDAY, MAY 7, 2013

FAITH/DOUBT

One question that a few have asked me – and perhaps many more have wanted to ask – is, "Are you afraid?" Actually, the second part of that question is left unstated; what people really want to know is, "Are you afraid *of dying*?"

I can answer that question with a clear, unambiguous, unequivocal NO! I certainly do not want to leave this earthly life, but I am absolutely not afraid of dying.

At least that is the way I feel today. The Dana-Farber doctors do not even know what kind of cancer I have, much less how to treat it. My lung tumors have not grown in the past month, and radiation has shrunk my vertebrae tumor. I have every reason at this point to think that I can beat this cancer – or at least beat it *back* – and stretch the amount of time I have on earth. And frankly, I spend very little of my time thinking about dying; as I have said before, thinking about dying is no way to live.

But that's today. I do not know how I will be feeling down the road if the doctors determine I have an aggressive or difficult-to-treat kind of cancer; or if the tumors start growing faster than can be treated; or if the chemo does not work; or if... if... if...

Perhaps if I start to slip toward the inevitable reality of death, I will be afraid.

On the other hand, maybe my absolute confidence in something beyond will prevail, bringing me peace and serenity as I walk through the valley of the shadow. I guess that is faith.

And faith is something people expect me to have. After all, I am a pastor. I have dedicated my life to God. I have spent the better part of the last two decades helping others develop life-transforming relationships with Christ.

I guess I had better have faith! But it took decades for my faith to develop.

The 20-year hiatus I took from organized religion proved to be essential to my faith journey, because during that time, I re-formed my theology belief by belief, and I made my faith my own as it was shaped and molded by real life.

The first "aha" moment I experienced was at Darcy's wake. As I stood by his casket and looked at his body, I knew instantly – deep in my heart and with an absolute certainty – that I was viewing only his earth suit; the essence that made Darcy who he was, his spirit, was now abiding with God in heaven.

Then, several years after Darcy's death, I felt the healing touch of God, who brought me out of a deep depression and made me not just want to live again, but blessed my life in ways I could never have imagined or hoped for – with a new marriage and two beautiful children. In other words, resurrection was not just something that happened to Jesus; I myself had experienced it in a tangible and authentic way. Hope out of hopelessness; joy out of heartache; new life out of death.

It was through these life experiences that I was able to forge a genuine and unwavering faith out of doubt, even unbelief.

But... what if sometime in the future, doubt starts to nibble at the perimeters of my brain? What if fear gains a toehold and finds a way deep into my heart? What if there comes a time when God seems absent to me? How can I face my illness – even death – if I do not have faith, if I cannot feel God?

Many seeking union with God have experienced darkness and struggles, from St. Augustine to St. Francis of Assisi to Mother Teresa. In scripture, Moses, Elijah, Job, and David all had crises of faith, praying to die or asking God *Where are you?* Jesus himself, as he was dying on the cross, felt abandoned by God: "My God, my God, why have you forsaken me?"[54]

And many more have been afraid. From the first time God speaks to Abraham in Genesis[55] to the final words of the risen Christ in the book of Revelation,[56] God says "Do not be afraid." The greatest figures of the Bible – Isaac,[57] Jacob,[58] Moses,[59] Joshua,[60] Elijah,[61] Jeremiah,[62] Daniel,[63] Zechariah,[64] Mary,[65] Joseph,[66] the disciples,[67] the apostle Paul[68] – are each, at one time or another, fearful. And God responds, "Do not be anxious,"[69] "Peace be with you,"[70] "I have heard you,"[71] "I will help you,"[72] "For I am with you."[73]

And I believe – truly believe – that God's words are meant for me, too – that I need not be afraid or anxious, whatever the future holds, for

God will be with me, upholding me, strengthening me, and bringing me peace.

FRIDAY, MAY 10, 2013

THROUGH THE VALLEY

A Sunday school teacher decided to have her young class members memorize one of the most quoted scriptures in the bible – the 23rd Psalm. She gave the youngsters a month to learn its six verses.

Little Ricky was excited about the task – but he just could not remember the Psalm. After much practice, he could barely get past the first line. On the day the children were scheduled to recite the 23rd Psalm in front of the congregation, Ricky was nervous but ready. When it was his turn, he stepped up to the microphone and said proudly, "The Lord is my shepherd – and that's all I need to know."

What a nice story. I used it in a sermon a few years ago.

It is interesting to go back over my old sermons and read them through the lens of Stage IV cancer. It is a kind of reality check. It seems that in so many of my past sermons, I have dropped phrases like "devastating diagnosis" and "terminal illness." Now those phrases have taken on new significance because they pertain to me.

If there is one scripture I have read more than any other as a pastor, it is the 23rd Psalm. I have used it at every funeral I have ever conducted, inviting the assembled mourners to say it along with me (and call me old-fashioned, but I have always used the King James Version).

The one line I quote most often from this beloved psalm is "walk[ing] through the valley of the shadow."[74] It's not just the valley of the shadow of death we might walk through; it could be the shadow of heartache, of loss, of failure, of regret, of estrangement. And what I say is that the valley may be a place of dread, but it is not a place of defeat; we walk *through* the valley, not into it, for God will be with us and lead us to healing, wholeness, and new life on the other side.

I think it is a good image and a good message – at least I used to. And the question I am asking myself now is: do I believe this? Do I truly believe that God is with me, at my side, as I walk through this valley called Stage IV cancer?

I will admit that, even as I have gained physical strength over the past couple of weeks, I have been on a bit of an emotional roller coaster. It is disconcerting that doctors at the finest hospitals have yet to figure out what kind of cancer I have. Which means I am in a holding pattern. Which means that chemo cannot begin. Which means that right now, nothing is being done to fight the cancer that is inside me. I will admit that the tears have come a little too easily the past couple of days.

I do not think this means I am feeling abandoned, forsaken, or deserted by God. Rather, I think serious illness, whatever it may be, can take an emotional toll on a person and all his/her loved ones – and that includes me. While I do truly believe God is with me, holding my hand and accompanying me as I spend time in this desolate valley, I am beginning to think that maybe it is not a straight path that we walk; it is not linear. Rather, it is two steps forward, one step backwards. It is both advancing and then retreating; progress and regress.

The Good News is that, even if my time in the valley seems prolonged, I am still walking *through* it and not into it. On the other side, we can be assured there is Light – otherwise, there could be no shadow. On the other side, I will find healing and wholeness and new life.

As I continue to walk *through* the valley, I know I am not alone, because God is there with me, and God will never leave my side. And that's all I need to know.

"All We Need to Know"

A Sermon Preached by Rev. Jean Niven Lenk

May 15, 2011

Text: Psalm 23, John 10:1-15

A Sunday school teacher decided to have her young class members memorize one of the most quoted scriptures in the bible – the 23rd Psalm. She gave the youngsters a month to learn its six verses.

Little Ricky was excited about the task – but he just could not remember the Psalm. After much practice, he could barely get past the first line. On the day the children were scheduled to recite the 23rd Psalm in front of the congregation, Ricky was nervous but ready. When it was his turn, he stepped up to the microphone and said proudly, "The Lord is my shepherd – and that's all I need to know."

Today the universal Christian church celebrates "Good Shepherd Sunday" with the reading of the 23rd Psalm, perhaps the most familiar and beloved verses in all of scripture. Nineteenth century Congregationalist clergyman Henry Ward Beecher called this the "nightingale" of the psalms, and indeed it has sung to the souls of people through the ages. Even those who don't know a thing about the bible have at least a passing familiarity with the musical cadences of the 23rd Psalm. We said together the King James Version today, and for most of us, the archaic "runneths" and "leadeths" and "maketh" spill onto our tongues so naturally and so easily that we could describe this text as one of the ties that binds us to each other, to our faith, and to God.

Not only are these the first verses of scripture many of us ever speak, but they are, for many, the last words we hear. I have recited them at countless bedsides, and I include the psalm at funeral and memorial services – inviting people to say it along with me, much as we did this morning – for it witnesses to God's guidance, encouragement, and life-long care. It is fitting this psalm accompanies us from the beginning of our lives until the end, because the words themselves speak of God's abiding presence with us.

"The Lord is my shepherd..."[75] My shepherd. My protector. My caregiver. The one who watches out for me. Many of us find comfort in the image of God as Shepherd, which can be found throughout the bible. In the New Testament, Jesus takes the title of shepherd for himself. In Luke [15:3-7], he speaks of the concerned shepherd who leaves his 99 sheep behind to go out looking for the one who is lost. In Mark's gospel [6:34], we are told that Jesus has compassion on the crowds because they are like sheep without a shepherd. And in today's Gospel reading from John, Jesus says, "I am the Good Shepherd. The good shepherd lays down his life for the sheep."[76] "I know my sheep and they know me..."[77]

The pastoral images of God as the shepherd who guides, protects, and provides for his sheep is at once engaging, encouraging and inspiring. We can, however, get overly sentimental about the serene image of Jesus in a flowing white robe holding a cuddly little lamb in his arms, and – to be honest – the childhood pictures we have of the Good Shepherd are sanitized and romanticized.

The reality is that, at the time of the writing of this Psalm, shepherds were marginalized people – needed but not always respected, for the work they had to do was dirty and often dangerous. The job required leading the flock to pasture, seeking strays before they fell victim to predators, and accounting for the well-being of the whole flock. The law was such that if a shepherd lost any of the sheep to wolves, thieves, or carelessness, the shepherd was personally responsible for replacing that which was lost.

It is easy to see why really good shepherds were in short supply in Palestine. It was neither an easy nor a glamorous job, and the sheep were completely dependent on the shepherd and on his sense of responsibility and love for the flock. Shepherds were even expected to become martyrs for the sake of their animals.

But the words of the 23rd Psalm touch us for other reasons, too.

We live in a world of uncertainty, a place of terrorism, a place where war can rage in the holiest of lands, where children can be unsafe even in a school. One wonders how we can recite and truly believe the words, "Yea, though I walk through valley of the shadow of death, I will fear no evil." The 23rd Psalm's image of green pastures and still waters live in tension with the pictures from the nightly news... images of suicide bombings, of shooting rampages, of kidnappings and brutal beheadings. It is not a simple melody, but rather a strangely dissonant song that we sing to God in this Psalm.

But the psalmist doesn't say that our world is without danger or trouble, nor does he say that we will be able to avoid the valley of the shadow in our lives. And that is why this Psalm undergirds our faith and stirs our souls. It is not a Psalm about comfort and ease, but a song of confidence, love, and faithful trust in the midst of the challenging, difficult, and terrifying places of life. Because difficulties will arise; danger is present; enemies are real; death will come. What the psalmist does proclaim is that we can live without fear because we can be assured that, through it all, God is with us – sheltering, leading, and providing for us.

A relationship with the shepherd will transform you, because when you know – truly know with every fiber of your being – that "thou art with me,"[78] then you can live your life differently. When "The Lord is my shepherd"[79] and your Shepherd, we can be assured that we will not be left in the valley alone. So powerful is the love of God that we no longer need fear danger, or enemies, or the realities of life; we need not fear even death. When we can say, "The Lord is my Shepherd,"[80] we can rest in the assurance that, no matter how far we stray from the flock, we will be sought after until we are found, rescued, and brought home.

The deepest needs of our life – the need for love, peace, joy, and comfort – can be met through a relationship with Christ. Know that the Good Shepherd is nearby. Know that he loves us. Know that he will come when we call to him in prayer, when we are frightened, or anxious, or in pain. Then we will be able to say with confidence and trust "The Lord is our shepherd. And that's all we need to know." Amen.

SUNDAY, MAY 12, 2013

WHAT A DIFFERENCE A YEAR MAKES

I remember well Mother's Day 2012. It was a beautiful spring day, and after church our combined families gathered at Joe's American Bar and Grill in Franklin. My mother – who favored plain, simple food – had selected the restaurant because she liked the menu. And it was a glorious gathering: not just my mom, but also Peter's mom, Connie; our children Tim, Lizzy, Beryl, and Ian; Peter's sister Susan, her husband

Charley, and their daughter Marisa. We had a great meal and a lovely time. I only wish I had savored those moments just a little bit more.

What a difference a year makes.

We never anticipated that my mom would not be here this year. Or that I would be so sick.

So Mother's Day 2013 has been decidedly different.

First, I have no mom to go visit, or to buy a card for, or to have Mother's Day dinner with. (Although, as I said in a previous post, if my mom were still here, my diagnosis would have devastated her, and I am so very very glad she is being spared all of this.)

Peter took off early this morning for a visit to his mom on the Cape.

Lizzy and Ian ordered Chinese take-out, did the food shopping, and folded laundry for me.

Tim and Beryl popped in to visit me and give me some sweet presents.

Yes, today has been a much different – but still precious – Mother's Day.

But I wish I had savored last year's Mother's Day celebration even more than I did.

But we did not know. Do we ever know?

And so we need to savor every precious moment.

Medical Update: My (second) biopsy is scheduled for 7 o'clock tomorrow (Monday) morning, at Brigham and Women's Hospital. The doctors will be sticking a needle into my lung tumors and hopefully extracting enough tissue to determine my primary cancer (the tumors in my lungs are not lung cancer; they are my primary cancer which has spread to the secondary location of my lungs). Mercifully, I will be under "conscious sedation," which means I will be able to respond to their commands about breathing ("hold your breath," "now breathe") but out of it enough so that I won't grab their arms in a panic as they try to stick that needle into me.

The doctor who called me Friday to answer my questions told me to expect to spend the entire day at B&W, since they need to watch me for several hours in recovery. He also told me to pack an overnight bag just in case my lung collapses during the procedure and I have to be admitted.

It will take 7-10 days for the B&W radiologists to analyze the tissue samples and come up with some answers. Then, hopefully, we will be able to commence with chemo.

TUESDAY, MAY 14, 2013

YESTERDAY

Hoooo-weeee, yesterday was a doozy! But the operative word of that statement is *yesterday* – we made it through, and today is a new day!

Yesterday, Peter and I got up early and were at Brigham and Women's at 6:30 a.m., a half hour early. We are both "better-an-hour-early-than-a-minute-late" kind of people, and since I have gotten sick, I particularly hate having to rush.

Anecdote: I knew Peter and I were perfect for one another when I arrived at his home to watch the 2004 Super "Wardrobe Malfunction" Bowl. It was only our second date (although we had first met at age three), and when I drove into his driveway at precisely 5:00 p.m., he opened the front door, looked at his watch, and declared, "Right on time!" A man who was not only punctual himself, but who also appreciated my punctuality!

Anyway, back to yesterday... Unfortunately, I had awoken with a wretched headache. I have been having them daily for almost two weeks, and they can sure put a damper on my day. I am a migraine sufferer and for years was on a wonderful medication called Amitriptyline which kept them in check. I found out too late they also cause weight gain – my doctor at the Mass. General Weight Center, where I was going for a while, said they were to blame for an extra 50 pounds. As soon as I heard that, I immediately went off that pill but have not yet found a good replacement. With no migraine preventative as I am going through my current treatments and stresses, it is no wonder I am headachey.

Every day, my headache has been a little different – over my eyes, back of my head, middle of my forehead. Yesterday's was at the base of my skull, and it was not helped by the fact that I could not eat after midnight. ("When did you last have something to eat or drink?" "11:58 p.m. – I had a cupcake and a glass of milk"!)

The biopsy took place in the Ambulatory Unit located down in the bowels of Brigham and Women's. I was taken into a pre-op room, changed into a johnny, and waited. Peter left at 7:30 a.m., and I tried to relax. The nurse gave me some Tylenol for my headache, and it seemed to help a smidgen. A doctor then came in and went over the procedure and risk factors, which included air leaks and a collapsed lung. I signed the consent form and was then wheeled into the operating room.

I would be lying on my stomach during the biopsy, and the doctor told me it was very important that I find a comfortable position because once things began, I would not be able to move for an hour (they even bound my arms with a large Velcro strap!). Let me tell you, it took a few pillows and a lot of shifting around to accommodate the zaftig attributes of this full figured gal, but I finally found my happy place, made all the more blissful when they started pumping the "conscious sedation" meds into my IV.

The procedure may have taken an hour, but it seemed like only five minutes to me. I never felt a needle going in and only remember being told to hold my breath a couple of times. (Gotta love those meds!)

Unfortunately, I did suffer one of the aforementioned complications: an air leak. The steroids that I was on for a month thin the lung's outer tissue, and it is common for the relatively large biopsy needle to cause an opening that does not immediately close upon removal.

After the biopsy, I was wheeled into another room where they took a chest x-ray to monitor the leak; then around 9:30 a.m. back to recovery where I alternated between napping and posting on Facebook (I was not allowed to talk because it could make the leak worse).

At 11:30 a.m., I was wheeled back to x-ray. It was hoped that the air leak would have sealed on its own and I could go home. No so fast. The leak was the same size, if not a little bigger. Another x-ray was scheduled for 12:30 p.m. By then, Peter had arrived to take me home, and I was getting hungry. My headache was also getting worse. But we waited.

The third x-ray showed that the leak had not gotten bigger, so the doctor felt comfortable letting me go home. (The air that has leaked into my chest cavity will dissipate in a few days.) I was given discharge instructions; among other things, I was to avoid for the next 24 hours three of my least favorite activities: housecleaning, vacuuming and flying!

First stop: Au Bon Pain in the B&W lobby. But the delicious chicken salad sandwich and Pepsi (I prefer Coke) did nothing for my headache, which had blossomed into a full-fledged migraine by the time we arrived home. I took my medicine of last resort: a very strong pain pill that usually makes me feel sick, stupid, and sleepy. But I was willing to suffer the side effects if it would vanquish my migraine. Peter darkened the parlor, Lizzy got me a cold compress, and Grandpa sat quietly in the chair next to me. The only noise was the hammering of the workmen who are replacing our roof.

I slept for an hour or so, but my headache was intractable. I then took a generic migraine relief pill, and it occurred to me that maybe one of its ingredients, caffeine, was the key to easing the pain. Since I do not drink coffee, I take a caffeine tablet every morning, but did not do so this morning since I was not supposed to eat. That is probably one of the reasons why I got the migraine in the first place. So I took a caffeine tablet and had a nice big Coke on ice, rested some more, and slowly the migraine portion of the headache faded away.

This morning, I saw my local oncologist. He is concerned enough about my headaches (yes, I woke up with another one today) that he has scheduled another brain scan for tomorrow; he thinks it unlikely that my cancer would have spread to my brain in the month since my last brain scan, but he wants to eliminate any doubt before moving on to other possibilities and treatments.

It will take about a week for the radiologists at Dana-Farber/B&W to come up with some results from yesterday's biopsy. We expect to see my Dana-Farber sarcoma specialist later next week, and hopefully we will finally learn the identity of my primary cancer. Then we can move to the next phase of treatment and conquer this enemy.

THURSDAY, MAY 16, 2013

AFTER EFFECTS

Yesterday...

I woke up per usual, but as the morning progressed, I just could not muster up the strength to get dressed. In fact, I went back to sleep for a couple of hours. It got to be 2 p.m., and I was still in my PJs (that *never* happens!). I wondered why sweat was pouring down my forehead... why my back hurt... why I was having trouble taking deep breaths... why I was feeling, in a word, crappy. I asked Peter to take my temp, and sure enough I had a slight fever.

Under normal circumstances, this would not be cause for alarm, but our circumstances are anything but normal. So Peter called my oncologist, and he told us to get down to the local hospital for a chest x-ray. I was scheduled for a brain scan there later in the day anyway, so off we went.

I had the chest x-ray, then blood work (I am beginning to feel like a pin cushion), and waited for the brain scan. When my name was called, a nurse brought me into the changing area to go over my medical history. As I began to recount the last seven weeks (got the diagnosis on March 29... cancer in my vertebrae, lungs, and thyroid... it's been almost seven weeks and the primary cancer still has not been identified...), I started to break down. It was just all so unbelievable.

The nurse started to comfort me as I sobbed and so did Peter, who was waiting outside in the hall and came in when he heard me crying.

I do like to think of myself as a brave person, and I am trying so hard to be strong and optimistic. But I am overwhelmed by how my life has changed so dramatically in such a short time. How could this have happened? Why? Is this just a nightmare from which I will wake up? Will life ever be "normal" again?

And although I hate to think of myself as a vain person, I guess I am, because looking in the mirror is particularly discouraging. It is not just my swollen face, huge double chin, and chipmunk cheeks; I now have a "buffalo hump" at the base of my neck from the steroids. Although I was not particularly happy with the way I looked before (that darn Amitriptyline!), I would give anything to look like that now – at least when I looked in the mirror, there was a "normal" person in the reflection, not the freak who now stares back at me.

The nurse then brought me into the brain scan room, and the machine was the dreaded tube! I have been so preoccupied lately – between Monday's biopsy, my constant headaches, and then feeling so lousy yesterday – that I had not given a thought to whether a brain scan was done with the "donut" machine or the tube, the latter being a nightmare for claustrophobes like me. But there it was, and it was too late to take a tranquilizer, so I had no choice but to screw up my courage and get in. Fortunately, for a brain scan, I only had to go in up to my shoulders. They offered me headphones to listen to music, which I accepted – anything to distract my thoughts (I just kept telling myself, "don't open your eyes, don't open your eyes..."). Unfortunately, between the rock 'n roll that blasted in my ears and the God-awful noises that emanated from the machine itself, I thought my already-aching head was going to fall off.

Twenty long minutes later, it was all over, and I finally got to go home.

I am feeling much better today – my temp is normal, my headache (yes I did wake up with another one) is in retreat, and I am back to my "new normal" (which means if I have enough energy to bathe and dress, I'm doing okay).

The chest x-ray did show that had a very slight lung collapse – but no pneumonia. The lung will heal itself, but I need to go back on Monday for another chest x-ray, when hopefully things will be back to (the new) normal. I just need to take it easy.

It will take a few days to hear about the brain scan, and of course we're waiting with bated breath for the results of Monday's biopsy – they will come in next week.

Patients need to be... patient!

SUNDAY, MAY 19, 2013

TRIP TO THE SPA

Shortly after I received my diagnosis, Lizzy asked me if there were some things that I really wanted to do – not so much a "Bucket List," but rather some fun activities that I could enjoy despite my illness, because she wanted to make them happen for me. Immediately I said, "I need a pedicure!" A facial would be nice, too.

So, yesterday was the day. Our appointments were for 10:30 a.m. at a spa just three blocks from the house. It sounds so simple – go to the spa, sit in a chair for an hour while a manicurist massages my feet and paints my toenails. Then walk to another room and lie on the bed for another hour while an aesthetician gives me a facial. Piece of cake, right? But I had to gear myself up for several days leading up this outing.

First, the very act of going out in public is physically challenging. I always have the option of taking my walker to steady me – but not all buildings are handicap accessible, which makes walkers more of a nuisance than a help.

If I leave the walker at home, however, I then have to be very careful walking. Many places – be they supermarkets, retail stores, or spas – are set up to be, above all, visually appealing; accessibility seems less a concern. I remember my petite little mom was constantly aggravated that the very item she wanted at the grocery store would always seem to be on the very top shelf, far above her reach, and she would have to enlist some nearby stranger to retrieve it for her.

The physical safety of sick, handicapped, or elderly customers seems to be way down on the priority list of most merchants. So I just have to fend for myself: walk slowly, hold on to the wall, watch out for inconveniently-placed furniture, always be alert to unexpected obstacles and safety hazards (not to mention, I am perfectly capable of falling on my own; I do not need help from external hindrances). And, if possible, hold on to someone's arm.

Then there's the emotional aspect to all of this. One look at me and you know something is not right. I am almost looking forward to getting chemo and going bald, because then people will say, "Ah – cancer!" The side effects of radiation and steroids are less well known, but can also play havoc with one's appearance.

I certainly do not think I need to explain to people why I look the way I do; but over the course of an hour-long conversation with a chatty aesthetician, there is an opportunity to bring it up. "So, is this a mother-daughter post-Mother's Day celebration?" "Well, yes, but also I haven't been able to get a pedicure since January because I was recently diagnosed with cancer..." It feels good to get it out in the open. I tend not to hold back these days, and I am all for naming the elephant in the room. It's not a sympathy grab by any means (Lord knows, I am receiving more than my share of sympathy). I think it is just less emotionally taxing to be forthright and frank than wary and guarded.

Lying on my back is uncomfortable due to my T6 tumor, so after my facial I had to ask for help to get into a sitting position. Then, the bed was so high I could not safely "jump" down, so I had to find a way to slide off (a move fraught with peril).

By the time I got home, I was aching and completely drained. I took something to knock out the pain and was essentially out of it for the rest of the day, but my hot pink toes and lovely smooth face made my trip to the spa totally worth it.

TUESDAY, MAY 21, 2013

FINALLY – A DIAGNOSIS!

1:00 P.M.

I see my sarcoma specialist at Dana-Farber later this afternoon. This is the day we are supposed to hear exactly what kind of sarcoma I have. It is difficult having to wait all day for answers, and both Peter and I have had to take tranks to keep our nerves in check. In the meantime, I have been imagining different scenarios of how the conversation could unfold. Here are some of the possibilities that have entered my mind.

Scenario #1 – The Miracle

"Well, Mrs. Lenk, I have amazing news for you. As a pastor and a woman of faith, you must have some special connection with the Big Guy, and all those prayers that I know your friends have been sending heavenward have obviously had an effect, because the radiologists found *no cancer cells* in your lung tissue! As you know, we found no overt features of malignancy in your vertebrae biopsy either. You'll remember that I told you I thought those results were a mistake because I saw systemic disease in multiple places; that is why we did the biopsy of the lung tissue. Well, I was wrong! No cancer in the vertebrae, and now no cancer in the lungs – those spots might just be a latent infection. And I have never really been worried about your thyroid, because things often show up there that aren't cancer. So – I have the most wonderful task of telling you that you don't have cancer after all! We're kicking you out as a patient of Dana-Farber, and we hope we never see you again in the thirty plus years we know you have left!"

Hmmmm... do I believe this is a possible scenario? Do I believe in miracles? The Gospel is full of miracle stories...

What about the Woman with the Hemorrhage? "Jesus turned and saw her. 'Take heart, daughter,' he said, 'your faith has healed you.' And the woman was healed at that moment."[81]

Or the Two Blind Men? "When he had gone indoors, the blind men came to him, and he asked them, 'Do you believe that I am able to do this?' 'Yes, Lord,' they replied. Then he touched their eyes and said, 'According to your faith let it be done to you'; and their sight was restored."[82]

Or the Canaanite Woman? "Then Jesus said to her, 'Woman, you have great faith! Your request is granted.' And her daughter was healed at that moment."[83]

Or Blind Bartimaeus? "'Go,' said Jesus, 'your faith has healed you.' Immediately he received his sight and followed Jesus along the road."[84]

In all of these scenarios, it is faith that heals these ill individuals. Perhaps these stories simply reflect a narrow world view in which the good get rewarded and the bad get punished, which was a first century understanding of the complicated process of affliction and healing. If you are ill, then it is your fault – your faith is lacking. If you are made well, then it is because of your faith.

But let's just say that it *is* faith that can make me well. Do I have that kind of faith, a faith that Jesus will recognize?

I would love to hear the doctor say the words, "No cancer." But I cannot get my hopes up, because I feel like I would simply be setting myself up for bitter disappointment.

So we move on to –

Scenario #2 – "Whack-a-Mole"

"Well, Mrs. Lenk, we have determined that you have ABC Sarcoma. This is a sarcoma that has responded quite well to chemotherapy. As always in deciding on treatment protocols, the challenge is to find a balance between response rates, survival rates, and quality of life. We believe that we can successfully beat back your tumors as they appear in order to maximize both your quality and quantity of life..."

I believe I will hear some form of this scenario. When new tumors crop up, we will whack them with more chemo or radiation. Surgery is not out of the question. Not a miracle, but not hopeless, either. We always knew I was going to have to work at living, and this diagnosis confirms it. I have a tough road ahead, but I can certainly have good quality time for who knows how long into the future?

And then, of course, there's....

Scenario #3 – "Are Your Affairs in Order?"

"I'm sorry, Mrs. Lenk, you have XYZ sarcoma, and there is not a good history of this kind of sarcoma responding to treatments... Are your affairs in order?"

Yes, yes, they are – my will is tucked away in my safe, my Funeral and Burial directive is written, my memorial service is planned, the bulletin done (if you know me well, you should not be surprised!) – but I am just not willing to go down this road unless and until I have to.

7:15 P.M.

We're back from Dana-Farber, and the scenario is... *Whack-a-Mole!*

After reading the radiologists' reports of my lung biopsy, the doctor believes we are now, in fact, dealing with leiomyosarcoma – the dreaded cancer I first heard about two and a half years ago when I had the hysterectomy. I find it unbelievable that there is no connection between that 2011 surgery and my current situation. However, a few weeks ago, we hand-carried all the surgeons' notes and documentation from my hysterectomy to Dana-Farber, and both my sarcoma specialist and the Dana-Farber pathologists reviewed them carefully. They also looked at tissue samples from that surgery. And it is their esteemed opinion that there is no connection.

Wow. It is not that I do not believe them... it is just that this is a coincidence beyond imagining. Fortunately, while leiomyosarcoma is often described as aggressive, my cancer is growing very slowly, so that is good news.

Now, it is on to chemo. The Dana-Farber doctor thinks something called Doxil (a combo of Doxorubicin and Liposome), will work well for me. Even better is that it looks like I will be able receive my chemo at the hospital near Foxboro rather than have to trek into Boston. More good news: it is administered only once a month, which means I might actually have some days (perhaps weeks?) of feeling well.

So... That's it. I am encouraged. The enemy has been named, there is a plan going forward, and no one seems ready to sign my death certificate yet. I am up for the fight. So bring on what you got, you old leiomyosarcoma, you have not met anyone like Jean Niven Lenk. Let this be a warning: you are in for a fight!

WEDNESDAY, MAY 22, 2013

PICKING UP MY CROSS

Okay, so now I have a name for the enemy: leiomyosarcoma.

And by being able to name it, it feels easier to contain, to control, to conquer.

But please do not let my upbeat attitude mask the reality of my situation. The fact remains that I am still dealing with Stage IV cancer. It is in my spine, both my lungs, and my thyroid. I also have cancerous tumors in my pelvis – that is the primary site – and my doctor does not feel that surgery is an option (it would be, in his words, a "big deal" – I guess that's another way of saying "inoperable").

In short, knowing what I have does not take it away or make my situation any less dire. I know the score – I am still in a fight for my life. That does not mean I don't have hope, or that I don't want to live, or that I am not going to battle this cancer with everything I've got.

But it reinforces what I have said before – that I am focusing on every single day rather than projecting too far into the future. Today is what counts; this is true whether you have Stage IV cancer or not, and my goal is to savor every moment.

I have also said repeatedly that I am not afraid of dying. And I am not, at least right now when death is still safely in the abstract.

But I would be lying to you if I said I was not worried about the immediate future – how will I tolerate the chemo? Will it make any dent on my tumors? Will it be successful in whacking some moles? Will I have any semblance of "normalcy," or will the chemo lower the quality of my daily life?

The cancer – and all the fear that emanates from this blasted disease – is my cross. And rather than running from it or leaving it lying there on the ground, I am reaching down, picking it up and dealing with it. Because if I do not acknowledge my cross, if I do not pick it up, then I deny God the opportunity to help me carry it.

One last thing – yesterday's chest x-ray revealed that my lung is still partially collapsed (and yes, it hurts).

THURSDAY, MAY 23, 2013

IT HAPPENS

This morning I saw my long-time primary care physician about my headaches. This was the first time I had seen her since my annual check-up on Valentine's Day, and we both burst into tears and hugged when we saw each other. So much has happened since mid-February, it is mind-boggling.

My yearly physical was scheduled for the day after Ash Wednesday, and in my homily at worship that evening, I actually anticipated how the appointment would go. As I re-read my words, however, I get chills. If I had only known then what I know now.... Well, there is no sense going down that road.

My doctor said that she has been going over and over in her mind what she could have done differently so that this would not have happened. Of course, it is not her fault. It is no one's "fault."

But I think it is human instinct for us to want to find someone or something to blame – especially when it is a calamity.

In fact, if there is anyone to blame for my cancer, I could just as easily look in the mirror. I have probably been walking around with cancerous tumors for over two years. Wasn't there anything – an ache, a twinge, a swelling – that I should have noticed? If I had been more in tune with my body, maybe we could have caught this before it had spread. But my tendency is to brush things off and explain things away. Unfortunately, it is a recipe for disaster when the "Queen of Denial" meets "The Anti-Hypochondriac."

And just as there is an instinct to lay blame – or at least find the responsible act or party – in medical situations, so too do we try to do so in the theological realm. It is the timeless question: if God is all-powerful, and God is also all-loving, why is there innocent suffering in the world?

And when things are reduced to this simplistic equation, it is easy to blame God.

But I think the whole thing is a useless pursuit. Will figuring out when and how and why things went awry with me take away my cancer? Will it make me feel better emotionally? Of course not.

The fact of the matter is (as I have said before) – fertilizer happens. In the medical realm. In the theological realm. In life. I do not blame anyone for my current situation, including myself.

I repeated to the doctor Barbara Brown Taylor's words: *the only thing worse than to suffer without reason is to suffer without God.*[85]

And I know I have God.

"Lent: Our Annual Spiritual Check-up"
An Ash Wednesday Meditation Preached by Rev. Jean Niven Lenk
February 13, 2013
Text: Psalm 51:1-10a

Tomorrow I go for my annual physical. I know pretty much how it will go. I will sit in the waiting room for about 15 minutes, and then my name will be called. First stop is the dreaded scale. Then it will be on to the examining room, where the nurse will take my vital signs. I will wait for another ten minutes or so before my physician comes in.

Then for about a quarter of an hour, the doctor will check me over, poking, prodding, asking questions, and pointing me in the direction of good health. "Pulse looks good; blood pressure looks good – that Lisinopril is working. Are you taking your Vitamin D and calcium? Belly feeling better? Hmm, how's that diet going? Are you exercising regularly?" And then about 40 minutes after I first arrived, she will send me on my way, saying "See you next year!"

At least that is what I hope. But sometimes at these annual check-ups I have been unpleasantly surprised. Sometimes she has said, "You've got to get this repaired," or "You've got to get that taken out." And suddenly doctors become both the last people I want to see and the ones I need the most.

Today, we enter the Season of Lent, which is another kind of check-up; it is when we spend some time with God and see how our health is, spiritually speaking. Ah, if only our 40 days of Lent were as easy as 40 minutes in the doctor's office.

"I see you made it to church more than half the Sundays; bonus points for Ash Wednesday; but hey, where were you on Maundy Thursday and Good Friday? I see you are a little behind on your pledge – try to get caught up, and while you're at it, how about boosting it a little. Served on a committee? Check. Washed dishes at the fair supper? Check. Said your prayers? Check. Good job! Now, keep singing in the choir, try to read your bible a little more this year, and remember – next year it's your turn to be on Trustees."

We might laugh, thinking that checklist hits a little too close to home. But you know, I don't think those are the things God is looking at to assess our spiritual health. Instead God might be asking us: How will you work on growing closer to me this season? How are you reaching out to my people in need? How are you treating your friends and family, and even more importantly, strangers and enemies? What are you doing to repair this beautiful creation I have put into your hands? How are you doing at becoming more patient and kind-hearted and slower to anger?

These are the kind of questions God asks us – not because God wants to learn (God already knows) but because God wants us to take a good look at ourselves. We need to face our failings, our shortcomings, our sins of commission and omission, so that we can repent, turn back to God, and become whole and healthy in our hearts.

In Psalm 51, King David's heartfelt prayer for cleansing and pardon, he is not coming before God for a checkup. He is not asking, "Am I doing okay, doc?" No, instead David says, "For I know my transgressions, and my sin is ever before me. Against you, you alone, have I sinned, and done what is evil in your sight."[86]

David recognizes the sorry state of his spiritual health. He is an adulterer and a murderer. There are no surprise diagnoses; David knows his heart needs major work. And he prays, "Create in me a clean heart, O God, and put a new and right spirit within me."[87] Listen to the verbs he uses throughout his psalm – *wash* me,[88] *cleanse* me,[89] *purge* me,[90] *deliver* me,[91] *restore* me,[92] *teach* me.[93] This is a man in anguish, and he knows that something radical must be done with his heart – something only the Great Physician can do.

And while going to God with his confession might have been the last thing he wanted to do, David knew that God was what he needed most. Yes, David had much to confess to the God who already knew all about his transgressions. But David also knew that it was only by turning back to God that he could begin the transformation toward healing and wholeness. Through God, his heart would be cleansed.

And how about us? Would God give us a surprise diagnosis about our spiritual health, or do we have a pretty good idea of where we need to improve? Lent is a time to go on a spiritual fitness program by looking at ourselves with honesty, confronting our ego and ambition and fear, just as Jesus confronted the Devil in the wilderness. It is a time to acknowledge both our capacities and limitations – our capacity to get angry or carry resentment or take offense or refuse to forgive – and what limits our capacity to love unconditionally, to forgive graciously, to give generously, to serve humbly...

And then to let them go by repenting – literally, turning around – and turning back to God. Such introspection is appropriate at all times within us, but Lent is that particular time in the church year when we need to pay special attention, because the Lenten journey that takes us to Easter's renewal and resurrection will not escape the shadow of the cross, where we are to acknowledge who and what we are.

And while going to God with our confession might be the last thing we want to do, God is what we need most for health and wholeness, for God is the one who can create in us a clean heart and put a new and right spirit with us. Amen.

FRIDAY, MAY 24, 2013

GETTING READY FOR CHEMO

Chemo.

The very word can strike fear in the hearts of both sick and healthy people alike. It conjures up images of weak, ailing, bald cancer patients enduring debilitating side effects in order to have a shot at living.

Indeed, it is a paradox that blasting one's body with chemical poison is the way to bring that body back to health (or at least extend that person's life).

Today Peter and I met with my local oncologist (we have seen four different doctors in five days this week) who went over the side effects of the chemo med Doxil and answered our questions.

I feel fortunate for a number of reasons. I can have these treatments at the local hospital; I love Dana-Farber, but traveling back and forth into Boston in the traffic (and there is always traffic) wears on our already-frayed nerves.

Doxil is administered only once a month. The total infusion time will be between three and four hours. After three treatments, I will undergo another CAT scan so the doctors can see if the cancer has progressed, stayed the same, or gone into retreat (whack those moles!).

The side effects sound fairly tolerable. I spent this morning doing online research and then discussed them further with the doctor this afternoon. The best news: very few people experience nausea and vomiting, but the doctor said "don't be shy" about asking for anti-nausea meds if I need them. (I admit, I hesitate when it comes to taking drugs. I remember after my hysterectomy, the doctor came in to my hospital room and said, "You're not pushing the morphine pump enough!") The side effects that seem to be most common with Doxil are skin rashes and heartburn. I think I can handle this.

Although speaking with the doctor allayed many of my fears regarding my upcoming chemo treatments, the fact remains that even if the side effects were horrible, I really have no choice. I must endure them if I am going to have any chance at life. It's my only shot, and I must marshal all my strength, all my courage, and soldier forth.

Once again, I need all your prayers. And I need to pray myself, for myself. But sometimes I find that hard to do. The words don't come easily. I dissolve into tears. My prayers feel ineffective and weak. But... "if [I] don't know how or what to pray, it doesn't matter. [The Spirit] does our praying in and for us, making prayer out of our wordless sighs, our aching groans."[94]

And I know that in my weakness – whether my weakness is fear, anxiety, doubt, or inadequate prayers – God is my strength.

SATURDAY, MAY 25, 2013

EXHAUSTION

If you asked what is the chief difference between the "then" me and the "now" me, I would have to say it is exhaustion.

All things considered, I do not feel sick. My back pain is more or less under control, my headaches have eased up a bit, and I do not have any obvious symptoms from my thyroid or lung tumors. Yes, my legs are weak and shaky, but I can deal with that.

But the least amount of exertion leaves me weak and worn out, and it seems to be getting worse every week. For instance, after each of my four doctor visits this past week, I stumbled back into my recliner and fell asleep within seconds. A nap does not bring me back to life; it simply brings me back to consciousness.

If I were a religious cynic, I would blame this on God's rascally sense of humor. After all, I used to be a ball of energy. I was an over-achiever, an over-functioner. I found it hard to relax (it made me feel guilty!), and if I was not doing something productive or constructive, even while resting, then I thought I was wasting time.

My, how things have changed.

Radiation knocked the stuffing out of me, and I have not yet recovered. I have been warned to expect to be fatigued for a couple of weeks after my chemo treatments, so I do not see me returning to my old self anytime soon.

While my exhaustion manifests physically, a good deal of it is rooted in the emotional. And how can I not react emotionally to the way my life is now? My loved ones, too. Ian comes home from school and heads straight upstairs for a nap. Peter falls asleep during the afternoon and still does not last beyond the second inning of a Red Sox night game. Cancer, and the emotional exhaustion that comes with it, is a family illness.

Before my diagnosis, I had no idea that there would come a point in my life that I would happily spend my days relaxing in a recliner, watching TV, and not feeling one scintilla of guilt. Of course, it took Stage IV cancer to get me to that place. I wish I had learned the lesson earlier, when I was healthy. But perhaps the lesson is not for me to learn myself, but for me to teach others.

SUNDAY, MAY 26, 2013

TOMORROW

By the time I start chemo next Thursday, it will have been nine weeks since my diagnosis. Nine weeks.

And it would be easy to think of those nine weeks as nothing more than a stretch in which I was in a holding pattern, treading water, biding my time while I waited for the doctors to figure out what kind of cancer I had. It would be reasonable to say that I could not do much until I knew the name of the beast I was dealing with. It would be understandable if I said that, during this time, I was focusing on the future day when I could finally start treatment for the cancer I have.

But treading water, biding my time, staying in a holding pattern, focusing on the future but not doing a whole lot in the present – that's not what my life has been like at all.

Instead, over the past two months, I have been... *living.*

In the 59 days since I learned I had cancer, I have been enjoying each moment (okay, well maybe not so much when the needles have been inserted or my head has been throbbing...). And these have included visits from friends and loved ones. They have included delicious meals lovingly made by neighbors and members of our church family. They have included Get Well cards with cheery handwritten messages from caring people. They have even included gifts large and small (candles, books, stuffed animals, quilts, prayer shawls) generously given by people from all dimensions of my life. And most of all, these moments have been filled with spending precious time with my family.

This morning, Peter went to church; he feels surrounded by love and support by our church family and rejuvenated by having some quiet, peaceful time with God. Ian stayed home, and I didn't even bug him about skipping church, because he spent the morning in the chair next to me in our living room, just hangin' with Mom.

It is easy to want to look ahead and focus on tomorrow. But tomorrow never comes. And in the meantime, life happens. If we focus too much on tomorrow, we'll miss today – the precious gift of this day that the Lord has made. May we all rejoice and be glad in each one that we are graciously given by God.

TUESDAY, MAY 28, 2013

ZOMBIE

For the better part of this past Memorial Day Weekend, I was basically a zombie. Over a week ago, the pain across the mid-section of my back, which was really my only cancer symptom last winter, returned to the level it was prior to my radiation treatments. I am trying not to worry about what this may mean regarding the cancer growing and spreading; I am more concerned about handling the pain. But my oncologist is scheduling another MRI of my spine and will compare it to the one done on March 26.

In the meantime, it simply is not possible for me to function with this level of pain – it really is excruciating. So, my alternative is to take a pill that will provide me with some relief. I always feel like this is giving in to the pain. I would much rather be strong enough to withstand the discomfort, but it does not work that way. My doctor urges me to take the pain medicine. So does my husband, along with friends who have been in my shoes.

And so, I eat a little something and then take my prescription. And it works beautifully. In less than an hour, the pain is virtually gone. But the reprieve comes at a price. I can barely stay awake. For most of the day, I lie in my chair and doze off and on.

When I have had a few moments of consciousness, I have watched TV or checked Facebook. I see that a lot of people, my friends included, spent the Memorial Day Weekend at the Cape, or went to a parade, or enjoyed dinner at a restaurant. How I would have loved to have been up for any of those kind of activities!

Shortly after I received my diagnosis, I had hoped that Peter and I would be able to take the camper to the Cape for overnight, or at least for the day. Lizzy and I had hoped we could go up to the Clam Box in Ipswich for some chowder. Now, those modest plans seem out of the question.

My big Memorial Day event was getting dressed, and I did not muster up the energy to do that until 1:30 p.m. My kids thought it would be fun to have a cookout, so they did the shopping, grilling, everything. Lizzy helped me out to the chaise longue on the deck, covered with extra padding to make me comfortable. I had a lovely meal – cheeseburger, corn on the cob, potato salad – but was soon ready to go back inside to my recliner; the brief time outside was so draining that I soon fell fast asleep.

All of this has caused me to make changes to my routine and *modus operandi*. I ended up putting a new message on my phone; it basically says that I may very well not pick up, and if you need to reach me immediately, just call Peter. A lot of the time, I am just not up to speaking with people.

My Miss Manners training is suffering, too. I am falling behind writing thank you notes to people who have sent along or dropped off presents or extended some other kindness. I appreciate everyone's thoughtfulness more than words can express, and just because I am late extending my gratitude, it is no less heartfelt.

My chemo, which had been scheduled for Thursday at 12:30 p.m., has been put off until next week. This is so I can have a biopsy of my thyroid on Friday, to see if the nodules there are thyroid cancer or leiomyosarcoma. And on it goes...

WEDNESDAY, MAY 29, 2013

SLIPPERY SLOPE

Yesterday was the first day that I began to think that I am really, truly dying.

It started at dawn as I was trying to come out of my med-induced sleep. I had the sense that I was floating away from my body, slipping away from this earthly life. Even though it was a dream, it seemed so real that it haunted me for the rest of the day.

Not to mention the slippery slope I have been on the past two months. First, the increasing pain; what does it mean?

Add to that the fact that in the first weeks after my diagnosis, I would put on make-up, mascara, lipstick and blush. I would color-coordinate my clothes and find matching jewelry. None of that seems worth the effort now. I have not put on make-up in weeks.

It is almost 3 o'clock, and I have not had the energy to get dressed. Is this a slippery slope I am going to continue to slide down?

And I have to make a request of anyone who might think the appropriate response to my emotional state is to say things like "cheer up," or "adjust your attitude," or "stop thinking about dying." Please know that these are not helpful admonitions, and they certainly are not pastoral.

In seminary, we were taught never to tell people how they "ought" to feel. Whatever people feel is what they feel. If you want to help, go stand next to them in that emotional place; do not try to bring them to where you are.

So, thank you everyone who is worried that I am giving up. I haven't. No way. But I am tired. And in pain. And I am just fully human, period, feeling fully human emotions. I write as an outlet for myself. What I have to say is as likely to shock and disappoint as it is to inspire and uplift. But I will never sugarcoat my situation or my feelings. I will be honest, authentic, and unfiltered.

And today, this is how I am feeling. I ask that you give me the space to rest here for a little while.

FRIDAY, MAY 31, 2013

BC/DC

I am having a biopsy on my thyroid at 12 noon today. Then this evening, I am having a MRI on my spine. I have another MRI on my spine tomorrow. It is getting to the point that I cannot keep track of all the tests! I just know where I am supposed to be at what time and when I have to stop eating.

In the meantime, last evening I was reminded yet again how having cancer has improved my life in some important ways.

Before cancer (B.C.), our evenings would look something like this. Grandpa would be in his own room watching the Red Sox game alone. Ian would be in the parlor, simultaneously doing homework, watching a basketball game, and texting with friends (call me old fashioned, but I just do not get how he can multitask like that). Peter would be up in his office working (or playing) on his computer. I would either be out at an evening church meeting, or at home writing a sermon or doing other work on my computer.

Now, during cancer (D.C.), this is how our evenings look. Grandpa, Peter, and I are settled in the parlor watching the Red Sox game together. Lizzy is down from Salem staying with us for days at a time, cleaning up the dishes, folding laundry, or just hanging around downstairs. Ian is either with us in the parlor or in the kitchen with Lizzy doing his homework.

In so many important and beautiful ways, cancer has brought us together as a family. I am hoping that when we enter the "After Cancer" stage (and we *will* enter it), we will remember the lessons of this difficult time and never again take for granted the precious time we could be spending together.

SATURDAY, JUNE 1, 2013

TESTS, TESTS, TESTS!

It has been a full two days of testing and doctor appointments!

It started yesterday (Friday) at 12 noon, when I went to the hospital for a thyroid biopsy. The purpose of this biopsy was to see if the nodules detected there were thyroid cancer or instead my primary cancer, leiomyosarcoma. It is uncommon, but not unheard of, for someone to have two different primary cancers going on at the same time (at this point, I would not be surprised if I ended up being one of those people!). We want to figure what is going on before chemo commences.

The biopsy itself was quite unpleasant. Awful, actually. I had to lie on my back with my head tilted way back in order to expose my neck. Simple Novocain was used to numb the area below my Adam's apple, and then the doctor inserted a long needle into my thyroid and dug around in order to get a good tissue sample. Two more needles on the right side, and then the same process on the left. We should get the results the beginning of next week. I hope I do not have to go through *that* one again!

Then we went straight over to the office of my local oncologist to talk about my medications. I have been on very strong pain pills for about a week, and it is just no way to live. I can barely function, and I spend a lot of time crying. So we have a new regimen, and already I feel better.

Then last evening, we went back to the hospital for a MRI of my lower spine, this to see if anything new is going on in my back that might be causing my recent pain. The MRI machine is the dreaded tube, and I had to take two tranquilizers to get through it – but get through it I did.

Then back to the hospital at noon today for two more MRIs – one of my mid-spine region and the other of my neck. Two tranks, and I think I actually fell asleep in the tube. Came home and slept the rest of the day.

I am hoping that all the necessary tests are now behind me, and we can move forward with chemo sometime next week.

SUNDAY, JUNE 2, 2013

GRADUATION

Today, our niece Marisa graduates from high school. This is a significant milestone in the life of any young adult (not to mention his or her parents). However, what makes Marisa's graduation particularly meaningful is that her mother (Peter's only sibling), Susan, is here to see it.

When Marisa was only five years old, Susu (as we call her) was diagnosed with myeloma. Even though it was caught early, cancer is unpredictable. You never know how things are going to unfold. Susu had to undergo chemotherapy and extended steroid treatments which left her with permanent and painful neuropathy in her feet. But she is here, and today she has the joy of seeing her only child graduate from high school.

I had my son Ian when I was the ripe old age of 42. When he was in pre-school, I was sometimes mistaken for his grandmother. I was always amused by the fact that I would be 61 years old when he graduated from high school. It never occurred to me that I might not be here.

And now being here is my focus. I want to enjoy the college admissions process with him; I want to be here as he looks at schools and fills out applications and waits in anticipation for acceptances. Parents might find the process to be a tedious and stressful endeavor, but its prospect has become precious to me now that it is in jeopardy.

Ian will graduate from high school in two years, and it is my dearest hope that I will be there in the audience to witness him walking into the auditorium with his class to "Pomp and Circumstance," to hear his name be called and see him walk across the stage and shake hands with the principal as he receives his diploma. Is this a realistic goal? I say it has to be! I have to believe that I *will* be there, and Susu's story inspires me.

I regret that my health prevents me from joining the family at this afternoon's graduation celebration. But Susu is there to celebrate with her daughter – just as I hope to be celebrating with my son in two years, by the grace of God.

MONDAY, JUNE 3, 2013

HOW ARE YOU?

How are you?

You might be surprised at how often I get this question. Not (as we were taught in seminary to say to an ill person) "How are you feeling *today*?" or "How is your pain *today*?" or even "How are things going for you *today*?"

Just a generic, perfunctory, superficial "How are you?"

And here are some ways I could answer the question.

With a generic, perfunctory, superficial response: "Fine, thanks! How are you?"

With an answer I think some people expect of me: "Well, I have had some difficult moments, no doubt about that. But I know that God is walking with me, and that makes everything okay, and I have faith everything will turn out all right!"

With an answer I think my family would like to hear: "I'm good, honey. All I need is a nice nap, so you don't have to worry about me for a few hours."

With my usual response: "Doing okay, thanks."

With the following honest, authentic, and expletive-deleted response which has entered my thoughts (but not yet crossed my lips) in my particularly negative, fully-human-period moments: "How am I?? How am I?? I've got Stage IV cancer. How do you think I feel? I've had so many tests, I've lost count. I have so many prescriptions, I can't keep track of them. It took the doctors almost nine weeks to figure out what kind of cancer I have. I haven't even started chemo yet. Every day I wake up feeling like crap and wondering what happened to my beautiful life. And I may go through all of the pain and treatments and stress and heartache and still end up dying anyway. *How do you think I feel?!*"

But let me put my cynical self aside and answer the question in a more thoughtful way.

I have actually had several good days, now that I am off the pain meds and on to a regimen of acetaminophen, ibuprofen, and pain patch. No more lying semi-conscious in my recliner. In fact, I spent yesterday afternoon laughing uproariously at the shows on Animal Planet. This morning, Lizzy remarked, "The old Mom is back!" It feels good! *I* feel good!

And now we're playing (once again) the waiting game: waiting for the results of the thyroid biopsy, waiting for the results of the three MRIs, waiting to find out when chemo will begin.

But in the meantime, I am just very thankful to be feeling better and enjoying life.

TUESDAY, JUNE 4, 2013

PAIN, PRAYERS, AND PROGRESS

Every day with cancer is different. I may have a couple of great days in a row, followed by a bad day. This roller coaster ride is hard for a linear thinker to get used to!

Sunday and yesterday (Monday) were definitely good days – I had no pain, and my spirits were high. But I was awake most of last night, and although I finally fell back asleep, I woke up with considerable back pain. Even after my regimen of acetaminophen, ibuprofen, and lidocaine patches, the pain persists, and I find it difficult to be emotionally strong when I am feeling physically weak.

However, we just received some great news from my local oncologist, which has boosted all of our spirits – the biopsy on my thyroid came back *negative*! I do not have cancer in my thyroid; what first looked like a tumor is a cyst! Also, the tumor in my T6 vertebrae has shrunk a little since my March 26 MRI, which means the radiation worked.

Now that the test results are back, it is on to chemo, which I begin this coming Thursday, June 6, at 11:00 a.m.

Thank you to all of you who have kept us in your prayers; they have been answered with the thyroid news. Now I ask that you continue to keep me in your prayers, that the chemo knocks back the rest of the cancer ("whack a mole") so I can have many more days ahead, by the grace of God.

WEDNESDAY, JUNE 5, 2013

FUTURE FEAR

A number of years ago, just for a lark, I visited a fortune teller at the Topsfield Fair on Boston's North Shore. Her name was – coincidence? – "Miss Jean." For much more cash than I ever should have paid her, she told me (among other things) that I would live to be age 89. I remember at the time feeling shortchanged – "Only 89! I was hoping to reach my 90s!" Of course now, 89 – even 79 – heck, 69 – would be an answer to my prayers.

Funny, but "Miss Jean" evidently did not "see" in her "crystal ball" the cancer battle that awaited me. No doubt, this so-called oracle dispenses only good predictions – much better for business!

But let's just say we had the ability to look into our futures. Experts tell us that 40% of the things people worry about will never happen, so imagine how being able to see what is ahead might cut down on our anxiety. For instance, I am sure I could conquer my fear of flying by knowing ahead of time that the flight would go fine and that we would arrive safely at our destination. We could relax knowing that our baby would be born healthy, that the surgery would be successful, that the marriage would be happy, that the job was secure. I would be a lot more relaxed today if I knew that all will go well with my chemo treatment tomorrow.

Of course, being able to see into the future would be good only if things worked out well in our life. What if we looked into our futures and saw the heartbreaks, the losses, the suffering? Would we live life more focused on a negative future than a positive present? Would we even choose to go on?

What if I had known that John was a heroin addict – would I have still married him? If not, my two beautiful children would never have been born – something I do not even want to contemplate.

No, I think it is a blessing that we cannot see into the future; we should focus on today. That is why God instructed the ancient Hebrews to gather just enough manna for "that day."[95] That is why the psalmist proclaimed, "This is the day the Lord has made; let us rejoice and be glad in it."[96] That is why Jesus taught us to pray, "Give us this day, our daily bread."[97] Focus on today; do not worry about tomorrow.

And the Apostle Paul exhorts us to replace our worry with prayer – "Do not worry about anything, but in everything by prayer and supplication with thanksgiving let your requests be made known to God. And the peace of God, which surpasses all understanding, will guard your hearts and your minds in Christ Jesus."[98]

Replace our worry with prayer. Good advice. Excuse me now... I am off to have some time away with God.

THURSDAY, JUNE 6, 2013

CHEMO – ROUND 1

I have survived (so far!) my first round of chemo.

I will confess that I was rather nervous (okay – a wreck!) this morning, not really knowing what was going to happen or how things would turn out. I am grateful that Pastor Mary came by and prayed with me before I left for the hospital. She also brought all the cards that people wrote to me at last night's prayer service at the church – I am grateful to everyone for their loving and supportive words.

Peter and Lizzy (my entourage) accompanied me to the hospital; we arrived promptly at 11 a.m. and went into the Chemotherapy Department – one area of that hospital I had never entered before. I met Lisa, my infusion nurse who would be overseeing my treatment for the day.

First on the schedule: blood work. My BP was also taken, and it was unusually (but perhaps not surprisingly) high. The aide then took my order for lunch; I was starving and chose fruit salad, a turkey sandwich, and bread pudding – comfort food.

Lisa then took us all into a small conference room and spent about an hour going over loads of information about cancer services and resources, chemo in general, and Doxil side effects.

Finally, I took my place in one of the comfortable recliners in the large chemo room. There were about 10 chairs with patients in them (spanning, I would guess, from their 50s to late 70s), all receiving their treatments. Each chair has its own TV mounted on the ceiling, complete with a remote. My lunch arrived, and while Lisa was getting things set up for me, I ate and watched TV; Peter and Lizzy went down to the cafeteria to grab something for themselves.

The infusion did not start flowing until 1:30 p.m. The first medications in the IV were anti-nausea medication, steroids, and Benadryl. Then came the chemo: Doxil. In the plastic bag hanging on the IV pole, it looked like dark pink Kool-Aid. Relaxing back in my recliner-away-from-home, I actually fell asleep for an hour. Lizzy stayed by my side, watching shows on her laptop; Peter went home to check on Grandpa and do a few errands before returning a little later.

When I awoke, I started to feel hot and flushed and my BP went up, so Lisa stopped my IV and we took a break until things settled down. We then got back on track, and the bag was finally empty at about 4:30 p.m.

A little before 5:00 p.m. – after having my BP checked one last time, getting untethered from the IV, and receiving a few final instructions – I was free to go home.

I feel fine (not to mention relieved) right now, but any side effects will probably not kick in for another day or two or three.

I will be returning to the hospital weekly for blood work – they need to keep on top of both my white and red blood cell counts. My next chemo infusion is scheduled for Wednesday, July 3.

So... thank you for all your prayers! I am sure they helped get me through today. Of course, the easy part was getting the Doxil; now it must do its job – beat back the cancer. And now I need your prayers that the treatment will do just that!

I will end with one of the scriptures that Pastor Mary shared with me during her visit. She had read it at last night's Prayer Service, and I think it sums up things up beautifully:

From the Apostle Paul –

> But we have this treasure in clay jars, so that it may be made clear that this extraordinary power belongs to God and does not come from us. We are afflicted in every way, but not crushed; perplexed,

but not driven to despair; persecuted, but not forsaken; struck down, but not destroyed; always carrying in the body the death of Jesus, so that the life of Jesus may also be made visible in our bodies.

~ 2 Corinthians 4:7-10, NRSV

Amen and amen!

FRIDAY, JUNE 7, 2013

CHEMO #1 – ONE DAY LATER

So far, so good!

One day after chemo, I am feeling much better than I expected – especially considering that I had such potent chemicals infused into my body 24 hours ago.

I had a good night's sleep, although at one point I did wake up in the wee morning hours; when I did, I turned on the TV and noticed that I had terrible double vision – probably from the steroids that were administered to me as part of yesterday's infusion. It was much better today.

I was feeling well enough this morning to go out and do some errands with Peter for a couple of hours; it was recommended that I do get up and out rather than simply acting like a slug in my recliner. We went in the truck, which I had trouble getting into because of my weak legs, but Peter fashioned a step stool out of his tool box – so gallant!

This afternoon, I took a nap (as usual) – fatigue is a side effect of chemo, and the physical and emotional toll of the last couple of months continues to catch up with me during the day, especially today.

My appetite has been good (when *that* disappears, I will really worry!), and I am following the directions to eat "frequent, small meals" – kind of like non-stop snacking!

One side effect that I was warned to expect is facial flushing – and for most of the day, I have looked like I just finished running 10 laps around the track in 100 degree weather. Other than that, I have a little foot and ankle swelling – no big deal.

I have also taken steps to prevent "hand and foot syndrome" (redness and rashes) by moisturizing, and also mouth sores by using alcohol-free toothpaste and mouth rinse.

That mischievous husband of mine did try to pull one over on me this afternoon – he got himself a Klondike Bar from the freezer, and I expressed a desire for one, too. "Oh no, you're not allowed to eat anything cold!" I had not remembered hearing this particular restriction, but my brain is not working on all cylinders these days, so I figured Peter was telling me the truth (I should know better!). Fortunately, my infusion nurse Lisa called a short time later to check on how I was doing, and I asked her about it – and she said of course I could eat cold food! I turned to Peter while still on the phone, and we all had a good laugh.

I am hopeful that over the next few days, I will continue to tolerate well the chemo's side effects; some kick in on day two or three or beyond.

But, for tonight, I am looking forward to special time with Ian, Peter, and Grandpa watching the Bruins game and simply enjoying – and being grateful for – every moment of feeling well and being with family.

SUNDAY, JUNE 9, 2013

CHEMO #1 – THREE DAYS OUT

I continue to have a few side effects from last Thursday's chemo treatment, but nothing too awful.

Today the fatigue knocked me flat for real. After eating breakfast and dressing, I fell asleep again for a few hours. Then I slept off and on all afternoon, throughout the Red Sox game. Later on this beautiful afternoon, Peter and I went out with Scooter for a little exercise. We went over to a nearby park, and I walked about a quarter of a mile. This might sound unimpressive, but my mobility has been compromised by steroid myopathy (not to mention the knee I twisted in that fall last month), and this was a good start. We will continue to get out and hopefully increase the walking distance – and my leg strength – little by little.

Other than blood work, I have no tests scheduled until August; no CAT scans, no biopsies, no MRIs, no x-rays. And my next chemo treatment is not until July 3. For the last two and half months, I have been in the "sick with cancer" stage – getting used to the diagnosis, going through tests and treatments, and so on. But now I am transitioning to a new stage – "living with cancer" – in which cancer is just part of my daily life.

I cannot spend the rest of my days in my recliner; I cannot use cancer as an excuse to do nothing. I need to motivate myself to get up and out and do things despite being ill. I think this will be as much a mental and emotional feat as a physical one.

There are things I would love to do – go down to the Cape, go up to Ipswich – and so I must stop thinking of myself as sick and begin this new phase of my illness, my life. Not sick with cancer. Not dying of cancer. *Living with* cancer. And by the grace of God, I will.

THURSDAY, JUNE 13, 2013

LIVING WITH CANCER

Some of you have noticed my silence of the past few days, since you have reached out to both Peter and me with emails, Facebook and text messages, and phone calls to make sure I was okay.

The simple truth is complete exhaustion has kept me offline for days. Such exhaustion is expected at this point post-chemo, but it has knocked me for a loop.

Today I went back to the hospital for blood work. The good news is that all of my results were within normal range, including red and white blood cell counts.

I have a bit more energy today, but not enough to come up with anything insightful or meaningful to write about. And I think there will be more such days, so if you do not hear from me every day, it means that I am moving into the "living with cancer" stage. There is nothing wrong (if there were, Peter would get the word out!), there is no need to be concerned – it is just a new phase of my battle.

Writing continues to be the method I will use to keep you updated, and it is the best way for you to find out how I am doing with all my tests and treatments.

Thank you for your continued love, support, and prayers!

FRIDAY, JUNE 14, 2013

WORST DAY YET

Today, nine days out from chemo, everything hit me.

I am not sure whether it was from the cancer itself, or from the side effects of last week's chemo, or from the side effects of one or more of my numerous medications, or from the side effects of medications prescribed to combat the side effects of my medications, or simply from the wretched migraine I awoke with.

Let's just say that this morning I experienced a full array of symptoms I would not wish on my worst enemy. The good news is that I have slowly felt better over the course of the afternoon.

No witty or creative observations... I just hope this day has been an anomaly that neither I nor my devoted husband and nurse Peter will have to endure again.

SUNDAY, JUNE 16, 2013

NADIR

Nadir: the lowest point; point of greatest adversity or despair.

Every once in a while, when the opportunity presents itself, I will use the word "nadir" in conversation. Sometimes I get puzzled looks in return, because nadir is just not a word one hears that often in common conversation.

Except if you are receiving chemo.

In the world of cancer, the word nadir is used a lot. It refers to that period of time following a chemo treatment when you hit the lowest point – of energy, of feeling sick, of everything.

I experienced nadir this past week.

I was warned it would happen on days 7 to 10 after my treatment, and that was pretty accurate. I had absolutely no strength. I felt wretched. I could barely move.

Mercifully, nadir is now behind me for this month. In fact, the improvement I experienced between Friday and Saturday was almost miraculous. Yesterday was such a beautiful day that Peter and I picked up some delicious egg salad subs at one of our favorite sandwich places in South Natick and then went across the street and had a picnic by the Charles River under a sycamore tree. Perfection!

It was a huge outing for me, and when we got home at about 1:30, I napped until the Sox game (they won!). Then Grandpa, Peter, Ian and

I spent a lovely evening watching the Bruins. (They won, too!) Only Ian and I stuck it out to the bitter end, and it was a lovely mother-son time.

Between the games, we were all just hanging out in the parlor. Ian was fiddling with his iPod, looking for some songs to purchase, and he started asking Peter and me questions about music of the 60s. "Have you ever heard of 'Sitting on the Dock of the Bay' by Otis Redding? How does it go?" Of course, Peter and I could not help but launch right into a rendition, along with an enthusiastic recommendation to buy it ("Fantastic song!"). Ian continued through "Beautiful Morning" by the Rascals, "Be My Baby" by the Ronettes, "Crystal Blue Persuasion" by Tommy James and the Shondells, "Hold On, I'm Coming" by Sam and Dave, "Reach Out" by the Four Tops. On and on and on. Every time Ian named a song, Peter and I sang the first couple of lines. We had Ian in stitches, but he was definitely impressed that we knew all these fabulous songs from the 60s – our era. I think it was the most fun I have had in months.

So... life with cancer continues. I am looking forward to a couple of good weeks before my next chemo treatment on July 3. And I am looking forward to those weeks being full of more fun and precious family time, just like yesterday.

THURSDAY, JUNE 20, 2013

MACRO/MICRO

When Peter and I talk about my illness, he speaks in macro terms: that the chemo is working in me right now whacking those cancer moles, and that my August scan will show that the tumors have shrunk, and before we know it, we'll be back to living our lives and be able to put this difficult episode behind us.

Curiously, I do not think much about the chemo, or my tumors, or about my long-range future; I think more on the micro level. That's because every day has turned out to be a struggle.

With the "nadir" stage now behind me, I was hoping to feel better every day, that soon I would be up to going on those trips to Ipswich and the Cape. But it has not turned out that way at all.

My worst time of day is when I wake up, because having taken neither food nor pain killers for a while, that is when I am feeling especially vulnerable. I can tell pretty quickly whether or not it is going to be a good day. Will it be back pain that gets me down today? Maybe it will be a migraine that lays me flat. Or maybe I will just feel all-around exhausted and sick.

I feel like a person half again my age. I have difficulty walking and sometimes need a walker for support. I wear Depends. I am more concerned with my bodily functions than my cancer. Sometimes I cannot even swallow correctly; yesterday I had a scary choking session that lasted about 10 minutes, and all I had done was inhale the tiniest crumb down my windpipe. Really?

Unfortunately, my worst time of day coincides with Ian's being downstairs eating breakfast, so he is a witness to it. And then he has to go off to school, not knowing until late in the afternoon whether I am feeling better. That has got to mess with his head.

This has not been a good week. My back pain has returned to pre-diagnosis levels, and I have been forced to start taking pain pills again during the day. Today, however, my back pain was overshadowed by a searing migraine which forced us to cancel my blood work appointment. In fact, my migraines have been so bad lately that I have made the decision to go back on Amitriptyline – if it prevents further migraines, it will be worth the extra pounds I might gain.

Thanks for coming to my pity party. And I ask that you join me in praying that I have better days ahead.

SUNDAY, JUNE 23, 2013

GUILT AND SOLIPSISM

Guilt: A feeling of responsibility or remorse for some offense, crime, wrong, etc., whether real or imagined.

Over my years in ministry, I have had parishioners express guilt for a variety of reasons. “I feel so guilty I haven’t been to worship the past month.” “I feel so guilty I had to say ‘no’ to serving on the committee.” Etc., etc.

To such laments, I have usually replied (with tongue half in cheek), “Stop, stop, there is no such thing as Protestant guilt!” (the Calvinism of our Puritan forebears notwithstanding).

And I would often add, “Guilt is a useless emotion that we inflict upon ourselves.”

Of course, guilt is not limited only to people of certain religious traditions; we Protestants can do guilt with the best of them!

And guilt can be useful. It can move a person to extend an apology, or to right a wrong, or to repay a debt.

I did not realize it at the time, but much of my life "BC" (before cancer) was motivated by – or at least racked with – guilt. Real or imagined, I thought I was not working hard enough. Or, I was working too many evenings, at the expense of my family. I was not visiting enough parishioners. Or, I was not seeing enough of my ailing mom. I was not a good enough pastor, or parent, or wife, or daughter. And my response was to work harder, which just continued the vicious cycle.

And then I got sick. And 95% of my guilt disappeared.

It was replaced by solipsism.

Solipsism: extreme preoccupation with and indulgence of one's feelings, desires, etc.; egoistic self-absorption.

I did not even know this word until my friend and colleague Molly mentioned it in terms of her own battle with cancer (she has now been cancer free for three years!).

It is the perfect word, because it's all about me now. Which means I only answer the phone when I feel like it. Which means I only check my email once or twice a week. Which means I only go on Facebook intermittently.

And which means I write only when I am inspired and am feeling up to it. When writing stopped being something I looked forward to and started to feel like an obligation (in other words, I felt guilty when I did not do it), I knew I had to back off. So please do not worry when you do not hear from me. Believe me, if there were something to report, we would get the word out!

A few updates:

I have had a few fairly good days. Friday evening, Peter took me for a short ride in his sports car (a red 1980 Fiat Spider), and it was a blast. I was surprised how comfortable the bucket seats were on my back – better than my Chevy Malibu. It was great to get out with the top down and take in the earthy summer fragrances.

I have developed mouth sores. This is a side effect of the chemo, and I have to go through a special mouth care routine to make sure they do not get worse. It feels as if the inside of my mouth is sunburned.

I awoke at 3 o'clock this morning with a(nother) migraine. I waited until 5 a.m., and then woke up poor Peter for some medication. Fortunately, the early intervention worked, and the headache disappeared early this afternoon.

I still have back pain, but its level fluctuates from day to day.

I am still plagued by extreme fatigue from the chemo and also my medications. But fortunately, the solipsist in me simply sleeps whenever I need to – *no guilt*!

WEDNESDAY, JUNE 26, 2013

BEST DAY YET!

We did it! We did it! Today, we spent the day at the Cape!

I have been feeling the best yet over the past couple of days, thanks in large part to a slight adjustment of my medications.

On Sunday evening, Grandpa, Peter, Lizzy, Ian and I all gathered outside to watch the "Supermoon" come into view. At one point, I got out of my lawn chair and started walking, bad legs and all, down the street to get a good shot with my phone camera. Peter sent Lizzy to chase me down to make sure I did not trip and fall on the uneven sidewalk– "Oh no, she's walking down the street! Lizzy, go get her! Go get her!"

Yesterday, we made it to the polls to vote, and then to an appointment with my local oncologist. We also stopped at the mall so Peter could run into Sears (I stayed in the car). Later, we went to Fidelity in Braintree to take care of some financial stuff – a trip we have been trying to make for months, but I just was not up to it.

Having survived that busy day and with my next chemo a week away, I suggested to Peter last evening that we go to the Cape while I was in this good stretch. There is no time like the present!

So we left this morning at 10 and first on the itinerary was a drive around my old stomping grounds in Harwich Port. We went to an overlook at the stretch of beach I spent every summer of my childhood near Allen Harbor – what memories!

A drive by my family's old cottage on Northern Avenue, and then on to Chatham, where we met up with Peter's mother, who lives on the Cape in Mashpee.

In Chatham we drove around the Hardings Beach area where the Lenk family cottage used to stand; after Connie sold it a few years ago, it was torn down and replaced with a beautiful year-round home.

Then off to the Chatham Lighthouse, where the contour of the beach looks considerably different from last year, thanks to Superstorm

Sandy. We picked up lunch at our fave sandwich place, and Peter – who knows all the nooks and crannies of Chatham – took us to a hidden jewel of a beach at the Town Landing. We had packed beach chairs, but it was too hot to sit outside so we enjoyed our meal in the air conditioned car.

Heading into today, I had hoped against hope for the opportunity (and ability) to put my toes in the water, and this beach was a perfect place to do it. After eating, I was able to navigate – with Peter's help – the short walk from the car to the shore. Feeling the sand between my toes and the cooling water around my feet was glorious!

Then off to Emack and Bolio's for ice cream (I made quick work of a chocolate chip cone turned upside down in a cup) before saying good-bye to Connie and heading back home.

I am tired but exhilarated – a week ago a trip like this seemed impossible. And it is not just a physical thing; there is a psychological aspect to it. Yesterday, as we were heading to Braintree, I actually started to feel a little panicky being "so" far away from the sanctuary of my home. But I quickly got over my anxiety, and it set me up for today's excursion.

At the appointment with my oncologist yesterday, we reviewed my chemo side effects, which have actually been quite minimal: mouth sores and fatigue. But my biggest complaint to the doc was my blasted knee – the one I twisted in that early morning fall on May 1. I have waited eight weeks for it to feel better, and there has been no change, so it is time for further action. If my knee did not hurt, I would be much more inclined to try taking walks (even with my radiation neuropathy), or even to climb stairs. Therefore, I am going to see my primary care physician on Friday so she can order up a MRI.

Of course, this knee problem – which has nothing to do with the cancer – leads to some questions. If there is, say, a ligament tear, how would that be treated? Can I have laparoscopic surgery while undergoing a course of chemo? Will I have to endure this pain until chemo is done (not for another five months)?

Life with cancer is complicated.

But life is also beautiful – especially today at the Cape. Thank you, thank you, thank you Lord!

MONDAY, JULY 1, 2013

MYSTERY, PLANS, AND RANDOMNESS

I have long recoiled at the idea of "God's Plan." As I have said before, I do not believe for one second that it was "God's plan" for my husbands Darcy and John to die so that I would be a better pastor. I could not worship, much less devote my life to, a God like that. But the fact of the matter is, I *am* a better pastor because of those losses in my life, for they have given my ministry breadth and depth and have helped me to better understand suffering and offer compassion. And that is how I have made meaning of those losses – by seeing the good that has come not just *in spite* of them but indeed *because* of them. New growth springing from the fertilizer of our lives.

But recently I have started to wonder if perhaps there actually might be a Divine Hand behind my life-threatening leiomyosarcoma. The reason is because I cannot think of one thing I could have done differently in my life to have prevented this cancer.

Consider the following:

- I have never smoked.
- I have never used street drugs.
- I have imbibed alcohol minimally (one to two glasses of Chardonnay at holidays and special occasions).
- I keep up with my annual check-ups, mammograms, colonoscopies, etc.
- There is no family history of cancer, much less leiomyosarcoma.

Moreover, while researchers have not yet identified any specific causes of leiomyosarcoma, there are risk factors associated with this cancer.[99] These include radiation therapy (never had it before my diagnosis); race (the odds of getting leiomyosarcoma in the uterus doubles in African-American women as compared to white and Asian women; I am white); and Cyclophosphamide therapy (CP), a medication-based therapy used in the treatment of Wegener's granulomatosis (never had it).

Leiomyosarcoma is rare, affecting only four out of every one million people. I have won the lottery; I think I will start buying "Lucky for Life" tickets (an ironic name, since all the money in the world could not change my circumstances).

Put in sacred terms, my question is: When God knit me in my mother's womb, did God say, "I will have her develop a rare cancer in her late 50s"? If so, why? What is the purpose of my having leiomyosarcoma?

Put in secular terms, my question is: Is life this random? A person can try to do everything "right," and it is no defense against misfortune and heartache?

Or perhaps we can have glimpses of Sheol while here on earth. That is not to say that every moment is torment, but just as we can experience heavenly "Kingdom Moments" during our earthly lives, so too can we experience The Abyss. I believe that in the last few years of his life, my husband John was trapped in the purgatory of his heroin addiction.

I am not expecting answers to these questions, at least not right now – perhaps not even in this earthly life. As Saint Paul tells us, "Now I know only in part; then I will know fully, even as I have been fully known."[100] And for the time being, I simply need to enter into the Mystery and relax in God's arms.

WEDNESDAY, JULY 3, 2013

SLAYING THE DRAGON

Today I underwent my second chemo treatment. I was much more relaxed than I was for the first, since this time I knew what to expect and had taken a tranquilizer before I left the house.

As I have reported recently, I have had some good days over the past week, but unfortunately yesterday was not one of them. I had shooting pains through my pelvic region and from both shoulders down my sides to my hips – really uncomfortable; I would call them an 8 or 9 on the 1-10 pain scale. My rib cage also hurt, especially when I coughed.

Today, we got an idea of where those pains were coming from. The first thing I undergo before a chemo treatment is blood work. We have to wait for the results before moving forward. We were surprised that today's tests showed that my red blood cells were way down; they should be at least 10, and they were at 7. The nurse said that this low red blood count could be from internal bleeding caused by one of my medications and could explain my pains.

To address the low blood count, I had my first-ever blood transfusion. I received my chemo infusion first, and then the transfusion, so it made for a long day (I slept most of the afternoon, thanks to a second trank). We left for the hospital before 10 o'clock this morning, and we arrived home shortly before 5:30 p.m. My loyal Peter spent most of the day next to my side, taking short breaks only for meals and quick errands.

I am feeling quite well right now. I had a nice lunch of chicken pie and chicken soup (chicken is a great chemo food – we're having roast chicken for dinner). I know that the side effects will start kicking in over the next week, but I am not afraid. If they are no worse than last month, I will consider myself fortunate. Anyway, this is how I must whack those moles.

Actually, I think the correct term is "slay the dragon." I was surfing the net yesterday for more information on leiomyosarcoma, and I came across the website for the National LeioMyoSarcoma Foundation (http://www.nlmsf.org). They have adopted "Slay the Dragon" as its slogan and purple as its cause color. Leiomyosarcoma is known as an orphan cancer; it is so rare that it does not get the publicity or the research funding as does, say, breast cancer. Peter's doctor said he had only seen one case of leiomyosarcoma in his entire career – and it was in an 88 year-old woman.

Perhaps there is an opportunity for me – and *you* – to help get research funding for this horrible cancer. Because we need to whack those moles and slay those dragons!

MONDAY, JULY 15, 2013

AMBITION – NOT!

When the early morning sun is breaking over the horizon, and I first open my eyes to the new day, I lie quietly and take inventory to determine what I need to do – or, more accurately, what I need to *take* – to fully enjoy the day. The list will vary in content and length depending on how many days it has been since chemo.

Am I feeling nauseous? A little Prochlorperazine will settle down the queasiness.

Where is my pain? If my temples are pounding or my neck is aching, some Fioricet will do. If my knee is throbbing, or my back is hurting, it is time for the really strong pain meds.

If I am retaining water, Furosemide will help.

If I am feeling anxious, I will take a trank.

And that does not even cover the medications I take no matter what: ibuprofen, acetaminophen, anti-depressants, vitamins, Omeprazole, Lisinopril, and lidoderm patches. Not to mention the things I am too private to list.

Some days, these meds will give me enough get up and go to shower and change into new clothes (although three out of the last seven days, I stayed unwashed and unchanged). Some days, this cocktail of drugs will allow me to feel almost normal – meaning I have the energy to tackle a doctor's appointment, or the appetite to eat a sandwich, or the wherewithal to write.

Other days, this regimen will do little more than allow me to lie on my recliner and passively watch TV. Some days, I do not even have the ambition to change the channel on the remote.

Ambition. I used to have a lot of it.

Add in competitiveness, drive, motivation, determination. That was me. If there was a recognition to achieve, a level of excellence to attain, a goal to accomplish, or a contest to win, I would work my butt off to land on top.

Now I lie in my chair going back and forth in my mind whether the effort needed to reach over and lift my water glass to my lips will be worth having my thirst quenched. I will soon be getting a bit of a breather, however. When we saw my oncologist last Wednesday, he suggested that we take a break after chemo #3 (July 31) so I can get my knee fixed.

We will be finding out on August 20 how well the Doxil has been whacking moles and slaying dragons. And then when I have recovered sufficiently from surgery, we can continue on with the next rounds of chemo, which – depending on what the August 20 scans reveal – may be just Doxil or Doxil combined with a trial drug.

This is what life with cancer has come to. Tell me a date post-chemo, and I can pretty much predict how I will be feeling. Last week, one week after chemo, was not so great. This week is an improvement. Next week should be even better. And then the cycle begins all over again.

TUESDAY, JULY 16, 2013

SYMBIOSIS

I suspect there are as many different reactions to a cancer diagnosis as there are people. Peter has always been a pragmatic realist, whereas I have always looked to the future with unabashed optimism. If things weren't so great today, they would surely be better tomorrow. Everything would work out.

It took a long time for me to see that my optimism was really a form of denial. And that Peter's approach to life could reap rewards. I told him when we got married that one of his jobs was to keep me financially solvent, and he has done a superb job at that (along with his other job: to make me laugh every day).

But now, as we deal with cancer, our roles have reversed. I am facing my diagnosis, treatments, and prognosis with stone-cold sober realism. It's not that I do not have hope; rather, I am aware of the odds and find no benefit in denying the reality of my situation. At the very least, it helps me to treasure every moment.

Peter, on the other hand, grasps at every possible sign that the chemo is working and the cancer is receding, and he tries to spin every development into good news (it is really quite dear).

For instance, after each of my chemo treatments, I have developed low grade fevers lasting several days (it feels odd to be shivering under four blankets during a heat wave). The doctor said this could be an infection. OR it could be irritation caused by the chemo drugs working on those tumors. While I feel pretty crummy during these fevers, Peter enthusiastically greets them as good omens.

Here are some others:

Am I having pain in my spine? That's irritation – sure evidence that the radiation and chemo treatments are doing their job! OR is my back pain-free? That's because the tumor has shrunk!

Am I exhausted? That's because my body is working hard to eradicate the cancer! OR am I energetic? The tumors are not sapping as much of my strength because they have gotten smaller!

Is my breathing clear? The lung tumors are shrinking! OR am I wheezing? That's the remains of dead tumors being expelled from my lungs!

Etc. Etc.

I guess it is part of the symbiosis of an intimate relationship that when one falls, the other uplifts; when one despairs, the other hopes; when one weeps, the other laughs. And so for Peter and me, this give-and-take of our relationship does not just feel natural; I am truly grateful for it.

I don't want to take one bit of hope away from my beloved. At the same time, it is important to face reality. But Peter shows me that reality does not always have to be negative, downbeat or depressing; in fact, it can be full of good news and encouraging developments – if you are looking for them.

FRIDAY, JULY 19, 2013

A DAUGHTER'S A DAUGHTER

"A son's a son 'til he takes a wife, but a daughter's a daughter for all of her life."

As I was growing up, my mom frequently repeated this little couplet. I am not sure whether it was to instill this idea into my impressionable brain, or to affirm what already seemed obvious. After all, the adage seemed tailor-made for me. In my family, I was the only girl and also the baby – my brother Dave is eleven years my senior, and Andy is seven years older.

While Dave and Andy went off to distant lands decades ago (and are currently living out their retirements in Los Angeles and Guam, respectively), I could never imagine moving far from my parents. I attended an in-state college, UMass Amherst. And except for a homesick-riddled year at The Pennsylvania State University (while first my husband getting his MBA) and an equally miserable 18-month stint in Rochester, New York, I have lived my entire life in Massachusetts – never more than 100 miles from my parents.

For all of my life, my parents have been there for me. Even when I was well into adulthood, I knew I could call upon them in times of trouble. In return, I tried to be there for them, especially as the fragility of years took their toll.

I fully expected to take care of my parents as they became frail elders. What I did not expect was that *my* daughter would be taking care of *me* when I was still middle-aged.

Since Peter and I married in 2005, I have lived in a testosterone-heavy household. While my mom and daughter Lizzy stayed in Ipswich so she could finish high school there (class of '07), Peter, Ian and I moved down to Foxboro, and I began my pastorate in Stoughton. Five years ago, my Dad moved in with us. (After graduating from Ipswich High School, Lizzy went off to college, finally settling in Salem on the North Shore of Boston.)

I got used to my guys not noticing when I came back from the hair salon with a sleek new 'do. I could understand if they did not appreciate the particular elegance of new, full set of acrylic nails or the singular beauty of freshly pedicured toes. I grew resigned to enjoying a new outfit based not on their compliments but on how I myself felt in it.

Then I got cancer, and Lizzy moved back. Sort of. You know that stage of growing up that is sandwiched between high school graduation and the day the baby bird has finally, once-and-for-all, left the nest? This is when you complete both the "current address" and "permanent address" lines on forms. When you still slip and call the place your parents live, rather than where you live, "home." When it is not unusual to go through multiple roommates and move a couple of times a year.

Lizzy comes down from the Witch City for several days each week, and I have found myself looking forward to her visits with a mixture of giddy excitement and breathless relief.

When Lizzy is here, she offloads Peter from his heavy load of responsibility. When Lizzy is here, she will spend two hours patiently explaining to Grandpa how to use his new phone. When Lizzy is here, she will make dinner and serve it, too, and then clean up afterwards. When Lizzy is here, she will do all the laundry, and then fold it and put it away. When Lizzy is here, she will just sit with me in the parlor – my companion.

But it is more than that.

When Lizzy is here, there is another female with whom to do girly-girl things with. Having remembered that I mentioned in passing a new nail product, she will go out and buy it for me, and we will get lost in the fun of a Mani/Pedi Evening. She will run out to Kohl's and find the perfect jersey based on my vague description. She will give me a foot massage, moisturizing my chemo- and radiation-ravaged feet.

I keep thanking her for all she does, and she brushes me off. "*Of course* I'm going to take care of you, Mommy!" But this is not what I pictured for my little girl. At 24, she should be out having fun, enjoying the single life, with no responsibilities. I used to think that maybe when I was 85 or 90, she could help me out a little. But not now.

Cancer changes things. It upsets plans. It dashes dreams. It hastens adulthood.

But it can also do beautiful things... like bring a mother and daughter closer together in precious and unexpected ways.

SATURDAY, JULY 20, 2013

CANCER BY THE NUMBERS

For a little change of pace (all stats based on the period 3/26/13 to present unless otherwise noted):

54 The number of days from the time I was given the diagnosis of Stage IV Cancer (3/29) to when I was told the identity of the primary cancer (leiomyosarcoma on 5/21).

16 The number of tests and procedures I have undergone, including MRIs, CAT scans, x-rays, and biopsies.

9 The number of new doctors I have seen because of my illness (this includes only the ones I have consciously met, not the ones who performed tests or procedures on me while I was anesthetized).

1,456 Number of miles we have traveled on cancer-related business, from picking up prescriptions at CVS to travelling into Dana-Farber.

1,167 Estimated number of job-related travel miles I have *not* incurred because I am out on Medical Leave.

15 Number of radiation treatments I received on my spine.

2 Rounds of chemo I have endured thus far.

17 Trips to local hospital.

11 Trips to Dana-Farber/Brigham and Women's in Boston.

3 Maximum number of hours of uninterrupted sleep Peter gets each night (he is either lying awake worrying about me, or coming downstairs to check on me).

24 Number of medications I am currently taking (includes patches, chews, sprays, liquid medicines, and pills)

TOO MANY TO COUNT Times I have been stuck with a needle.

Medical update:

My recent blood work has come back normal, so my July 3 transfusion did the trick.

I am going to have a port implanted under the skin of my chest next Wednesday; it is a procedure that requires me to be anesthetized. The port will eliminate the need for nurses to try to find a good vein (which is becoming harder and harder to do) for chemo, blood work, etc.

I have developed a dreadful chemo rash – raw and painful. Definitely the worst chemo side effect so far. I went to my primary care physician yesterday and am now on antibiotics and a soak/spray routine.

SUNDAY, JULY 21, 2013

FACE TO FACE

(NOTE: The following is a work of fiction.)

I am so tired. Sick and tired. Dead tired.

Not the kind of tired that a turbo shot or a nap or a vacation will fix. It is a tired-to-the bone fatigue. Physical, yes, but also emotional and mental.

For as long as I have been sick, I have had my bouts of exhaustion, but I always had the will to fight back, to fight for "normalcy," to fight for life. But now, I think it is time to rest. I have fought the good fight, like the Apostle Paul; I have kept the faith; now I think it is time to finish the race.[101] I am done.

The cool sheets of the special hospital bed caress my skin. The hospice nurse makes sure I have enough Ativan and morphine to be comfortable.

People slip in and out of the parlor, with hushed voices and unobtrusive footsteps. To them, I appear unresponsive. But I was always told that hearing is the last sense to go, and it is true.

I can recognize the voices – my husband, Peter; my daughter, Lizzy; my son, Ian; my stepchildren, Tim and Beryl – gathered in a Death Watch. Soft weeping. Short whispers. But mostly silence. What is there to say at this point?

Then a new Voice ... I can't place it, and yet it is both familiar and comforting. "Jean, my daughter. Jean."

I remember that when my mother was on her deathbed, she kept asking, "Who's calling 'Olive'?" I had not heard anyone then, but now I understand.

"Beloved Jean, it is time to go home. Be not afraid. I am with you and will guide you to the other side."

His words bring me a peace that no medication could ever deliver, and the nurse notices the change in my breathing. I hear shuffling and movement in the room, and then one by one, my husband and children whisper loving good-byes into my ear.

The Voice speaks again. "It is time. Take my hand." And suddenly I am floating, floating beyond the dimensions of time and space, beyond earth and matter, beyond the beyond. And then the Voice says, "You are home, my beloved Jean."

I am startled to hear barking, and I open my eyes to a half-dozen dogs making a bee-line for me. Their enthusiasm knocks me over as they cover my face with kisses, but I feel no pain and revel in the joyous reunion. Then the cats, in a more subdued but just as tender gathering.

Suddenly I catch a familiar scent, and my eyes look up to see the face of the most beautiful woman I have ever known. "Jeanie, dear. It's mother." "I know, I know." I fall into her arms, with tears of joy cascading down my face.

The Voice speaks again, and for the first time I see him, face to face. At once striking, rugged, delicate. But his features are inconsequential compared to the light emanating from his being – the light of peace, of joy, of comfort, of healing. I now know there was no reason to be afraid.

"Is it like you imagined?" he asks, with a wry smile.

"I could never have imagined this," I marvel. "It's beautiful, wondrous, perfect."

He begins to walk away, then turns and pauses. "Welcome home, beloved Jean. Welcome home."

MONDAY, JULY 22, 2013

TABOO

I started to write because I knew it would be the best way to get news about my health to as many people as possible as quickly as possible. It is tiring and tedious to have to keep repeating myself.

But I realized early on that writing gave me the opportunity to not only keep you up to date on my latest tests and treatments, but also to articulate my various thoughts and feelings as I battled Stage IV cancer. And although this is the place for people to catch up on what is happening with me health-wise, the rest of my musings and reflections have really been for myself.

I have always loved to write, but never before did both a compelling subject matter and the luxury of time align simultaneously to create the opportunity. Writing has provided me a creative outlet, much as writing sermons used to. I find it therapeutic to put my thoughts and feelings into words. I also think it is healthy to do some serious self-examination ("The unexamined life is not worth living for a human being" – Socrates), and writing on a regular basis prompts me to do that.

I share my ponderings because, for me, having a public rather than private journal forces a discipline and structure I need these days. And maybe something I say will resonate with someone, somewhere.

Okay, so having said all that...

I am quite bemused at the reaction I have received to yesterday's piece of fiction. People either hated it or loved it (the latter tended to be clergy or people of deep faith). I guess it felt too real for some people. Others figured I must be giving up if I have such a finely-tuned vision of dying.

Why such a disparate response?

I suspect that it is because death is a taboo subject and uncomfortable to contemplate. How many people put off writing wills for this reason? Of course, in the pastor biz, we talk about death a lot, but usually in terms of everlasting life. Resurrection is the fundamental tenet of our Christian faith; death does not have the last word!

It is my faith – *not* any loss of the will to live – that enables me to write such a descriptive narrative.

I will say that the part about my mom hearing someone call her name – that actually happened. I was sitting at her bedside as she lay unresponsive, and suddenly she opened her eyes and slowly formed the words to the question: "Who's calling 'Olive'?" I told her that I did not hear anyone, but she was insistent. "Someone is calling 'Olive.'"

My friend Paula swears that when her daughter was taken off life support, she saw her spirit leave the hospital room following the figure of a man.

The partner of a woman whose funeral I conducted a couple of years ago told me that a few days before she died, she insisted she saw the figure of a man in the bedroom mirror.

Look, I can't say for sure what this all means, but I know what I believe. I don't know for sure what it is like to die or what awaits us beyond this earthly life (and I don't want to find out anytime soon), but I have a vision of how it might be.

And that gives me great comfort in the midst of fighting this battle.

TUESDAY, JULY 30, 2013

DIALOG

Yesterday I had a visit from Mary, who is Acting Pastor at UCC Stoughton. Mary served as Student Pastor at the church two years ago, and we have remained close. I consider her my colleague, friend, and pastor.

Mary asked me yesterday if the cancer has changed my faith. Hmmm, well yes it has, actually. For starters, I have a lot of questions. And yes, I am rather angry. But perhaps most of all, I can now see how inadequate and wanting are the answers I might have offered as Pastor Jean to Patient Jean's questions. I have an on-going conversation in my head that goes like this.

Patient Jean: You know, Pastor, I have one question for God, just one question: "What were you thinking!?"

Pastor Jean: Oh Jean, I can understand how you might ask that question. But God, through the prophet Isaiah, tells us that "My thoughts are not your thoughts, neither are your ways my ways."[102]

Patient Jean: That's for darn sure! Okay then, I don't understand why I had to get cancer. I don't deserve this! Why am I being punished?

Pastor Jean: It's not a matter of who "deserves" cancer and who doesn't, Jean. Scripture tells us that God "sends rain to the righteous and the unrighteous alike."[103]

Patient Jean: But Pastor, I have tried to be a good person and a faithful follower of Jesus. I've dedicated my life to God, for crying out loud. And this is my reward?

Pastor Jean: You can't earn God's favor, you know that. It's a little thing called grace – God loves us before we can do anything to earn it or deserve it.

Patient Jean: Well, then, am I being punished for some sin I committed? Which of the many was the "cancer sin"?

Pastor Jean: Ours is a merciful God, Jean. Just as grace is getting what we don't deserve, mercy is not getting what we do deserve. God doesn't dole out punishment in some hierarchy of sin. Ours is a God of love and compassion.

Patient Jean: How can I believe that – I've got cancer! Not very loving and compassionate if you ask me!

Pastor Jean: Sounds like you're blaming God for your cancer, Jean.

Patient Jean: Of course I am blaming God! Where else did it come from? God is all-powerful, after all.

Pastor Jean: But God is also all-loving. Do you think our loving God would inflict this kind of pain and heartache on you?

Patient Jean: You mean this isn't God's doing?

Pastor Jean: An important part of my theology, Jean, is that fertilizer happens. It's not God.

Patient Jean: Well, if this isn't God's doing, who can I get angry at? I am bitter, and I need to direct my anger at someone.

Pastor Jean: God is big enough to receive your anger so that you don't have to carry it around in your heart. In some ways, anger can be as detrimental as cancer, Jean. Let God lift that burden from you.

Would Pastor Jean's responses satisfy me? Would they you? Or do they leave us wanting?

Medical Update:

For the past several weeks, I have been dealing with three different kinds of skin infections which look to be chemo-related. This means yet another doctor: a dermatologist. After two antibiotics, special body wash, and two different kinds of ointment, the rashes are finally starting to recede.

Last Wednesday, I had a port implanted. It was supposed to be fairly routine surgery, but it ended up being complicated. I was on the operating table (and under full anesthesia) for twice as long as expected (nothing is simple!). When I saw the surgeon this morning, she did not like the way the wound was healing, and so my chemo has been postponed a week, from tomorrow to 8/7. That means I had to push my quarterly scans appointment with Dana-Farber back also – it is now rescheduled for 8/27.

The good news is that the "good week" I usually have this time of the month (boy, has *that* phrase taken on a new meaning!!) but lost due to my rashes and port surgery has miraculously been given back to me. So I have been able to schedule an appointment with the orthopedic doctor about my knee before my next chemo knocks me down again.

MONDAY, AUGUST 5, 2013

GOING – NOT

(If you have ever been on prescription pain medications for an extended period of time, you might understand the following.)

I wish I could go.
That's not the same as
I wish I could leave.
Leaving means
Getting out of my chair

Exiting the parlor
Departing the house
For faraway places,
like CVS and the doctor's office.

I pray I could go.
No, seriously.
With prayer beads in hand
I beseech the Almighty
"Let me go."
Not quite the same as when
Moses confronted Pharaoh
About his people.
But in a very basic way,
Just as important to me.

I yearn to go,
and I have an army behind me.
Pills and powders and prescriptions,
Fluids and fiber
Liquids and laxatives
And other weapons that even I
am too self-conscious to name
All lined up like soldiers in this epic battle
Against the unseen enemy.

It has come to this.
I long not for a cure
Or whacked moles and slain dragons.
I plead not for an easy chemo
Or relief from the pain.
I covet not another person's good health
Or feeling well enough

to work, to play, and to fill
my head with frivolous thoughts and
my days with inconsequential acts
that have nothing to do with cancer.

No, my whole life
has been reduced to this:
I wish I could go.

TUESDAY, AUGUST 6, 2013

RELIEF!

Today I have received relieving news on several fronts.

First, my port surgeon was pleased with the way my wound has healed since last week, and she took out my stitches. The port should be ready for testing when I go for chemo tomorrow morning.

Also, I saw my orthopedist about my knee. This was the doctor who did my rotator cuff surgery in 2009, not the one who last winter misdiagnosed my spinal tumor as a muscle pull. The MRI results show that I have a full tear of my Posterior Cruciate Ligament (PCL) as well as a partial tear of my meniscus. The doctor feels that we can hold off on surgery for now, which means we will not need to delay any chemo treatments (a PCL tear is less debilitating than an ACL). He says rest might be enough to heal my knee – and I am certainly getting enough rest these days.

And – it seems that my use of the term "go" in yesterday's "poem" was misinterpreted as "die" and scared the daylights out of some people! I thought for sure the reference to fiber was a dead give-away, but evidently it was too subtle, so I have added a line about laxatives – and yes, I have received relief on this front (or should I say rear?), too!

Thank you all for your love and concern!

WEDNESDAY, AUGUST 7, 2013

CHEMO – ROUND 3

I am getting to be an old pro at this chemo deal. Peter brought me in for my 11 a.m. infusion today and then took off for home with my blessing so he could get some of his woodworking jobs done.

The infusion nurse checked my new port and said it worked "beautifully" (good news after the hassle of having it implanted). I thoroughly enjoyed my lunch of chicken noodle soup, turkey sandwich, and vanilla pudding, and then promptly fell asleep.

I awoke just before Peter arrived with Ian, who had wanted to see what goes on in the "Chemotherapy Suite." Their timing was perfect, for after they returned from lunch in the caf, my infusion was complete, and I was okayed to go home – I was back in Foxboro by 3 p.m.

Here's a pleasant surprise: I've lost 20 pounds since my last infusion 5 weeks ago. I know that sounds impressive, but it was all water weight. The nurse warned me not to lose so much weight next time (I guess it is good to have a few pounds to spare!).

The downside, of course, is that I know I will start feeling lousy in a few days. It is just part of the deal. The upside is that, while I am down for the count, the chemo will hopefully be whacking those cancer moles.

Please pray that this is what happens.

WEDNESDAY, AUGUST 21, 2013

DIFFICULT DAYS

On Thursday, August 8, I was enjoying a post-chemo high. I knew it would be short-lived, but I was relishing it all the same. And then the crash came; I grew more exhausted with every passing day. I had no energy, no creativity, and no inspiration, and every day I felt worse.

On Wednesday afternoon, August 14, I had blood work done at the hospital and then saw my local oncologist. He said my kidney function was way down, and I would need another blood transfusion the next day. So Thursday it was back to the Oncology Suite, but while there I began to suffer some intense pain around my shoulders and ribcage. I had experienced this kind of pain the last time my red blood cells had dropped, but a transfusion had taken care of it. Not this time. So they wheeled me over to the Emergency Department for an evaluation, and it turned out that neither of my kidneys were working. Needless to say, I was admitted.

My six days in the hospital are pretty much a blur, but here are the noteworthy points:

The tumors in my pelvis, the primary site of my cancer, were impinging on my ureters and preventing a smooth flow of urine from my kidneys to my bladder. So my newest doctor, a urologist, implanted stents into my ureters so they can withstand the encroachment of the tumors.

I had a total of four blood transfusions, which brought my red count up a little bit.

I had a CAT scan which revealed that the tumors in my lungs and the one in my spine have grown. The chemo drug Doxil has not worked. Of course, this is not the result we had hoped and prayed for. My oncologist has consulted with my Dana-Farber sarcoma specialist, and the plan is that I will be started on a new chemo regimen within the next week or so. I will know more tomorrow.

Today, I had my first visit (of many, no doubt) from a VNA nurse. We also had a hospital bed delivered as well as a commode (with my bad kidneys, I cannot quite make it to the bathroom these days).

I will not lie, these have been difficult days. I am certainly not ready to throw in the towel, but I feel like my health situation has slipped precipitously these past two weeks.

That is all I have the energy for now. Will write again when I am up to it.

Thank you for all your love, support, and prayers.

FRIDAY, AUGUST 23, 2013

LIVING ROOM/DYING ROOM

We live in a Victorian style house that was built in 1878. In keeping with the architecture of the period, there is a front parlor graced with a floor-to-ceiling bay window. In modern parlance, this room would be called the living room, and until recently it has functioned as a gathering place for entertaining friends and family.

However, over the course of the last five months, our parlor has evolved into a space designed less for hosting guests and more for our own comfortable day-to-day living. The first change was removing our sofa to make room for my electric-powered recliner. We rearranged some tables and wingback chairs, and the parlor was still able to convey a sense of welcome to visitors.

More recently, we added a second recliner, this one for Peter. Especially after his recent bout with hives, his well-being is paramount (he needs to be well to take care of me!), and now we can both sit and relax in comfort. These recliners take up a lot of space, and we had to sacrifice more guest seating to accommodate the second chair.

And then two days ago, a commode and a hospital bed were delivered. I do not find the bed very comfortable because of my spine tumor, but it helps Peter's finicky back, so now he spends the night with me downstairs in the parlor. This is just as well, since upstairs he would sleep fitfully, listening for my voice and coming down several times during the night to check on me.

Now, our parlor looks nothing like a place to entertain. Rather, the room bears the awkward mark of trying to be something completely different than its intended function. The first thing one would normally see when entering the front door of a Victorian home would be a gracious and inviting foyer, not a commode. But that is the way it is in our home now. The parlor, where I can picture guests through the generations enjoying tea and crumpets, should not be overpowered by a mechanical bed. But that is the way it is in our home now.

As a pastor, I have walked into a number of these retro-fitted living rooms. The addition of hospital beds and commodes, along with other similar accoutrements, have turned them into dying rooms. And that is what I fear our front parlor is becoming – a dying room. That does not mean I have given up. That does not mean I don't have hope. But please please please do not tell me how I ought to feel or not feel. It's just the way it is right now. My time in the hospital, the shutting down of my kidneys and subsequent surgery, the failure of the Doxil to stem the growth of my tumors, have all combined to bring death into closer focus.

My oncologists now want to put me on new chemo regimen of Gemcitabine and Taxotere, on a "2 on/1 off" schedule. I will have infusions on September 4 and 11, and then take the 18th off. Then back on 9/25. I pray that these new medicines will keep our living room from becoming a dying room, and I ask that you do, too.

SUNDAY, AUGUST 25, 2013

BODY BETRAYAL

I weighed only 6 pounds when I was born. That was the last time I could be considered "small," and over the ensuing six decades, I have had a love/hate relationship with my body.

I quickly grew to be a chubby child, and wishing on the night sky's first star failed to stretch out my stubby legs or skim off my layer of baby fat.

Throughout my school years, I was envious of the perfectly proportioned and athletic figures of my female classmates, and no amount of dieting seemed to reverse the fact that I had a weight problem.

I think I have tried every diet known to humanity. The Water Diet, Cabbage Soup, Stillman, Diet Workshop, Weight Watchers, Atkins, Jenny Craig, Nutrisystem – you name it, I've tried it. When the diet worked (or I worked the diet) and I was able to get down to a small size (I was actually a 4 Petite at one point), I was proud of the way I looked. But when I let things get out of hand and the weight came back on, I felt like a colossal failure.

At the beginning of this millennium, I worked hard and lost 85 pounds. I will say it: I looked hot! But within a few years, I got lackadaisical about what I put in my mouth, and foot problems (plantar fasciitis) interfered with my exercise regimen. Before I knew it, all the weight I had struggled to lose had found its way back onto my body. I consider this one of the greatest failings of my life – not keeping that weight off. In fact, I was so mortified that I decided I would never diet again – what was the point if I did not have the emotional and mental fortitude to keep the weight off?

Other than my weight problems, I have tried to take good care of my body. Could I have done anything to change the circumstances under which I am now living? All indications are no – nothing I could have done would have prevented the cancer, including keeping my weight in check.

So, have I betrayed my body, or has my body betrayed me? Moreover, is it even possible to divide the body from the spirit – without our bodies, our souls have no house in which to dwell in this earthly life.

Someday, I will be set free from this earthen vessel. Of course, I must die for that to happen, and I would rather live in this decrepit abode for a while longer than face the alternative anytime soon.

But when the day does come, I will be cremated – finally shedding this earth suit that has brought me both pleasure and pain. I will not need it where I am going – and my spirit will be able to soar unencumbered by earthly concerns.

THURSDAY, AUGUST 29, 2013

DANCING ON GRAVES

Yesterday I read with surprise and delight that actress Valerie Harper has signed on for this season's "Dancing with the Stars." Harper, who played Rhoda Morgenstern on "The Mary Tyler Moore Show" and "Rhoda" decades ago (both of which I watched religiously), announced in March that she had a rare form of brain cancer and that doctors had given her only three months to live.

And now she is defying that grim prognosis by undertaking the grueling regimen of weekly dance routines. In the past I have not had the time to watch "DWTS," but now I do – and maybe I will tune in to root for this most courageous and gutsy woman.

I think it is a natural human tendency to want definitive answers – what will happen and how and when? I remember when my husband

Darcy was in the last week of his life, I asked the nurse, "When do you think he will die?" It was not enough to know that he was actively dying; I wanted to know the day and time. In the midst of almost two years of uncertainty regarding his prognosis and our future, I needed something concrete to hold on to – even if it was something as heartbreaking as time of death.

But the nurse would not, could not give me a definitive answer, saying in effect, "Your husband is imminently moribund, but we cannot know with any precision when his organs will cease functioning."

I suppose somewhere deep in my heart, I too would like to know when I am going to die. Living in a state of unknowing can be exhausting. And it would make planning ever so much easier! I would no longer drive myself to tears wondering whether I was going to be present for Lizzy's college commencement next May, or Ian's high school graduation in June 2015. I would no longer wonder whether – with my recent hospitalization and failed chemo – if I am currently on a downward spiral towards the inevitable, or simply hitting a bump in the road.

Alas, despite the certitude sometimes displayed by the medical community, we just do not know when the organs will fail, when the heart will stop beating, when the brain will stop functioning.

And the best way to respond is to live fully into each moment, regardless of the prognosis.

Valerie Harper has made the decision not to yield to the grave, but to dance on it instead. I pray I may display the same strength and grace in the face of death.

WEDNESDAY, SEPTEMBER 11, 2013

MEDICAL UPDATE

It has been a while since I have written, so here is what has been going on with me medically.

On Labor Day Sunday, I awoke with a terrible ache in my lower back (lumbar region). My main physical complaint with cancer has been mid-back (thoracic region) pain, so the lumbar pain was unusual.

I tried to ignore it and not say anything, since we had family visiting for the weekend. But when I started to cry, everyone knew something was drastically wrong. The thermometer registered a temp, and after a telephone call to my primary care physician, Peter took me down to the hospital around noontime. The Emergency Department was expecting me, thanks to my doctor, so I did not have to spend too long in the waiting room.

A series of tests revealed I had a raging urinary tract infection (UTI), so they infused me with antibiotics, and I was able to return home around dinner time.

I had never before had a UTI, so I was not prepared for how absolutely wretched I ended up feeling. Of course, it could have been as much from the antibiotic Cipro as it was from the UTI itself. Fortunately, I finished the course of Cipro this past Sunday (9/8) and felt really quite well this past Monday and Tuesday.

In fact, on Monday, I was able to attend Ian's home opener football game, and the Foxboro Warriors won 21-0 against Walpole. Woo hoo!

Then yesterday, I had a wonderful visit from my forever friend Dee-dee, who had travelled from her home in San Diego to bring her daughter to college in Providence. Dee-dee and I were inseparable friends beginning in Kindergarten, and it was wonderful seeing her again!

Today, I started my new chemo treatment of Gemcitabine and Taxotere. I will receive infusions twice in a three week cycle – on/on/off. I am delighted to report that today's infusion proceeded without a hitch – I am back home feeling quite well. I know this good feeling will not last, but I am living into the moment.

I will have six weeks of this new cocktail, and then it will be time for another scan. Please pray that the GemTax will shrink my tumors – I really need some good news!

TUESDAY, SEPTEMBER 17, 2013

THE HOUSE OF OUR HEART

This past Sunday, I attended a birthday party for Michele, the mother of my step children. The party was held at Michele's house which, coincidentally, is my old house. (See my entry of April 15, "I've Already Got My Happy Ending!").

I lived at that house in Hopkinton from 1983 to 1985 – between marriages – before selling it to Peter and Michele and moving closer to my new job in Dedham. Two years seems like a short time to live in a house I owned, but when I think back over all the homes I have had, I can see a pattern of restlessness. Four years in Webster, six years in the Medfield log home, two years in the colonial in Medfield, four years in Quincy, six years in Ipswich....

Certainly the circumstances of my life – the deaths of Darcy and John, attending seminary, being called to a church – played roles in my decisions to move. But I think the deeper reason for my restiveness was an unsatisfied yearning in my heart. Something was missing from my life (love, peace, fulfillment, God) that prevented me from being content. And this yearning was revealed in my desire to change my external surroundings.

I particularly remember my years in the Medfield colonial. It was a stately five-bedroom house on a cul de sac in one of the town's most desirable developments. From the outside, it looked as if I had "made it." But the external trappings belied the chaos that raged within. John's addiction was out of control, and I had neither the heart nor the wherewithal to stop my co-dependency and make the tough decisions that would get us both on the road to health. Add in a stressful and meaningless job I detested, and – except for the joy of my baby girl – I was completely miserable.

And how did my despair manifest? Almost every time I walked into that house, I thought of how I wanted to change it. Knock down a wall here. Remodel that. Add a bathroom. Bring the washer and dryer up from the basement. There was no end to the projects I envisioned, and I felt I could not be comfortable in that house until they were accomplished; if I could just get my house to my liking, my life would follow suit. Alas, we did not have the money to tackle such projects, and it is probably just as well – no amount of changes to the house would satisfy my heart. I had to undertake a remodeling of my life to accomplish that.

Fast forward to the present. Peter and I have lived in our Foxboro house for eight years, and I am completely content here. It is not a perfect house – some rooms certainly need redecorating, and I am still waiting for that second bathroom upstairs – but it is a comfortable house. Or am I the one who is comfortable?

Isn't that a kick? When I was physically healthy and had the world by a string, I was miserable. Now, when I am fighting for my life, I have never been more contented in my own skin, never more joy-filled. It does not mean that I am not ticked off about my diagnosis, or that I don't wish things were different, but in my heart of hearts, my emptiness has been fulfilled and my yearning satisfied. And I am grateful.

THURSDAY, SEPTEMBER 19, 2013

IT'S ALWAYS SOMETHING

When I was much younger and had the stamina to stay up late, I loved watching "Saturday Night Live." One memorable character from the original cast back in the '70s was a frizzy-haired, obnoxious personal advice expert named Roseanne Rosannadanna played by Gilda Radner. Roseanne often concluded her bits with the catchphrase "It just goes to show you – it's always something."

Later in the 80s, Radner penned an autobiography entitled *It's Always Something*, which was published a few months before her death in May 1989 from ovarian cancer at age 42.

And yours truly can say the same thing about living with cancer: it's always something. I never know from moment to moment what minor or major health issue is going to pop up.

Consider the following:

For weeks after my August hospitalization, I had painful, bloody, weeping sores up my arm where the phlebotomist had used adhesive tape, to which I am allergic (doesn't anyone read the "allergies" list?).

The compression boots I wore during that hospitalization left deep gashes in my ankles which are still healing.

If I am not careful, simply brushing my teeth will turn into a 15-minute bout of dry heaves.

For no reason at all, I will swallow (usually just saliva or water) the "wrong way," and a gagging fit will ensue.

Not to mention that I am regularly irregular (see my August 5 blog).

And just this past Tuesday, I started peeing blood. This was disconcerting, especially because hematuria was the first symptom of Darcy's kidney cancer. I called the Oncology Department at the hospital to report this development, and they passed it along to my oncologist. He determined that the bleeding was probably related not so much to my cancer per se, but rather to my kidney problem which put me in the hospital in the first place last month.

So this morning I saw my urologist. Peter and I spent two hours in the waiting room (good thing there was a TV!) before getting in to see the doctor, just to have him say that bleeding was normal. Oh.

We then saw my oncologist, who was delighted to hear me say that I felt "terrific." And it is true – I feel unbelievably well considering I have had two chemo treatments in the last eight days. It would be wonderful if this is indicative of how easily I will be tolerating the

Gemcitabine/Taxotere cocktail over next couple of months. It is great to feel (relatively) great, but I am not getting my hopes up.

Because, you know, it's always something...

FRIDAY, SEPTEMBER 20, 2013

ONE DAY VS. DAY ONE

My mornings start slowly. I can wake up anytime between 4 and 8 a.m. (but I *do* wake up, which is what matters), and I take a few pre-meal pills. Then a little breakfast, chased by the rest of my morning pills.

I do this while watching the morning news. I have settled on WCVB for local news, followed by "Good Morning America," which is on the same station. But it is more than convenience that has me watching GMA. It's Robin Roberts.

Robin was a standout basketball player in college and went on to ESPN as a sportscaster before joining GMA. But she is perhaps as well known for her courage in the face of health challenges.

In 2007 Roberts was diagnosed with an early form of breast cancer, which was treated with surgery followed by chemo and radiation. Then in 2012 she was diagnosed with myeldyplastic syndrome (MDS) – also known as "pre-leukemia"– and underwent a life-saving bone marrow transplant which took place one year ago today. So today, Robin is celebrating her "one year birthday" – one year since she received a new beginning.

Today, Robin is radiantly healthy, and although our illnesses are different, she inspires me. This morning she said that so many people talk about "one day" – "one day.... I will be happy... or healthy... or fulfilled." Robin exhorts us to turn that around and say today is "Day One" of feeling happy, healthy, fulfilled.

I know the score about my situation – there are no "life-saving" options available for me like there were for Robin. But there are life-prolonging treatments – and I am prepared to undergo every one available in the never-ending hope that something will work. But I have not put my life on hold until I feel better. I do not spend my days thinking "one day, I will be healthy" any more than I spending them thinking "one day, I'm going to die." I try to live each day to the fullest – and the funnest.

Hence, my new pink hair, thanks to my hairstylist niece who visited from Virginia over Labor Day Weekend. And in a few weeks, I will be bald. In fact, I am thinking of speeding the process along by shaving my head. When I mentioned this to Peter, he gave me a look, but I said, "Hey, if I've gotta go through this, I'm going through it *my* way! I've even toyed with the idea of getting a tattoo, but have not yet settled on a design compelling enough for me to take this major step.

Yesterday my oncologist said attitude is so important. "The ones who give up tend not to make it." Well, I am not giving up by a long shot, and I am trying to eke out as much life and as many laughs as possible from my situation.

Is cancer fun? No, but there can be fun and funny aspects to it – if you look hard enough.

Is cancer good? No, but good can come from it and can be experienced in the midst of it – if you keep your heart open.

Is cancer going to get me? My body, maybe, someday. But never my soul. Never my spirit. Never what makes me me.

That's the way it's been since Day One, and I am never giving up.

MONDAY, SEPTEMBER 23, 2013

MY TENDER SPOT

Today, my baby boy turns 17.

He is 6 feet tall, weighs 177, and wears size 14 shoe. But he will always be my baby boy.

He has many gifts, most of which he does not recognize in himself. He has got a great sense of humor and is fun to be around. He is a wonderful writer. He is a talented drummer. He can dance! And I know he is hiding a lovely singing voice.

The sides that he is willing to project to the world are that of athlete and history buff.

He is a three sport athlete in school – last year, it was football, winter track (shot put) and spring track (javelin), and he also played basketball in the town league. He will be playing on the high school basketball team this coming winter.

He loves history. He has always had a mind like a steel trap, and he eats up dates, facts, and figures (which he also puts to use with sports minutiae).

But what makes me so proud is that he is just a wonderful kid. I know that sounds like the gushing of a very partial mom, but his friends' parents and his teachers have always raved about his good manners and respectfulness, and he truly has a heart of gold. When he found out that one of his best friends might not have enough money to go to college, he asked us if he could give him some out of his own college fund.

I cannot imagine the last 17 years without my boy. But Ian would not be here were it not for his sister Lizzy.

I had Lizzy when I was 35 years old – pretty old for a first-time mom. I was wrapped up in my (pre-ministry) financial services career, and Lizzy was in daycare from 7 a.m. to 6 p.m., five days a week. The years went by, I was getting older, and I gave no thought to expanding our family, until one day...

Lizzy was in the den watching "Sesame Street," and I was standing quietly in the doorway behind her. On the TV was a segment with a little girl extolling the virtues of being an only child. "I love being an only child!" she concluded. To which Lizzy responded, shouting back at the TV, "Well, I *hate* being an only child!"

Lizzy's passion caught me off guard, and I asked her about it. She wanted siblings – a brother or a sister, preferably four of each! If Lizzy had been happy as an only child, I would never have thought about adding to our family. But at the ripe old age of 42, I gave birth, and Lizzy got a beautiful little brother.

I have often shuddered at what a lonely life it would have been for Lizzy without Ian. After John died, it would have been just her and me. But having Ian made us a family.

Ian, who was just a baby when John died, never had the chance to know his Daddy, although we are all blessed that he has a Dad in Peter. And now Ian is facing the real possibility of losing his mother.

It's not fair! Ian should not have to worry about whether I am going to be around to attend his football games, or see him off to his prom, or go through the college application process, or watch him graduate. But here we are. That is the reality we are dealing with.

And it's my tender spot.

I can contemplate dry-eyed my own death. I know that Peter will be heartbroken, but he will make it okay. Lizzy is mature beyond her years, and while I know she will miss me terribly, she will be fine.

But even thinking about leaving Ian before he is out of high school causes me literal pain in my heart and makes me weep. My poor baby. This is not how I wanted things to be, my sweet boy. I would do anything to change our circumstances. I am so sorry, honey, so sorry so sorry.

And so, my baby is 17. I pray I will be around to see him turn 18... and 19... and beyond. But we have all been blessed that he has graced our lives for 17 years, and I am grateful I have seen a delightful little boy grow up into a wonderful young man. So that is what I am focusing on today, not what tomorrow might bring. Today is a day to celebrate and to thank God for the precious gift of my son.

MONDAY, SEPTEMBER 30, 2013

COLLATERAL DAMAGE

One of the most difficult aspects of having Stage IV cancer is seeing the toll my illness is taking on my loved ones.

Beryl has cancelled her plans to spend another winter in Steamboat Springs, Colorado, so she can be near us.

Despite my efforts to disabuse her of the notion, Lizzy is wracked with guilt because college prevents her from spending more time in Foxboro.

Peter is still breaking out in hives, a stress reaction which has plagued him for months.

And this morning, Ian came home ill from school with sharp stomach pains. Peter took him right to the doctor and the diagnosis is strep. A few weeks ago, Ian had a terrible sore throat, and at that time, the doctor said it was a virus and he was just going to have to wait it out. Now he is on antibiotics, which hopefully will knock this bug out of him once and for all.

Ian is rarely sick. But we are not even out of September, and he has already been absent four days, with more to come. I am sure the root of the problem is stress. School is stressful (he's in that all-important junior year). Football is stressful (Coach isn't happy with the Warriors' 1-2 start). And home is a hotbed of stress because, rather than providing a sanctuary from his troubles, it is where he comes face to face with them.

Even though I am the one who is sick, in many ways I think I have got it the easiest. Oh, it is not fun to wake up dry heaving, or to sneeze and feel like my back is going to explode. But I have come to the conclusion that I am having an easier time dealing with cancer – and facing my mortality – than others are.

Caring for a seriously ill person can be taxing. And even though I try to do things for myself when I am up to it, I am afraid I can be demanding without even meaning to be. If I do not get my medications on time, the pain can get away from us. Peter needs to help me bathe. I can be a baby about taking my pills. I can get too comfortable in my chair and not want to move.

Cancer has collateral damage. And so I ask that you pray not so much for me, but for my family members who lovingly and uncomplainingly care for me, despite the toll it is taking on their hearts, minds, and bodies.

FRIDAY, OCTOBER 4, 2013

PURPLE POWER!

October is Breast Cancer Awareness Month, which means we will be seeing a profusion of pink and a proliferation of related articles, news stories, and promotions over the next several weeks.

Worldwide, breast cancer accounts for 22.9% of all cancers (excluding non-melanoma skin cancers) in women. In 2008, breast cancer caused 458,503 deaths worldwide (13.7% of cancer deaths in women).

Compare those stats to leiomyosarcoma, the cancer I have. Less than 10% of cancers are sarcomas (soft tissue cancer), and of that small number, only 5-10% are leiomyosarcoma. Put another way, only 4 in 1 million people get leiomyosarcoma. How did I get so lucky?

Leiomyosarcomas are aggressive tumors and among the more difficult soft-tissue sarcomas to treat. The prognosis is poor, with survival rates among the lowest of all soft tissue sarcomas.

I have Stage IV leiomyosarcoma, which means it has spread from my pelvis where it began to distant sites – in my case, my T6 vertebrae and both lungs.

Leiomyosarcoma is a resistant cancer. Currently there is no cure for Stage IV, which is not very responsive to chemotherapy or radiation. The best outcome occurs when the cancer is removed surgically, but my tumors are inoperable.

Not very pretty, is it? I have a cancer that almost no one has heard of, is hard to spell and pronounce, and has a pretty grim prognosis, especially for Stage IV patients like me.

No wonder there is no "Leiomyosarcoma Awareness Month" (or week or day). No wonder there is no profusion of purple, its cause color.

Sometimes I think it would be easier to have a more common cancer; certainly it would be easier to have one with a more positive prognosis.

But here I am. It took me a few months, but I have finally gotten used to the fact that I do not have decades, perhaps not even years, left. I am resigned to the fact that I probably will never hold a grandchild or even attend a child's wedding.

This does not mean I am giving up! It just means my dreams are more modest. Lizzy's college commencement this coming May. Ian's high school graduation in June 2015.

And yet, life is good – very good! Because I cannot count on a future, I do not focus on it, which gives me more time to enjoy the here and now.

For instance, there are four – *four* – baseball play-off games on TV today (including the Red Sox) – heaven for a baseball junkie like me. I have friends coming to visit. Ian is almost fully recovered from his bout of strep. Lizzy is coming down tonight.

And after four hours of chemo this past Wednesday, and then five hours yesterday of being transfused with two units of blood, I am feeling pretty well!

To paraphrase the late, great Lou Gehrig, you may think that I've had a bad break. But I've got to tell you – I am feeling very blessed.

TUESDAY, OCTOBER 8, 2013

MY WAY

I have become almost obsessed with my hair.

Back in April, not long after my diagnosis, I had my hairdresser chop off my shoulder-length bob, which had become more than I could handle; washing, blow drying, straightening was all too much work. Anyway, I figured it would all fall out once I started chemo.

But it did not. Write-ups on the side effects of Doxil, my first chemo med, stated that thin hair would go bald, but thick hair would thin. I had thick hair, and while it did thin, most of it held tenaciously to my scalp. It also turned gray since there was no sense in coloring it any longer.

I figured if I was going to have hair after all, let's have a little fun. That is when I got the pink/purple/teal dye job. I must tell you, it is liberating not having to groom to meet someone else's expectations. If I had dyed my hair this way while I was still working, no matter the job, I think people would conclude I was a little off my rocker, or at least too edgy for my own good. But under my current circumstances, my multi-colored hair has met with universal approval – and, in some cases, envy.

But it was not enough.

When the Doxil did not work and I went on to the Gem/Tax cocktail, I was assured that I would lose my hair. So I waited. And waited. Again my hair held on.

I know I am in the minority of cancer patients who actually *want* to go bald. For many, especially women, hair represents health, normalcy, and beauty. But for me, going bald was going to be a kick! When else could I go hairless and not be considered a total whack job?

So I decided I would force the inevitable by going to the barber shop. I spent a week vacillating between having my head completely shaved and simply cropped short. I was pretty much settled on a total shave job when Lizzy pointed out that if we left a little hair, we could reinvigorate the color with a new dye job. That's how I came to sport a "high and tight" with purple highlights.

I know Peter shakes his head at the crazy way I am handling my illness, but he is very tolerant. I just feel strongly that I have to travel this journey my way.

And now I want a tattoo; I just have to get the okay from my oncologist. I have settled on the design: I want on my left inner forearm (so I can see them) the words, "...then we will see face to face..." which is from 1 Corinthians 13:12, my favorite scripture passage. (Lizzy said she's going to get a matching tat.) They are also words I hang on to. "For now, we see in a mirror dimly, but then we will see face to face..."[104] The face of God. The face of Jesus. The face of my mother. That is what's awaiting me beyond this life, and it is a comforting promise.

And so, I am on a wild ride, but on my last day on earth, I know I will be able to say that I travelled this final journey my way.

THURSDAY, OCTOBER 10, 2013

RIGHT BELOW THE SURFACE

Yesterday I had another chemo treatment, and it went very well. Because I had stayed up late the night before cheering on the Sox (yay!!), I was exhausted. Add in my before-chemo trank, and I was more than ready for a little shuteye. So after eating a nice comfort-food lunch (soup, chicken pie, carrot cake), I snuggled down and slept for two hours while poison was infused into my body. By the time I woke up, it was almost time to go home.

And today, I am feeling quite well, although the steroids that were part of yesterday's treatment kept me wide awake until 3:00 a.m. But today I have no appointments, no visitors, nothing on the docket, so I am just going to take it easy.

When I walked into the Chemo Department (the hospital calls it a "suite," but that just may be pushing things) yesterday, all the nurses smiled at my "high and tight" and purple dye job. I think, after four months, they have become used to Crazy Jean. But I really try to put on an upbeat demeanor when I enter the infusion room. Despite the nurses' smiling faces and compassionate, attentive care, it is not the most cheery of places, as you can imagine.

Some patients face their treatment with a matter-of-fact air that belies their health challenges. But yesterday there was a 31-year-old fellow across from me, and it was painful to look at him. He lay with his hand covering his closed eyes, his father sitting next to him offering support and companionship. (I knew it had to be his Dad, because they looked exactly alike – except his father had hair.) I do not know what cancer he is battling, but I can understand if he is wondering how his future will unfold and asking why he has to spend a beautiful autumn day getting chemo.

So I make it a point of putting a smile on my face and letting my hair and my purple "Leiomyosarcoma SUCKS" button quietly do the rest when I am in the infusion room. I mentioned this as I was describing my yesterday to Lizzy on the phone this morning, and she dropped the word "brave." And I burst into tears.

Because I'm not so brave.

Right below the surface is a hurting, confused, and rather angry woman who is wondering what happened to her beautiful life.

Right below the surface is a pastor who does not have a great relationship with God right now.

Right below the surface is a wife and mom who is heartbroken because her future has suddenly been pulled out from under her, and her loved ones' altered forever.

Right below the surface is woman of faith who believes strongly in eternal life but very much wants to stay in this earthly life.

Oh, thanks to anti-depressants and pain pills, I can come across as courageous and fearless and upbeat. But I'm not, really. The tears are there, right below the surface.

SATURDAY, OCTOBER 12, 2013

THE NIGHT THAT CHANGED MY LIFE

As someone who pays attention to dates and anniversaries, I wish I had had the energy to write this entry yesterday. Alas, chemo side effects got the better of me, so I am celebrating one day late.

Ten years ago yesterday, October 11, 2003, I attended my 30th high school reunion. Actually, it was my 30th reunion one year late; I was in the class of 1972, but it took a while for the organizers to get their act together. And so, on a beautiful autumn evening, I drove down from my home in Ipswich to the Wellesley College Club to catch up with old high school chums.

It had been a busy day for me. I had already attended the wedding of good friend Paula earlier in the afternoon in Chelmsford. It had been a difficult decision for me to go to the ceremony but skip the reception, but that was the only way I was going to be able to attend the reunion.

And so, after Paula and Tony's ceremony, I drove back to Ipswich, showered (again), put on fresh make-up and a different outfit, and hit the road for Wellesley.

I entered the reception hall where the festivities were taking place, and a familiar face stood out among all the others: the tall, skinny redhead I had sat next to during tenth grade Algebra. He was still tall and skinny, but not quite the "hippie" I remembered. I made my way over to him and started to chat (see my entry of April 15, "I've Already Got My Happy Ending!").

Turns out, Peter had hemmed and hawed about attending himself because he had not been feeling well that day. But he pulled himself together and made it to the reunion.

By the end of the evening, I was completely smitten. And I guess he was, too, because he got in touch with me the next day.

Nice story, huh? Well, it was a little more complicated than that. I had been in a relationship for a couple of years, but by 2003, I was ready to move on. (Had our 30th reunion been held on time, our story might have had a different ending.) It took a few more months to work things out, but – finally! – on January 23, 2004, Peter and I went out on our first date, and we were married 14 months later.

I have often thought – usually with a catch of my breath – of how close Peter and I came to not connecting that night. What if he had decided to stay home? What if I had decided to attend Paula's wedding reception? What if we had just somehow missed talking to each other at the reunion? What if he had not been encouraged by his friend Jerry to get in touch with me the next day? What if I had not reached out to him once I was single again? What if he had changed his mind about me?

What if... what if...

We can "what if..." ourselves to distraction about life. But what if I did not have Peter in my life now? I would be completely lost. I cannot imagine going (and I would not want to go) through my current situation without him. A magnificent man of honor, integrity, and decency. A wonderful father for my children. He is my strength, my heart, my best friend, my partner, the love of my life.

We came *so close* to not re-connecting that I truly believe the Hand of God was with us that night ten years ago, bringing us together, and changing our lives forever.

MONDAY, OCTOBER 14, 2013

UNWELCOME INTRUDER/MERCIFUL HEALER

A few days ago, I learned of the sudden death of a former co-worker.

We had not been more than work colleagues, had not seen each other in ten years, and her death actually occurred almost two years ago. Nevertheless, I was shocked.

The last couple of days I have been pondering why her death hit me so hard.

Because she always seemed so vital and full of life? Because she was a couple of years younger than me? Because it was sudden and there was no warning? Because it reminded me – once again – of the fragility of life? Because I have no wake or funeral where I can express my condolences to her family or deal with my own feelings?

This woman's passing does not change my life one iota, and yet it has moved me.

And that is what death does. It catches us unexpectedly. We react with unanticipated feelings. We are caught emotionally flat-footed, not knowing why we respond the way we do, sometimes not even knowing how to respond at all.

I have conducted too many funerals of people who died suddenly. And their loved ones seemed to be in shock, unable to process the awfulness of it all. Mothers and brothers and girlfriends unable to even bring up tears, because their protective mechanisms were just trying to get them through those first dreadful days.

In such cases, I included these words in the funeral homily:

Death comes through many doors. For some it slips through the door marked "Merciful Healer" and liberates a person from pain, illness, and a worn-out body. In these cases it is easy to see how death fits normally into the circle of life.

Then there are those times when death bursts through the door marked "Unwelcome Intruder." It comes as a vicious thief and robs the victim and his family of the life that was God's intention. These deaths make no sense, and they frustrate our attempts to provide easy answers when hurting people ask "why?"[105]

When a loved one is taken from us abruptly, the imposition of death onto our lives is almost unbearable. We are struck by the fragile nature of our existence, and we are frightened to know how quickly life can be taken away from us. And of course, we are brokenhearted and stirred at the deepest level of our emotions with pain and grief.

I know firsthand that an anticipated death is no less difficult to deal with than a sudden one. It's just different.

I found this out the hard way when Darcy died. He had been labeled terminal from his diagnosis because his cancer had spread, and treatment protocols back in the early '80s were relatively limited. For almost two years, we knew he was dying. That did not mean we had lost hope. But the radiation failed in slowing down the death train. And every three months, the scans would show a new metastasis: to his bones, to his lungs, to his brain.

I grieved so much before his death that I naively figured his passing would be a relief rather than a heartbreak. But I was wrong. That is one of the things about death – we are never ready, even when we think we are.

I remember officiating at the funeral of a 103-year-old woman, and her family was bereft. Of course they were – grief does not respect age or cause. It just comes. It just is. We cannot control it, and we cannot avoid it, and that is why I included the following in all the funerals I conducted:

I don't think any of us are ever truly ready to say good-bye to a loved one. No matter how death happens, suddenly or slowly due to illness, nothing can prepare us for the actual sense of sorrow and loss we feel. We wish we could have held onto our loved one just a little bit longer. Even when we see death as a friend who brings an end to suffering, there is still something in us that wishes we could have stopped time, before illness took its toll.

Despite my efforts to get back to "normal" (or to find a "new normal") after Darcy's death – developing new friendships, finding new hobbies and interests – I felt like I was spinning my wheels. I could not move forward, no matter what I did. Grief enshrouded my life, and there seemed to be no escape. And eventually I slipped into the black abyss of depression.

It took a couple of years, but with the help of medication and therapy, I was able to get on with my life. And I learned a valuable lesson: each person must do the hard work of grief for him- or herself. No one can do it for you. The only way to get *over* the grief is to work *through* the grief.

Fifteen years later, John died suddenly. He walked out of the house perfectly healthy (except for the little problem of his heroin addiction) and never returned. This time I knew what I had to do: the hard work of grief. And it was a much healthier recovery from loss, despite the shock and circumstances of his death. In both losses – expected and unexpected – my heart was broken, my life interrupted. It was how I dealt with my grief that made the difference.

And now, I ponder how people will react to my death when it happens. I hope that people will remember my laugh and sense of humor, how I loved every minute of my life (even the difficult times, which taught me to appreciate every good moment), how I felt so blessed to have such wonderful friends and family and a vocation that gave my life meaning and purpose.

I do not want people going around with a pain in the pit of their stomachs, trying to absorb the awfulness. I do not want awfulness. I want fond memories, smiles, a renewed appreciation for health, and a gratitude for life.

For me, my death will be liberating! It will free me from feeling sick all the time and enable me to fly unencumbered by a diseased body.

I do not want to leave this earthly life, but when I do, I know I am going to be fine. I just want everyone else to be, too.

FRIDAY, OCTOBER 25, 2013

SCANXIETY

Okay everyone, I need your prayers! Next Thursday morning – yes, Halloween – I will be undergoing a scan to see how my tumors have (or have not) responded to my latest chemo cocktail. The results will determine how we move forward and will also give a good indication of what my future may hold. I would be happy if the tumors have stayed status quo, delighted if they have shrunk.

So please start sending those prayers heavenward. I will get the results when I see my oncologist on Thursday, November 7, and will of course let you know.

In the meantime, Lizzy and I are going to get matching tattoos tomorrow!

THURSDAY, NOVEMBER 7, 2013

NEWS

Hey everyone, Lizzy here. I came down from Salem to accompany Mom and Peter to her visit today with her local oncologist. This was the big day where we were getting the results of last week's CAT scan.

She has asked me to write today's blog, because she continues to be wiped out from chemo.

(Note: I asked her if she wanted me to just type what she said, and she said no. She wanted me to type in my own words. She then began to tell me, word for word, exactly what to say. Even the worst chemo side effects can't stop her from finding something to micro-manage. Haha.)

Here are the results in a nutshell:

The tumors in her lungs have not grown. We don't have too much information about the spine tumor, but as of right now, no news is good news. There seems to be an inflamed lymph node in her abdomen (near her aorta). However, it is unclear right now if the node is cancerous, or just inflamed. She will soon be having a PET scan to figure that out. If it is not cancerous, great; who wants more cancer? If it IS cancerous, that's not the worst. The doctor had wanted to do another biopsy, so the node could provide a really great sample. It would be much safer and easier to biopsy the lymph node as opposed to her lungs. Her oncologist will soon be consulting with Dana-Farber to figure out the next steps.

(This is where she became distracted with being a mom to Ian, so I will finish the rest myself.)

In other words, it's neither good nor bad, it just is. We always prepare ourselves for a black or white answer; whether they've grown, shrunk, and stayed the same. However, it's never like that. It's always complicated.

Knowing my Mom, I am not surprised. She never took the easy way in anything. If something was too easy, she would figure out a way to complicate it. She couldn't just get cancer, she had to get a super rare cancer. If that wasn't enough, it had to act abnormal for an abnormal cancer. We get it Mom, you like a challenge. Now quit showing off.

Thank you all for your continued love and prayers.

TUESDAY, NOVEMBER 19, 2013

I'M BA-A-A-CK

It has been ages since I posted, and I am not quite sure why I chose to be so silent.

I originally went on "hiatus" in mid-October when my laptop needed service, but it was returned to me fixed in days, not weeks as originally projected.

Unfortunately, I just could not motivate myself to get writing again, not even when the Sox won the World Series. I wanted to share the results of my October 31 scan and had my daughter Lizzy write it; I was just not up to it myself. In fact, it has been ages since I have checked my emails or Facebook – it just seemed to require more energy than I could muster up.

It has been three weeks since my last chemo treatment, and I am slowly recovering from the side effects. My appetite completely disappeared (a first!), and Peter was reduced to holding a piece of toast up to my lips, begging me to "Eat, eat!" But I just couldn't. Fortunately, food is starting to look good to me again, and my energy is slowly returning.

I have been plagued by other relatively minor health concerns. My blood pressure has periodically dipped while my heart rate has been elevated ("tachycardia") – signs of dehydration. I have been to the hospital twice over the last couple of weeks to receive IV fluids; then yesterday I visited my primary care physician who put me on antibiotics for a UTI.

Well, whatever the reason for my silence, I am back, and here's an update on what's going on.

Last Saturday (11/16), I had a PET scan (Positron Emission Tomography), which is a nuclear medical imaging technique that produces a three-dimensional picture of the body. My 10/31 CAT scan revealed a lymph node in my abdomen which was "making itself known" (my oncologist's words), and the PET scan will show whether the node is cancerous or simply inflamed. Hopefully, we will get the PET scan results within the next day or so.

But even if the node is cancerous, it is not all bad; in that case, the doctor would like to have it biopsied to see if the data it reveals will enable the doctors to find a chemo cocktail which will be more effective against my kind of cancer. After all, the Doxil (my first chemo drug) was a bust; the tumors in my lung grew. Then the Gemcitabine/Taxotere combo was only slightly better; the tumors did not grow, but they did not shrink either. In other words, there has been a net increase in tumor size since I was first diagnosed.

The other news is that I am no longer Pastor of the First Congregational Church of Stoughton. Once my Long Term Disability was approved last month, it was time to submit my formal resignation so that the church could move forward into a future which did not include me. So, this past Sunday, the church held a lovely "farewell" for me. It was the first time I had been to worship since Easter, which was my last Sunday in the pulpit. It was wonderful seeing all the people who mean so much to me, and they were gracious in their kind words and sentiments.

And while leaving is bittersweet, it is absolutely the right thing to do; I just do not see me regaining my health to the point that I can work again, no matter what the job.

But who knows what the future holds? I hardly think about it anymore. Eight months after my diagnosis, I am so used to life with Stage IV Cancer that I hardly remember what it was like to feel well. Life "DC" (during cancer) is still good – in many ways, better than life "BC" (before cancer). I would be happy living DC for many years to come.

SATURDAY, NOVEMBER 23, 2013

CAUTIOUS OPTIMISM

It has been a week since I had my PET scan, and I have yet to receive any definitive results. On Thursday, I called my oncologist's office to give him a little "goose." On Friday, a nurse in his office called me back to say that my abdominal lymph node had not "lit up" during the scan.

"Does this mean there is no cancer present in the node?" I asked optimistically.

"Not necessarily. The doctor is sending it in to Dana-Farber for their opinion."

And so the wait continues.

If I have learned anything in my eight months as a cancer patient, it is that, first, black-and-white answers are rare (Lizzy hit upon this in her November 7 post). That is why it took nine weeks for the doctors to finally decide that I probably had leiomyosarcoma. (As one doctor said, "The cancer isn't there waving a flag saying 'Here I am and I am leiomyosarcoma!'"). I do not think the radiologists were convinced, but the oncologists thought it was as good a guess as any, and at least it put a name to the beast.

The second thing is – you had better get used to waiting. Waiting is difficult under normal circumstances – waiting in line, waiting for payday, waiting for the mail. But when you are waiting for test results with life-threatening consequences, it is a whole different ballgame.

I could sit here and moan about how hard it is to wait, but I am actually okay with waiting. I think this is because I live and enjoy each day. If I am focused on tomorrow, or next week, or next month when I might be getting some answers, it takes my focus off of today, and today is what I have got.

Also, I could live in dread of what the test results may indicate. I was actually surprised that the node had not lit up during the scan (guess I am used to getting bad news), and I am cautiously optimistic that the final verdict will be good, but I am not heartbroken that the doctor was not ready to say it was not cancerous. If it is to be, it will be. If it ends up being cancerous, then we will face that challenge just as we have dealt with all the other bad news that has come our way these past eight months. God gives me the strength and courage. Otherwise, my life would be consumed with fear and dread. And that is no way to live.

WEDNESDAY, NOVEMBER 27, 2013

MORE NEWS

My local oncologist called me yesterday. He had conferred with my Dana-Farber sarcoma specialist and was ready to tell me how they have decided, together, to proceed.

He went over in greater detail the PET scan results. He said the expected areas lit up – the tumors in my lungs, and (to a lesser extent), the one in my back.

Surprisingly, the lymph node in my abdomen did *not* light up. (He referred to this node by the more ominous sounding terms of "mass" and "lesion.") When I asked if he thought the node was cancerous, he said he was "on the fence," but leaning a little bit toward it being not. That is not definitive enough for me to breathe a sigh of relief just yet.

Now they want to go in and extract tissue from these various sites so they can come up with a chemo cocktail that will better target my tumors. However, rather than calling this a "biopsy," my oncologist referred to it as "surgery," which sounds more complicated.

I have an appointment with my Dana-Farber sarcoma specialist next Tuesday. It has been months since I have seen him, and I am looking forward to hearing his take on my condition and to getting more details about next steps.

In the meantime, I am simply enjoying having my family around.

Lizzy had her wisdom teeth out yesterday and is recuperating here under my roof. She was adamant that she did not want to burden us with her neediness – we are already stressed to the max with Grandpa (who is now on oxygen), Peter (who continues to suffer debilitating hives, rashes, and pain), and of course me. But I just love having Lizzy here, and this is where she should be as she recovers.

Beryl has been a godsend, coming every couple of days to clean the house, do the laundry and grocery shopping, and just helping around.

And of course Ian. I was very proud of myself that I was able to attend his parent-teacher conferences on Monday evening. It involved a lot of walking, from one end of Foxboro High School to the other, but I held on to Peter's arm, and we made it through the seven meetings.

Tomorrow, all four kids – Tim, Lizzy, Beryl, and Ian – will be here for a very informal Thanksgiving. This is the first time in eight years that I am unable to host a formal family Thanksgiving celebration. But we will still have turkey – Beryl will be arriving at 7 a.m., and I am going to teach her how to cook one! The rest of the meal is coming from the prepared foods section of the local supermarket. And we have plenty of homemade desserts from the dear people at church.

If at all possible, I hope to go see at least a portion of Ian's Thanksgiving football game against Mansfield. It is here in Foxboro this year, and it is a thrill to see him run out onto the field under the gauntlet with all his teammates.

Holidays like Thanksgiving become markers of our lives. Last year was the first without my beloved mom, and she was sorely missed. And I could get caught up wondering if this will be my last. Who knows what the coming year holds?

But as I have said before, I have no interest in dwelling on what might be. Rather, this Thanksgiving I am grateful – perhaps more than ever – for life and for family. And tomorrow will be a day for savoring both.

TUESDAY, DECEMBER 3, 2013

REPRIEVE

Peter and I went to Dana-Farber this afternoon, and we are cautiously optimistic about what the doctor had to say.

First, he is giving me a reprieve from any treatments or tests through the holidays. This means two things: I have a good chance of feeling pretty well for Christmas, and the tumors must be growing fairly slowly for the doctor to give me so much time off!

Second, he still is not convinced that I have leiomyosarcoma, since my tumors are not growing as aggressively as expected. So he wants to get more biological information to see if my cancer can be identified with more certainty so as to better target my upcoming treatments. Therefore, in late January I am going to undergo a surgical biopsy on my tumors. This may be done laparoscopically but nevertheless will be more complicated than the needle biopsies I have had in the past.

Third, my Dana-Farber doctor believes that there may be no more cancer in my T6 vertebrae and that the pain I am experiencing in my mid-back is due to a compression fracture in my spine.

Fourth, he is not convinced that Doxil, my first chemo, was a failure. He said that my tumors may have grown prior to my treatments and that the Doxil actually held them at bay.

It is a lot of information to absorb, but I am feeling good about what I heard. If the tumors are growing slowly, then I am wondering if maybe my cancer is more of a chronic condition than a critical one. I do know that I felt completely different going to Dana-Farber today than I did the last time, which was a good six months ago.

Back then, I was still in shock about my diagnosis, was thinking I might only have months to live, and could not believe I was a Dana-Farber patient. Today's visit did not carry the same gloom and doom but felt more like a routine "no big deal" visit. In the meantime, I had a nice Thanksgiving weekend.

I got up early on Thanksgiving Day to make stuffing but tired quickly and sat while giving directions to Peter and Beryl on cooking the turkey. When we later took it out of the oven and started carving, there was no meat. We could not understand what had happened until we realized we had cooked the turkey upside down. We all had a good laugh about that!

Also, I was able to make it to a portion of Ian's football game. I saw the team run onto the field, and also watched as the senior members of the team were recognized in a pre-game ceremony. I vowed that I would be there next year when Ian is recognized.

Over the weekend, I felt up to doing a little cooking and then had a lovely visit from the church's youth group (along with some parents) on Sunday evening (they brought a delicious dinner, too!).

So, I am feeling physically and emotionally "up." I don't know how long it will last, but I am enjoying it for now because, as I have said before, now is what I've got.

SATURDAY, DECEMBER 14, 2013

THIS WEEK'S HOSPITALIZATION

So much has happened over the past couple of days that I am still trying to absorb it all.

In my last entry, I dared to think that perhaps maybe my tumors were growing so slowly that my cancer would be more of a chronic rather than critical condition. However, those hopes have been dashed.

On Wednesday morning, I awoke with a sharp pain in my lower pelvic area. This got my attention because my pelvis is the primary site of my cancer, not to mention that I have had on-going urological issues over the past several months. I took some pain meds, which took the edge off enough for me to continue with my planned visit from a dear colleague.

After he left, the pain got so bad that I called my primary care physician. I was frightened – I had never felt pain like that. While waiting for a call back, Peter got impatient and called my urologist because we thought the pain might be related to the stents which he had inserted in my ureters during my August hospitalization. The doctor told us to get right down to the hospital, and he would call ahead to tell them we were on our way. That was a great help because when we arrived about 4:30 p.m., we were seen immediately.

First on the docket was pain control. The initial dose of morphine did not touch it, but a second did the trick. Next was a CAT scan, which would show what was going on between my neck and my knees. But first, I had to down 32 ounces of the special drink, wait two hours, then drink another 16 ounces of it before I could have the scan. Unappealing, but I did it.

After endless waiting for the results, the emergency doc had the unenviable task of telling me that I had a new tumor in my pelvis. He also asked if I had my final directives and other instructions on file with the hospital. For a moment I was wondering if the end had come. He was very sweet and apologized for having frightened me but explained that hospital procedure required him to ask these questions.

In the meantime, my blood pressure was fluctuating in the low range (e.g., 90/60), and there was a question of a UTI, so I was admitted.

On Thursday, the medical staff was able to get both my pain and my BP under control. My urologist came by in the evening and said that it looked like the new tumor was sitting on a nerve, which was causing the incredible pain.

My local oncologist came by yesterday and said the new tumor "was a surprise," especially the swiftness with which it had appeared and the size – 10 cm. He was going to get right in touch with my Dana-Farber doctor to move up my surgical biopsy originally planned for January.

So here is where things stand: it looks like I will be going under the knife as soon as possible. The surgery has two purposes: (1) to get a good bit of biological data to use in coming up with a custom-tailored chemo cocktail that will specifically target the genetic make-up of my particular tumors, and (2) to extract some of the tumors in my pelvis; it is getting crowded in there, and they are impinging on my urological function.

I will be candid: I once again feel that I am on a slippery slope towards the inevitable. This does not mean that I have given up hope, or that I am in a depressive funk. I treasure every beautiful day. But I know my days are numbered. Despite everything, I am at peace – I have had months to get used to the idea of my own mortality. I am not afraid of dying. I am just not ready to leave yet. By the grace of God, I will have a little more time in which to savor my family, my friends, and my incredible life.

THURSDAY, DECEMBER 19, 2013

ANOTHER TRIP TO DANA-FARBER

Five days have passed since I last wrote, and once again, we are dealing with new developments and a new treatment plan. Surgery is now off the table, and chemo is going to begin again ASAP. Here are the details...

I was discharged from the hospital last Friday evening, and then Saturday I received a letter from Dana-Farber that my sarcoma specialist is leaving and my case is being transferred to another oncologist in the Sarcoma Clinic.

Our first thought was to ensure that I do not fall through the cracks of the medical establishment, so on Monday Peter hand-delivered a copy of the Dana-Farber letter to my local oncologist and expressed his sense of urgency regarding my situation.

My local oncologist got right in touch with my outgoing Dana-Farber oncologist to explain the new developments – pain, hospitalization, and a new pelvic tumor. He was able to fit us in yesterday, so it was off to Dana-Farber for the second time this month.

Whereas up to now the focus has been on my lung tumors, the doctor is now concentrating on my pelvic area, since that is where new tumors are growing. We discussed a variety of options – chemo, radiation, and another needle biopsy, and here is what we have decided.

I am going to start chemo again ASAP – within the next few days. We are going to try the Gemcitabine/Taxotere combo again, since my lung tumors did not grow while I was on this cocktail this past fall; hopefully it will have the same effect on my pelvic tumors.

After I have gone through three rounds (a round being once a week for two weeks, followed by a week off) of the Gem/Tax, I may undergo some radiation to my pelvis.

At the end of January, I will have another CAT scan as well as another needle biopsy, this time on one of my pelvic tumors. The idea of a surgical/laparoscopic biopsy is now off the table because the risk of inadvertently spreading the cancer is great. The doctor said that while most of my pelvic tumors are in difficult locations (one is toward the back near my aorta, another possibly attached to my intestine), there is one near the surface which should be fairly easy to access. The goal is to get some good biological data on my cancer which will help determine the next treatment steps.

Throughout our meeting with the Dana-Farber doctor, it felt obvious to me that there were things being left unsaid, things none of us wanted to acknowledge. A question was on my lips: "How much time do I have left, doc?" But I did not ask it because I did not think it was a fair question, and quite frankly I don't really want know, because I would be consumed by the answer.

So instead I burst into tears and said, "I am just trying to buy as much time as possible." The doctor's "all business" scientific approach suddenly softened, and he said quietly, "Of course, of course." And that is what we are trying to do – buy quality time so I can enjoy life and my family as much as possible.

After seeing my Dana-Farber doctor, I had an EKG, then some blood work, and we picked up my contrast drink mixture for my late January CAT scan. Dana-Farber was incredibly crowded – long lines and long waits. Whenever we go there, I am always sadly surprised at the number of people who, like me, are fighting this battle. And it was particularly heartbreaking to see the multitudes yesterday during this holiday season.

On the way home, Peter and I just cried. We are no longer couching our conversations in qualifications: "If I die..." Now it is "when." Peter knows he is facing a life without me. "I am going to miss you so much," he sobs. I want him to have a happy life. I bounced back from losing two husbands, and I know he will be able to rebuild a good life for himself. And he promises that he will take care of my children.

There are tears in my eyes as I write this. But despite everything, I am okay. I am grateful for each beautiful day. And while this Christmas will be laced with pain, it will be wonderful to have the family together. That is the hardest thing about this situation: I just do not want to leave my loved ones.

FRIDAY, DECEMBER 27, 2013

CHRISTMAS

A year ago, if I had known about someone suffering from Stage IV cancer which was "rare," "aggressive," and "resistant to treatment," I know I would have imagined that person having a somber and subdued Christmas.

Well, this year, I am that person, and I had an absolutely lovely Christmas.

Because my last chemo treatment took place on October 30, I was feeling really well in the weeks leading up to the holiday. With Beryl as my chauffeur and companion, I even got out to do a little shopping for presents and food; I used the motorized carts provided by the stores, and they made all the difference.

Not surprisingly, this year's celebration was different for a couple of reasons. First, because of my illness, we could not host our traditional formal sit-down Christmas dinner for the extended family. Also, because I no longer pastor a church, I did not have to "work" on Christmas Eve. Don't get me wrong, I loved leading worship on Christmas Eve and, when the calendar fell right, on Christmas Day, too. But it meant my family had to share me with the church.

When I was Associate Pastor at The Congregational Church of Topsfield (MA) from 1999 to 2005, I was unable to spend any part of Christmas Eve with my children, who were still young at the time. We had three services, including one at 11:00 p.m. It was sacred and sublime: candlelight, communion, a harpist, and "O Holy Night." But I would not arrive home until well after midnight, and then I would set up the stockings for my children, write the note from Santa, and take a bite out of the snack that had been left for him.

By the time I went to Stoughton, my children were older, and we only had one service at 7:00 p.m., so we developed a new tradition: on our way home we would order Chinese food, which became our late Christmas Eve dinner.

This year, I looked at our changed circumstances as an opportunity to do things in ways that had not been possible during the 14 years I served as pastor. So, with the help of Peter and the supermarket, we roasted a chicken and enjoyed delicious sides at a casual supper late Christmas Eve afternoon. Then we went to the service at UCC Stoughton; I was grateful to feel well enough to go, and also that I could simply sit in the pew. When we got home, we snacked on leftovers and watched our all-time favorite Christmas movie, "Mr. Magoo's Christmas Carol."

The next day, Lizzy made cinnamon buns for breakfast (a tradition), Peter and I put in a second roaster chicken to cook, and we opened presents. The best gift I received was not wrapped in paper; it was Ian exclaiming, "I'm so happy!" My boy has been understandably down for months, and his words were music to my ears (even if they may have been prompted by all the Ohio State swag he received).

Later in the morning, Beryl and Tim arrived. More present-opening and another delicious dinner. And then I closed my eyes and took a nap. Ahhhhhh.

This year, I could have spent my time thinking about how radically things had changed since last Christmas, how suddenly our lives were turned upside down by cancer. I could have spent my time contemplating next Christmas – will I be here, or will my chair be empty? I could have spent my time that way, but I didn't. Instead, I enjoyed every moment of *this* Christmas and spending a lovely time with my family.

The day after Christmas (yesterday), it was back to reality: chemo. The Dana-Farber sarcoma specialist thought we should try the Gemcitabine/Taxotere combo again since my lung tumors did not grow while I was receiving this cocktail last fall. Hopefully, it will have the same effect on my pelvic tumors.

On January 2, I will be going into Brigham and Women's for a biopsy on the pelvic tumor closest to the surface, in hopes that the tissue will help the doctors come up with a targeted treatment. Then on January 29, I will be heading back to B&W for a scan to see how the Gem/Tax has worked.

And it must work! The pelvic tumors must be stopped! And so I ask you to please pray that at the very least the tumors stop growing, and even better, that they begin to shrink. That would be the best Christmas present of all!

TUESDAY, DECEMBER 31, 2013

NEW YEAR BLESSINGS

When I was a little girl, waiting anxiously for my birthday or Christmas or summer vacation to come, I sometimes lamented, "Time goes so slowly! I wish time would go quicker!" And my Dad, with the wisdom of years, would answer, "Don't wish away your life, honey; the older you get, the faster time will pass by."

My father's words have rung truer with each quickly-passing year, and perhaps never more so than this year. When we welcomed 2013, I could not have imagined how the year would unfold. And as I stand on the brink of 2014, the last thing in the world I want is for time to go faster.

After all, I don't have a lot of time. Even if I were to live five more years (an unimaginable blessing!), I would still only be 64 when I died – a full 15 years less than 79, the average lifespan of women in the United States. Chances are I will get less than that.

But I wonder if I am looking at this time thing all wrong. In seminary, I learned that there are two words for "time" in Greek, the original language of the New Testament. One of those words is *kronos*, which refers to chronological or sequential time. With *kronos*, there is yesterday, and today, and tomorrow, and next week, and so on. We humans think in *kronos* time, and we go about our lives in *kronos* time.

But there is a second word for "time" in Greek – *kairos*. *Kairos* is the appointed time for God's purpose to be fulfilled; *kairos* is God's timing.

Yes, I do feel cheated that I am not going to have 90 years (after all, my Dad is 93 and my mom died six weeks shy of her 90th birthday), or 80, or even 70 years. But that is *kronos* thinking.

Rather, I am beginning to see my life through *kairos* time – that I have had a full lifetime in my (almost) 60 years. I am grateful that I have lived a life packed with meaning and purpose and significant relationships. But it was not always so.

I have always found New Year's to be a natural time to take stock of my life, and for too many years, it was a depressing analysis. What had I accomplished in the year just completed? Was I more joy-filled than a year ago? Was my life more meaningful? Had I made a difference in the world, even in some small way? Was I a better person?

For too many years, my answer to these questions was "no." No, I was not joy-filled. No, my life was not more meaningful. No, I had not made a difference in the world. No, I was not a better person. Ultimately, I got into right relationship with God, quit my meaningless job, attended seminary, and entered the ministry.

And in the ensuing 20 years, I have developed or renewed countless relationships which have enriched my life and filled it with meaning and purpose. And now, relationships mean more to me than ever. Since my diagnosis, people stretching all the way back to my pre-school days have reached out to me, sending me cards and messages and even visiting me.

These relationships are the greatest gift of my illness. Under "normal" circumstances, we would have gone about our lives with no compelling reason to re-connect. But serious illness changes things – and in my case, in so many ways, that change has been for the better.

For me, the opportunity to have so many people (back) in my life – offering their love, prayers and good wishes – is a godsend. And it is not *despite*, but *because of*, the cancer that I have been so blessed. New growth springing from fertilizer.

Time – and life – are clearly among the greatest gifts from God, and they are ever more precious as I feel them slipping through my fingers. The year 2014 may very well be the last I see. But rather than thinking in *kronos* time – that I am being cheated out of 20 or 30 years – I prefer to think in *kairos* time: that God has already given me a full life bursting with meaning, purpose, and loving relationships. And isn't that what life – no matter the length – is all about?

FRIDAY, JANUARY 3, 2014

TEARS AND RESOLVE

My 2014 has started off with a bang.

Yesterday, January 2, I went into Brigham and Women's for a biopsy on one of my pelvic tumors. This was the fourth biopsy I have undergone to aid my medical team in getting more information about my kind of cancer; the others were on my T6 vertebrae tumor (April), on one of the tumors in my left lung (May), and on my thyroid (also in May – which showed no cancer!).

For the T6 biopsy and the one on the lung, I was put under conscious sedation, much like when getting a colonoscopy. The thyroid biopsy was wretched – I was awake (and tears streamed down my face) the whole time as the doctor and attending nurse rooted around the base of my throat with two needles.

I was under the impression that I would be under conscious sedation for yesterday's procedure, but it turned out that, even though tranquilizers kept me at ease (sort of), I was wide awake the whole time. And I could feel what they were doing. It was not pleasant. Not as bad as the thyroid biopsy, but painful nevertheless.

As we had been leaving Foxboro to head into Boston, I started to get teary. How many tests and procedures must I undergo? Will this one yield any useful results, or are the doctors just grasping at straws? How did I end up in this mess anyway?

Then as I was in pre-op getting prepped, one of the nurses spotted my tattoo and asked me about it. I quoted to her 1 Corinthians 13:12, and I explained that I hold on to the words of my tat ("then we will see face to face") because that is what I know awaits me in heaven. And then I teared up again. (In addition to getting questioned about the words of my tattoo, I am usually asked if getting it hurt, and I respond, "Not as much as my thyroid biopsy!")

I think that subconsciously – despite my brave talk in my last blog – I am pondering what the New Year will bring. For many, the beginning of a new year offers a new start, a chance to wipe the slate clean and begin again. Unfortunately, my cancer carried forward from 2013 to 2014. The tumors are all still in my body, slowly killing me.

Today, as I was taking off my bandage from the biopsy, I took a moment to feel my pelvic region. I have long had a "pooch," but this felt different – it is no longer soft and flabby but rather hard and protruding. Full of all those tumors... And again I burst into tears. Those awful, evil things inside my body! I picture them looking like the leeches that covered Humphrey Bogart's back in "The African Queen." Vile, wretched, life-sucking things.

And today, chemo. When I arrived, the nurse asked if I was up for my treatment. She said I looked spent. I told her about yesterday's biopsy and burst into tears again. But I did not want to put chemo off and give those tumors any more chance to grow.

But it has had me thinking – how far am I willing to go? Will there come a time when I finally say, "Stop! Enough! Let me die in peace!" Or will I try everything, anything that might buy me some time?

At my last meeting with my outgoing Dana-Farber oncologist, he mentioned radical surgery as an example of one end of the possibility spectrum. It would involve taking out all my pelvic tumors, and all my organs down there, too. I would forever forward poo and pee into ostomy bags. I think he mentioned it as an illustration of a remote possibility that would require a long recovery period without good odds for a significantly extended life.

But what if such an operation would buy me six months, or even three months? Three more months of hearing my son's voice, of feeling my daughter's cheek against mine, of holding my husband's hand. Three more months of saying "I love you" and hearing those words returned to me. Aren't those worth anything I might have to endure?

I do not know if such a radical surgery will ever be presented to me as a viable option. But right now, in this season of resolutions, I am feeling the resolve to try *anything* that will give me a little more time on earth.

MONDAY, JANUARY 6, 2014

"YOU LOOK WONDERFUL!"

"You look wonderful!"

I cannot tell you how many times I have heard these words over the past couple of months.

Don't get me wrong – I am not complaining! But how I look barely registers on my radar screen these days, a victim of convenience, lack of energy, and rearranged priorities.

First to go was the hair (see April 18 entry, "Hair"); I had it cropped short and let it go naturally gray (although I eventually pepped it up with some fun colors). That was quickly followed by mascara (incompatible with tears) and then all make up, including lipstick. In recent months, I have even stopped plucking. It is all I can do to shower each day; everything else seems superfluous, or at least not worth the effort.

And yet, I still get "You look wonderful!" My sarcoma specialist said it when I went into Dana-Farber the other week. In fact, recently it has only been my chemo nurse who has expressed concern about my appearance; she wanted to make sure I was up for my infusion. Not five minutes before, I had run into a friend at the hospital, and she had said – you guessed it – "You look wonderful!"

Of course, I know what it is all about. I look wonderful for someone with Stage IV cancer. I look wonderful for someone on her third round of chemo. I look wonderful for someone who has numerous tumors growing in various parts of my body. I look wonderful for someone who is dying.

I can imagine that people who have not seen me for several months might expect me to be shrunken, balding, and weak. But I am deceptively robust; my face (and double chin) still show the effects of last spring's steroids, and my natural girth is working to my advantage these days.

It may not always be so. I am still hoping, in my twisted way, to go bald – and the Gem/Tax I am back on might do it this time. There may come a time that I start losing weight – hard to imagine, but certainly possible (file under "Be careful what you wish for..."). I will no doubt become weaker as the cancer overtakes my organs.

Remember Billy Crystal's "Fernando" bit on Saturday Night Live? "You look mahvelous!" and "'Tis better to look good than to feel good, my friends." It still makes me laugh, even though I don't necessarily agree with the "wisdom." Because the truth of the matter is that I would trade looks (but not personalities) with the Wicked Witch of the West if I could get my health back. That is the thing about cancer, or any life-threatening illness for that matter – it quickly rearranges priorities, and I think for the better. Love, generosity, compassion, forgiveness, faith – these are the dwelling places of true beauty; it is in the spirit, not the looks.

There will come a time when I won't look so wonderful. I will know it, and there will be no need for anyone to pretend otherwise. Just know that it is still me inside. And while cancer may take my looks, it will never break my spirit.

THURSDAY, JANUARY 16, 2014

THE NEARNESS OF DEATH

Twelve years ago, my beloved cat Sweetie Pie was dying. His kidneys were failing, he had stopped eating, and he was losing strength. When I was ready to bring Sweetie to the vet for the last time, my son Ian – who was five at the time – asked to come with me so I would not have to go alone. And the trip became a teachable moment.

"Why does Sweetie have to die?" he asked.

"Every living thing has to die some time," I said.

"It's not fair," Ian declared.

"Well, Sweetie has had a wonderful life, and he's old and sick." I explained. "It doesn't seem fair when someone dies too young, but this is the right time for Sweetie." I think I was trying to convince myself as much as I was Ian.

"Will Grandma and Grandpa die?" Ian asked.

"Yes, when it's their time."

"Will you die, Mummy?" he asked me, wide-eyed.

"Someday, yes, but hopefully not until I'm much, much older."

And then a shadow of fear passed over my son's face. "Will *I* die?"

"Yes, honey, but not for a very, very long time, when you're very very old."

"But I don't want to die!" he wailed and his face crumpled into tears as he faced his own mortality for the first time.

People – and pets – do not die until they are very, very old. That's what I assured my son, although I knew it is not always true, and so did he – his Daddy died at age 44, when Ian was only eight months old.

But I wanted my little boy to believe, at least for a little while longer, that the world is fair, that nice people live until they are very very old, and that bad things don't happen to good people. I wanted my son to think that, because I knew someday he was going to lose his innocence. Someday he would learn the truth: that you can do everything right and still get hurt, that you can be good and still suffer pain, that people – nice people – can die when they are much too young.

And that someday has come.

I think Ian must feel that death is very close these days. Not only is his mother terminally ill, but his friend and classmate Sam Berns died last Friday.

In the days since his passing, much has been written about Sam. He was born with a condition called Progeria, an extremely rare (1 in 4 million), fatal genetic condition characterized by an appearance of accelerated aging in children.

But Sam's life, personality, and achievements were always larger than the frail, earthly frame that tried to contain them. I think we all knew that Sam was living on borrowed time. The average life expectancy of children with Progeria is 13, but a new treatment seemed to be slowing the progression of the condition's worst effects in Sam. In other words, even though we all knew Sam had a fatal illness, his death was a heartbreaking shock.

And for me, Sam's passing has helped me put my situation in perspective.

Some day in the foreseeable future, Ian will don a jacket and tie and attend my funeral. And as sad as it will be for him, it fits into the cycle of life that a child buries a parent. A parent should not have to bury a child, and a child – even one on the brink of manhood – should not have to attend the funeral of a classmate and friend.

I lament that I might not be around to help Ian with the college application process. But whether or not I am here, Ian will be applying to colleges. Scott and Leslie, Sam's parents, will not have a son going to college.

I hope against hope that I will be at Ian's graduation. But whether or not I am there, Ian will graduate. Scott and Leslie will not have a graduate in the Class of 2015.

I have expressed feeling cheated out of 20 years of my life. But I have experienced a full life – career, marriage, children. Sam, for all he packed into 17 years, did not.

My heart breaks for Sam's parents, his family and friends. And my heart breaks for my strong and brave son, for whom death feels way too close these days.

SATURDAY, JANUARY 25, 2014

HAPPY NEWS!

I have much happy news to report, but chemo has sapped my energy recently, preventing me from writing. So I am going to write while I am still enjoying my "steroid kick" from yesterday's infusion.

Just to catch up – Back on January 8, Peter noticed a huge ugly purple discoloration, six inches wide, stretching around my waist from my navel to my spine – he said it scared the daylights (okay, that's not the word he used) out of him. I had not fallen or bumped my hip, and I am not on blood thinners, so the main concern was internal bleeding. After a call to my primary care physician, we went down to the hospital for another CAT scan. The scan itself is a piece of cake, but prep takes hours – 32 ounces of drink, wait two hours, another 16 ounces of drink, wait another 30 minutes; then after the scan, wait for the results. Fortunately, after spending most of the day in Emergency, the verdict was that a needle likely nicked a blood vessel during my recent biopsy, causing the sub-dermal bleeding. No big deal, and now the discoloration is completely gone. As I have noted before, "It's always something."

This past Wednesday, Peter and I went into Dana-Farber to meet with a surgeon in the Sarcoma Center. This appointment had been made in early December when my outgoing Dana-Farber doctor was considering a surgical biopsy on my pelvic tumors. After my mid-December hospitalization and the discovery of a new, large tumor, those plans were shifted to a "simple" needle biopsy. But Peter and I decided not to cancel the appointment with the surgeon because we wanted to see if she could recommend any surgical options.

I was quite weepy as we prepared to go to into Boston. The last visit to Dana-Farber was particularly discouraging, and I had come to associate the place with bad news. But my tears turned to smiles with the surgeon.

Right away, we were taken with her warm, friendly manner. She had reviewed my full file before the appointment and showed us pictures of my scans on the computer. A couple of things she said really struck me. First – speaking as a surgeon, not a radiologist – she said she saw little, if any, sign of the tumor in my spine. She showed us the pictures and kept saying, "I see nothing – I see nothing," meaning (as my old Dana-Farber oncologist had said previously) that the constant pain I feel in my back is most likely the result of a compression fracture in my vertebrae. Believe me, I will take the pain as long as there is no cancer!

Then, as she was showing us my pelvic scan, she said, "I've seen a lot worse – *a lot* worse." I know this statement does not sound all that reassuring, but it was a huge relief to me. When I am standing looking down at my toes, I can see a big bulge in my left pelvic region; I am sure it is a tumor, one of the several growing down there, and it is very discouraging.

I took this as an opening to ask The Big Question: "My daughter is graduating from college in May – do you think I'll make it?" And, waving her hand, she said something to the effect of "Absolutely!" Emboldened, I said, "My son graduates from high school in June 2015, and I want to be there." And she responded, "Then we'll do everything we can to make it happen." She went on to say that I was doing really well now (including a comment about how "wonderful" I looked) and said that if there were changes to my condition, they would be right on top of addressing them. And she gave us great big hugs at the end of the appointment.

You have no idea how the surgeon's responses have changed my outlook. I am not dying, at least not yet. I cannot be cured, but it sounds like I have some time left in which some of my hopes and dreams might be realized. Maybe buying a house on the Cape and having some real retirement time is within the realm of possibility!

This coming Wednesday, it is back to Dana-Farber for a(nother) CAT scan at 7:15 a.m., followed by our first meeting with my new Dana-Farber sarcoma specialist. The Dana-Farber surgeon says he is "great," and I am looking forward to this visit and perhaps additional (cautiously) optimistic news.

But even if that is not forthcoming, I am so grateful for the time I have had and the time that is yet in my future. Every moment is a blessing and a gift!

SATURDAY, FEBRUARY 22, 2014

BACK FROM THE ABYSS

Health is the greatest of God's gifts, but we take it for granted.
Yet it hangs on a thread as fine as a spider's web
and the tiniest thing can make it snap,
leaving the strongest of us helpless in an instant.
And in that instant, hope is our protector and love, our panacea.

~ Jennifer Worth, *Shadows of the Workhouse*

It's always something. I have said that several times over the past couple of months. But it sounds too flippant, too glib to describe my experience of the last three weeks. Yes, it does feel sometimes that cancer is the least of my worries, that other health complications move in to push it aside. But nothing could have prepared me for the ordeal I have been through the last couple of weeks.

It all started on Tuesday, January 28. I was feeling really punk. I had been exposed to the stomach flu and had had a chemo treatment the previous Friday, so my tummy was out of sorts. On top of that, I was exhausted and out of breath. Peter took my vital signs, and my pulse rate was a whopping 133. Normal is 70, and my "normal" had been in the 110-115 range for months. But 133 was off the charts.

Peter called my primary care physician, who told me to get right down to the Emergency Department (they know us there!). Before I could blink, I was undergoing an echocardiogram and prepping for a CAT scan. When the diagnosis came in, it was not good news: there was a lot of fluid around my heart, and something needed to be done about it ASAP.

A thoracic surgeon came to talk with me. He gave me the usual grilling: Do you smoke? *No.* Have you ever smoked? *No.* Do you drink alcohol? *No* (my Chardonnay days ended as soon as I was diagnosed). Street drugs? *No.* Any underlying health issues? *No diabetes, no Hep C, no HIV, nothing.* "Okay, then we can proceed," and he went on to tell me that I needed to undergo a "pericardial window" – a surgery which would allow fluid to drain from the space surrounding the heart into the chest cavity, from which it would eventually, and uneventfully, be eliminated. The thoracic surgeon also said that it was important that this surgery be done immediately, for the fluid build-up would most certainly "get me into trouble" in the future. Translation: without the surgery, I could die.

I was admitted to the hospital, and the next day, Wednesday, January 29, beginning at 1:30 p.m., I underwent the surgery.

I have always found waking up from anesthesia to be a most unpleasant experience, but when pain is thrown into the mix, it can be brutal. The pain that I felt coming to was intense – so bad that it has replaced childbirth as my "10" (as in, "on a scale of 1 to 10, what's your pain?"). The 11 staples, looking like railroad tracks running down between my breasts, did not help. All I could do was weep, but even that hurt. In my post-op pain and disorientation, I found myself in an intolerable physical and emotional place – a place worse than death. It felt like the edge of The Abyss, and if I had to spend an extended period of time there, death felt like the kinder, gentler option.

If life itself is God's greatest gift, then surely healing comes in second. Healing offers hope. Healing offers a future. And healing pulled me back from The Abyss. It was slow, to be sure. But every day, I was infinitesimally better. Still, it was an awful recovery. I hated being tethered to my IV pole. I hated not being able to get comfortable – either in my hospital bed or the recliner in the hospital room. I hated having to use the commode next to my bed and depending on the mercy of the nurses and Personal Care Assistants to wipe my butt. I felt – and was – completely enfeebled. But every day I felt a little better, and I held on to that hope, which kept me going.

On Monday and Tuesday following the surgery, I received blood transfusions which perked me up. And on Wednesday, one week from the surgery, I was discharged.

I was still very weak, so it was decided that I would go to a rehab facility for further recuperation. I cannot tell you how many times I have visited parishioners in rehab. And now here I was, a patient. Peter and Ian brought in my power lift recliner from home so I could finally be comfortable. And even though I really wanted to be home, rehab turned out to be the right move.

I received physical therapy and occupational therapy every day. Unfortunately, I was suffering from another UTI and the antibiotics so killed my appetite that I could barely eat. Nevertheless, with every passing day, I could feel myself getting stronger and more independent. There was just one thing – my pulse rate was not significantly lower than when I had entered the hospital in the first place. It registered in the 120s, even when I took frequent rest stops. I was breathless walking just a few steps down the hall or after getting myself dressed. The surgery was supposed to have rectified this. Nevertheless, I was discharged to home on Wednesday, February 12, a week after arriving.

It was so good coming home. I had been away two weeks and had missed my family terribly, including my pets. It was wonderful regaining my independence – being able to get a glass of apple juice when I wanted it, or taking a pill when I needed it. But my homecoming was short-lived.

The next day, I had a follow-up visit with yet another new doctor, my cardiologist. I had an echocardiogram and EKG in his office, and he came back with the disturbing results: my pericardial window was not working. Fluid (still or once again) was surrounding my heart. And something had to be done ASAP.

My cardiologist conferred with the thoracic surgeon and then called Brigham and Women's. He wanted me to go there to have the pericardial surgery redone, but this time using a different technique. We raced home, picked up a few things, and headed into Boston.

They were waiting for us in the Emergency Department at the Brigham. After spending some time being examined there, I was wheeled down to the bowels of the hospital, to the "PAC-U" – post-anesthesia care unit – which was essentially row after row of curtained cubicles (I was in PAC-U 60). I was going to have the surgery the next day, but in the meantime, I would be undergoing a pericardiocentesis to drain more fluid from around my heart.

I was awake throughout the procedure, and it was okay – no pain or discomfort. Because there were no hospital rooms available, I spent the night in the PAC-U, which was so bustling with activity that the nurse came around with ear plugs and eye shades. Without a TV to distract me, I had a lot of time to think about what the next day would bring. Would the second window surgery be as bad as the first? Would I feel a lot of pain? Would this one be successful?

I was half expecting to break down, or to scream out in panic. But an amazing thing happened. I was at peace. This was more than simply accepting the inevitable. I truly believe that the Holy Spirit was there with me in that little curtained cubicle, assuring me that all would be well.

The next day, Valentine's Day, I had heart surgery (you can't make this stuff up) – my second pericardial window. This time, rather than go through my chest, the surgeon went through my left side with scopes. And I remember thinking as I awoke from the anesthesia, "Hey, it's not so bad!" Even though I had two chest tubes and a lot of pain, it was not intolerable. Thank God.

I spent five more days at B&W recovering, and then I was able to come home for good on Tuesday, February 18. In the previous three weeks, I had spent a total of 22 hours at home. And I think being home has helped my (literal and figurative) heart heal.

I now have an oxygen machine. I don't really need it – my "sats" (oxygen saturation levels) – are in the 90s, which is good. But it is nice to have available after exerting myself such as taking a shower, and Peter says it cuts down on my snoring! I am also using my walker when I leave my chair. In addition, I have a visiting nurse and physical therapist working with me. The fact of the matter is I am not nearly as strong or as well as I was before this whole ordeal began a few weeks ago. My stamina is limited, and my energy level depletes quickly. For these reasons, I have had to put a moratorium on visitors until further notice. And when I am finally able to see people, the visits will have to be brief.

Yesterday, we met my new sarcoma specialist at Dana-Farber. We have been so pre-occupied with my heart over the past several weeks that treating the cancer seemed to have become a secondary concern; my last chemo was January 24. So we wanted to get back on track fighting the disease.

The bottom line from our visit to Dana-Farber: the Gem/Tax chemo which I was receiving in January was not successful – my lung tumors grew. So now I am going on a new chemo, which is taken as a pill. We will go back to Dana-Farber in three weeks.

So, there you have it. My journey to the edge of The Abyss and back. But I am back. Thanks be to God!

FRIDAY, MARCH 7, 2014

HEALING CONTINUES

I have spent the last two and a half weeks quietly healing from my surgeries. It is surprising what an assault on the body major surgery can be and the amount of energy the body needs to heal. For instance, yesterday I took three naps: late morning, early afternoon, and late afternoon.

And while my healing has continued apace, it has not been without incident. Two weeks ago, during my appointment with my new Dana-Farber oncologist, he noticed that my shirt was being stained by blood-tinged fluid coming out of my left side, where the tubes had been inserted during my second pericardial window. He bandaged me up, but the next evening, as I was getting ready for bed, the fluid starting coming out so fast that it actually formed a puddle on the bathroom floor.

I called for Peter, and although it would have been so much easier to go to the local hospital, we got in the car and drove into Boston to Brigham and Women's Emergency. They were very efficient and before I knew it, a member of the thoracic team that had operated on me was stitching up my side. Three hours after leaving, we were back home in Foxboro.

This past Monday, I had an appointment at Brigham and Women's with the thoracic surgeon who had done my second window. He has quite a personality and his first words to me were, "Do I know you?? You don't look anything like you did when I first met you! Give me a high five!" He was so happy with the results of the surgery that I do not have to see him for two months.

Then on Wednesday, I saw my cardiologist. He, too, was happy with my progress, especially the fact that my heart rate is now around 100, down 30 beats per minutes. I am so grateful to him for sending me into Brigham and Women's when he saw that my first window was not working, and I thanked him several times during the appointment. My cardiologist is a serious guy, but at the end of the appointment, as he was leaving, he turned to me, cracked a smile, and said, "You're beautiful!" I don't have to see him again for two months either.

Fatigue is really my only complaint. The pain in my back is under control. My appetite is good, and I have yet to feel any side effects from the Letrozole, which is the chemo pill I am now taking.

I will say it again: healing is a miracle. And I feel so blessed that God continues to heal me from my surgeries. Will healing from cancer be next? We can only hope and pray.

TUESDAY, MARCH 11, 2014

"IN SICKNESS AND IN HEALTH"

I am a little embarrassed to admit that I watched "The Bachelor" finale last night. I did so with a healthy dose of cynicism, however, because I do not think those kinds of shows are a great way to find a future spouse. My personal experience has no doubt affected my attitude.

I used to be a hopeless romantic, believing in "one true love" and "happily ever after." Well, 40 years and four marriages later, I see things a little differently now. As a pastor, I officiated at countless weddings, and at most of them, I could not help but thinking, "Do they have any idea what they're getting into?"

Marriage is hard even under the best of circumstances. But throw in complications like job loss, money problems, in-law issues, even children, and things can get tough. And a terminal illness can test even the best of marriages.

Twice I have dealt with the terminal illness of my spouse. Only eight months into our marriage, Darcy was diagnosed with terminal kidney cancer. We barely had a chance to enjoy married life before our lives were turned upside down. For 21 of the 28 months we were married, he was dying. And all I could do was be there for him.

My marriage to John was a little different. Addiction is treated as an illness, with one major exception: the addict is responsible for his/her addictive behavior. It is "terminal" because unless the addict gets clean, the addiction will surely end in death. I found it a challenge to be compassionate and understanding as I watched John destroy himself and our family. Every day I asked myself, "Are the kids and I better off with him or without him?" and the answer was always "with him." And I had taken a vow when we were married: "In sickness and in health."

Now I am the one with the terminal illness. Cancer has certainly tested my marriage to Peter. But in so many important ways, it has made it stronger. We know our time is limited, and so we try not to waste it on small stuff and disagreements but instead cherish every moment together. Peter is my rock and completely devoted to me, and I to him. He is my soul mate, my best friend, and the love of my life, and I am so very blessed to have him as my husband.

Nine years ago today, we pledged ourselves to one another "in sickness and in health." We could not have imagined how our lives would unfold or how that vow would be tested. And even though our time together has been shortened, I feel incredibly blessed.

Happy Anniversary, sweetheart. I love you.

THURSDAY, MARCH 20, 2014

VISITS TO DANA-FARBER

In the past week, Peter and I have made two visits to Dana-Farber.

Last Friday (March 14) was a "touch base" with my new oncologist. One new development I discussed with him is a problem with my right foot, which has lost some mobility and feels numb and tingly. He was concerned enough with this "drop foot" as he called it, as well as some other pain in my right leg, to schedule some additional testing; is this new pain being caused by a new tumor?

So two days ago (March 18), Peter and I spent a long day at Dana-Farber. First up: two MRIs beginning at 7:00 a.m. in an annex building on Longwood Ave. As usual, I had to take tranks before I was inserted into the dreaded tube, and mercifully, I fell asleep while I was in the blasted thing. Good thing, too, since the tests took well over an hour.

Next stop was a CAT scan in the basement of Brigham and Women's. I was groggy from being tranked, but fortunately Peter pushed me around in a wheelchair. After the CAT scan, it was on to blood work in Dana-Farber's Yawkey Building. I actually fell asleep waiting for my name to be called. We then had a break and got a bite to eat (my beverage of choice: Coke!) before meeting with a Dana-Farber nurse practitioner. Once again, I fell asleep in the waiting area.

The nurse practitioner went through the results of the tests I had undergone that morning, and the great news is that one of my pelvic tumors has actually shrunk! I was too mellowed out at the time to get overly excited by this good news, and it was tempered by the fact that another tumor had grown slightly. Still, the fact that a tumor has actually shrunk means that my current chemo drug, Letrozole, seems to be doing some good. Yahoo!

I will be returning to Dana-Farber in early April to meet with an orthopedic doctor about my drop foot.

In the meantime, I am having some routine doctor appointments. This afternoon, I had my annual physical with my primary care physician (why bother, I wondered, except that I just love seeing her). I asked her if she had told the gynecologist who had performed my hysterectomy about my cancer. "Oh, yes. We talk about you all the time." She said that everyone involved in that surgery had gone over and over what they did, what they might have missed, and what they should have done differently. No one could come up with anything.

This was followed by an appointment with my urologist, and then tomorrow it is my semi-annual date with my dentist. It is the first day of spring, the Red Sox season will be starting soon, and I am finally feeling recovered enough from my heart surgeries to have visitors again.

Life is good.

MONDAY, MARCH 24, 2014

THE YEAR OF LIVING MORBIDLY

A year ago this coming week, the life I had been living – filled with pastoral visits, clergy meetings, funerals, Sunday worship, plus all the tasks of being a wife, mother, and daughter – ended suddenly and without warning. It was replaced by a totally new life full of doctors, hospitals, tests, and treatments, and my 2013 calendar starkly reflects this sea change.

Sunday and Monday, March 24 and 25, 2013, were important but uneventful – Palm/Passion Sunday worship, bible study, Youth Group, my semi-annual dentist appointment.

On March 26, a Tuesday, a barely perceptible shift began to take place: I underwent a MRI, which my orthopedist had finally ordered to get to the root of the back pain which had dogged me for two months. Afterwards, I returned to work for a Worship and Music meeting.

The next day, I knit with the prayer shawl ladies in the morning and attended a Christian Ed meeting in the evening, gatherings which book-ended a disturbing afternoon call from my primary care physician. "Do you have a few minutes?" she asked ominously, and proceeded to tell me that the MRI revealed "something funky" – a tumor – in my spine. "When you say 'tumor,' are you talking cancer?" I asked. "Yes," she responded simply. And then she gave me my marching orders: go right down to the local hospital to have blood work done and to pick up the prep drink for my CAT scan, which would take place the next morning, Maundy Thursday.

She had also set up for me an appointment with an oncologist for Thursday afternoon. Surely she meant *next* Thursday, I concluded. I did not have the time for a doctor's appointment, much less to even think about my own health, on such an important day on the Christian calendar – I had a worship service at a local nursing home to do, followed by a supper and service at the church I served!

Late Thursday afternoon, I received a phone call: it was the oncologist's office, calling to tell me I had missed my appointment. "But I am a pastor, and today's Maundy Thursday. I could not possibly have come in today!" "Then come in tomorrow morning at 9:30." "Tomorrow" was Good Friday. Why were these doctors being so pushy when I had holy work to do?

The next morning, Good Friday, Peter and I found ourselves sitting in a sterile examining room listening to a new doctor, an oncologist, explain what the tests revealed: cancer that had started in my pelvis and spread to both lungs and my T6 vertebrae. Stage IV.

The next three days were a blur: phone calls and emails to those who had to know; arrangements for coverage at church; and the heartbreaking task of telling my children. I made it through Easter Sunday worship and then began my new life. No more Pastor Jean. I was now a full-time cancer patient and all my effort and all my strength was going to be focused on fighting for my life.

My calendar for the first week of April 2013 reflects this new life: daily radiation treatments, a pre-op appointment, a biopsy on my spine, another meeting with my oncologist. And the 50 weeks since have been similar: trips to Dana-Farber; a procedure to insert a port for infusions; four rounds of chemo using three different drugs; biopsies on my thyroid, lungs, and one of my pelvic tumors; surgery to insert stents in my ureters, thereby getting my urological function back on track; a pericardiocentesis to drain fluid from around my heart; two "pericardial window" surgeries to prevent fluid from building up again; and endless doctor appointments with a full range of specialists, including four different kinds of oncologists, two thoracic surgeons, a urologist, and a cardiologist.

When I got the Stage IV diagnosis on Good Friday, March 29, 2013, I had no idea how much time I had left. And for the first few months, I think I just curled up in my recliner waiting to die. It was comforting (and comfortable) to do nothing but watch TV. When I had the energy, I put my affairs in order: updating my will, writing out my final Funeral and Burial Directive, planning out my funeral, and putting together the worship bulletin.

Spending my days like that may sound morbid, but I just wanted to wrap myself in my own misery and drop out of life.

Peter has a different perspective. He thinks I was so exhausted after working for forty years (and raising two children, mostly as a single mom), that I needed a year off just to unwind and recover. He may be on to something, because as long as I take my pain meds, I actually feel better now than I have since early January 2013 before my back pain started. And I am still very much alive! We are even daring to talk about retiring to the Cape – it becomes more of a possibility with every passing day.

I have had a lot of time this past year to try to make sense, or at least meaning, of my cancer diagnosis. Keeping on track with Peter's theory, I look back and can see that I was indeed completely burned out, especially from my vocation as a pastor. In fact, in the Fall of 2012, I was actually floating the idea of leaving the Stoughton church to become an Intentional Interim Minister. But I am not a quitter, and I would never just walk away from my position at the church without a compelling reason. Stage IV cancer was a compelling reason.

I have a tendency to think every little ache or pain is related to the cancer, but it is not necessarily true. A few months ago, I mentioned that I thought I could see a great big tumor bulging out of my pelvis. At my annual check-up this past week, my doctor said no no, it's a hernia, and she tucked it back in just to prove it. (It causes me no pain, so we are just going to leave it be.) She said it would pop out again if I laughed, which I did about five seconds later.

Because, as I have said most of my life but perhaps never more so than during this past year of living morbidly, "I can laugh or I can cry. I choose to laugh."

SUNDAY, APRIL 6, 2014

YEAR TWO BEGINS

April 1 marked the beginning of my second year of living with cancer. And if I knew then what I know now, I would not have expended so much time and energy thinking about death.

Of course, that is easy to say now. During the first few months of being a cancer patient, I walked around stunned at my diagnosis, shocked that suddenly my life expectancy had been reduced by 20 years, and staggered that I had gone from a seemingly healthy person to a terminally ill person in a matter of days.

But I haven't died. I am still here, on the sunny side of the grass!

In fact, I feel better these days than I have since before I was diagnosed. My back pain is virtually gone – could it be that draining all that fluid from around my heart relieved pressure on my T6 vertebrae?

I have more energy – I can go out and do a few errands, or go for rides in the car (I have not driven in a year due to the powerful painkillers I take), although I still love a nap in the afternoon.

I no longer need Peter's help showering or dressing. I can even bend over to put on my socks and shoes! I can do things around the house, such as getting my own meals, which helps take the load off his shoulders.

I have once again taken up my favorite pastime: reading. This past year, double vision and sheer exhaustion limited me to passive activities such as watching TV. But now I am deep into three different books simultaneously.

Yesterday, Peter and I attended a stamp club brunch. And last Sunday, I attended church – what a balm for my soul!

It's funny, but these days I often forget that I have cancer. Because I get my chemo in pill form rather than an infusion, it is easy to think that my joint pain and sore feet (both side effects of Letrozole) are simply due to my age.

And I am daring to think I have a future, one that includes a few retirement years down at the Cape. The very thought lifts my spirits and fills my heart with joy-filled anticipation!

MONDAY, APRIL 21, 2014

LOOKING TO THE FUTURE

"This has been an Easter day full of a range of emotions: tears... fear... hope... joy... love..." I wrote those words a year ago, just two days after I had received the devastating diagnosis that changed my life.

This year Easter, yesterday, was markedly different – full of hope, joy, and love, but no tears and no fear.

In a poignant twist, Easter 2014 fell on my 60th birthday. Just as my life seemed to be taken away from me on Good Friday, 2013, I feel it has been given back to me on Easter, 2014. And so it was a day to celebrate not only Christ's resurrection but also my own coming back to life. Because dying no longer occupies my thoughts. Instead, I am allowing myself to dream that we will have some retirement years on the Cape.

In fact, Peter and I spent today driving around the Cape looking at houses – that was the only birthday present I wanted. We did not go inside – that is still a year off – but we are daring to anticipate our lives by the ocean.

Are these dreams realistic?

I just finished *The Emperor of All Maladies: A Biography of Cancer* by Siddhartha Mukherjee. The author describes watching with wonder as a fellow oncologist gently spoke to a patient about her recently-removed lung tumor which was likely to recur. The most important task was to give the patient hope, while at the same time telling the truth of her prognosis:

> [The oncologist] emphasized process over outcome and transmitted astonishing amounts of information with a touch so slight that you might not even feel it. He told [the patient] about the tumor, the good news about the surgery, asked about her family, then spoke about his own. He spoke about his child who was complaining about her long days at school. Did [the patient] have a grandchild? he inquired. Did a daughter or a son live close by? And then, as I watched, he began to insert numbers here and there with a light-handedness that was a marvel to observe.
>
> "You might read somewhere that for your particular cancer, there is a high chance of local recurrence or metastasis," he said. "Perhaps even fifty or sixty percent."

> She nodded, tensing up.
>
> "Well there are ways that we will tend to it when that happens."
>
> I noted that he had said "when" not "if." The numbers told a statistical truth, but the sentence implied nuance. "We will tend to it," he said, not "we will obliterate it." Care, not cure.

As I read these words, I realized that I, too, had been on the receiving end of such nuance. When we saw the surgeon at Dana-Farber at the end of January, she was equally deft with her words. "My son graduates from high school in June 2015, and I want to be there," I had stated. And she responded, "Then we'll do everything we can to make it happen." I left the appointment feeling encouraged and optimistic, although she had made no promises.

More recently, I had an appointment with an orthopedic oncologist at Dana-Farber about my "drop foot." As we sat in the examining room with him and his Physician's Assistant, Peter started to tell them about our plans to retire to the Cape in another year. They looked at us and nodded but said nothing. Are our plans within the realm of possibility, or are we simply deluding ourselves? Their faces were inscrutable, but I wonder if internally they were shaking their heads, knowing that our dreams would never be realized.

Perhaps I am overthinking this. The fact of the matter is, I feel well, and there is nothing like feeling well to give one hope. And hope is so important. As my local oncologist told me months ago, "Those who give up tend not to make it."

Well, I am not giving up, no matter how unrealistic my dreams may be. I heard the other day about a fellow who had been given six months to live; that was eight years ago. At the recent stamp club brunch, we sat with a woman who was diagnosed with Stage IV breast cancer four years ago – and now she is cancer free. And then there is Jackie, who volunteers at the Oncology Suite where I get my chemo infusions. Two years ago, she had Stage IV rectal cancer that had spread to her liver. She had 90% of her liver removed, and now the cancer is gone.

I hang on to stories like these.

Maybe one day people will be talking about me: "Yes, that Jean – she was diagnosed with a rare and aggressive cancer, Stage IV. That was ten years ago. Now she spends her days feeling the gentle off-shore breezes, breathing in the sweet salt air, listening to the water gently lap the shore, and thanking God for every beautiful moment."

EPILOGUE

So there's my story, up to now. As the first anniversary of my diagnosis came and went, I decided it was time to gather my blog posts and turn them into a good old-fashioned printed page book.

Why?

Because I wanted my loved ones – family, friends, colleagues – to have my story in a more permanent form.

Because I wanted future grandchildren to be able to hear me in my own voice.

And because I wanted to see and hold this book in my own hands before it was too late.

How will my story end?

As with all of us, in death. In the meantime, I look forward to seeing how the rest of my life unfolds!

Jean Niven Lenk
Foxboro, Massachusetts
May, 2014

(Above) The Niven Family gathered for Mom's 80th birthday, November 2002.
(L-R): My brother Dave, me (during a thin stage),
my dad David, mom Olive, brother Andy.

(Left) Darcy in 1980. He had already received his diagnosis and wanted a good picture for his obituary.

(Right) January, 1997 – John holding baby Ian.
This is the last picture of them together.

March 11, 2005 – 47 years after first meeting, Peter and I were married. (L-R) My father David, me, mom Olive, Peter's mom Connie, Peter. (Peter's father Walter died in 2001.)

Love makes a family. (L-R) My son Ian, 8; my daughter Lizzy, 15; me; Peter; Peter's son Tim, 18; Peter's daughter Beryl, 14; Peter's niece Marisa, 9.

(Left) Lizzy and I (sporting my "high and tight") show off our new tattoos: "...then we will see face to face..." from my favorite Scripture verse, 1 Corinthians 13:12.

(Below) A closer look at my tattoo.

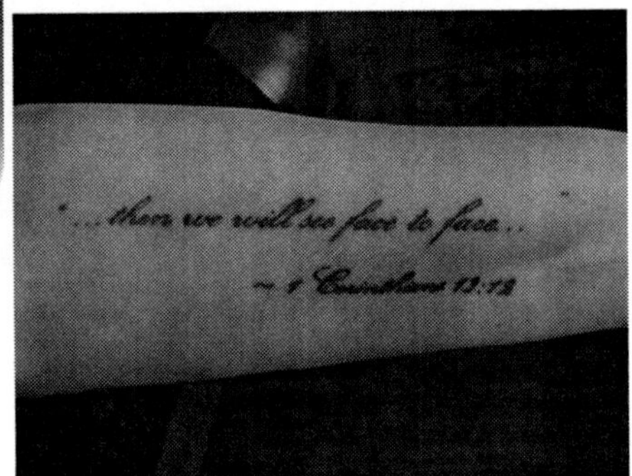

November 17, 2013 – My farewell as pastor of the First Congregational Church of Stoughton. (L-R) Michele (mother of my stepchildren); Jill (Lizzy's girlfriend); Greg (Michele's husband); Lizzy (my daughter); Ian (my son); Charley (Susan's husband); Tim (Peter's son); Susan (Peter's sister); Beryl (Peter's daughter); Peter. That's me holding the cake.

May 17, 2014 – So grateful to be at Lizzy's graduation from Salem State in the morning...

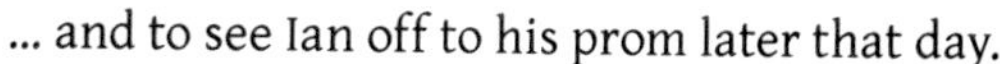
... and to see Ian off to his prom later that day.

ABOUT THE AUTHOR

Jean Niven Lenk grew up in Wellesley, MA, and after a 20-year career in business, attended Andover Newton Theological School, Newton Centre, MA. She served as a United Church of Christ pastor for 14 years before being diagnosed with Stage IV cancer on Good Friday, 2013. She lives in Foxboro, MA. This is her first book.

ENDNOTES

1 John 1:20, NRSV.
2 John 20:13, NRSV.
3 John 15:12, NRSV.
4 John 20:15, NRSV.
5 John 20:16, NRSV.
6 Diana Butler Bass, *Christianity After Religion* (New York: HarperCollins, 2012), p. 97.
7 New Revised Standard Version.
8 William Sloan Coffin, *Credo* (Louisville, KY: John Knox Press, 2004), p. 168.
9 Prof. J. Earl Thompson, now retired Professor of Pastoral and Family Studies at Andover Newton Theological School, Newton Centre, MA.
10 http://www.time.com/time/magazine/article/0,9171,910501-4,00.html
11 Acts 9:36, NRSV.
12 Acts 9:38, NRSV.
13 Jon M. Walton, "Living by the Word," *Christian Century*, April 17, 2007, p. 16.
14 Based on Numbers 6:24-26.
15 Barbara Brown Taylor, "Out of the Whirlwind," *Home By Another Way* (Lanham, MD: Rowan and Littlefield Publishers), pp. 164-165.
16 Job 1:1, NRSV.
17 Job 1:7, *The Message.*
18 Job 1:7, *The Message.*
19 Job 1:8, *The Message.*
20 Job 1:9-11, *The Message.*
21 Job 1:12, *The Message.*
22 Job 1:21, NRSV.
23 Job 2:4-5, *The Message.*
24 Job 2:6, *The Message.*
25 Job 23:6-7, *The Message.*
26 Job 38:4, NRSV.
27 Job 38:12, NRSV.
28 Job 39:19, NRSV.
29 Job 39:26, NRSV.
30 Ibid, p. 168.
31 Matthew 5:4, NRSV.
32 Job 42:5, NRSV.
33 Ibid, p. 167.
34 Isaiah 55:2, NRSV.
35 http://www.foxnews.com/story/0,2933,236706,00.html
36 Ibid.

37 http://abclocal.go.com/wls/story?section=news/consumer&id=7186413
38 http://www.nytimes.com/2009/03/27/business/media/27adco.html
39 New Revised Standard Version, pew edition.
40 Isaiah 55:3, New Life Version.
41 Rev. Fred R. Anderson, whose March 11, 2007 sermon "The Eternal Question," serves as my inspiration.
42 I have changed the gender of the child in the story to ease its telling.
43 John 6:35, NRSV.
44 John 15:11, NRSV.
45 John 16:22, NRSV.
46 John 15:10-11, NRSV.
47 Michael W. Foss, *The Disciple's Joy: Six Practices for Spiritual Growth* (Minneapolis: Augsburg Fortress, 2007), pp. 6-8.
48 Habukkuk 3:17-18, NRSV.
49 Anthony B. Robinson, "Congregational Spirituality: From Givers to Receivers Who Give," *Transforming Congregational Culture* (Grand Rapids, MI: Wm. B. Eerdmans, 2003), p. 66.
50 Charles J. Sykes, *San Diego Union-Tribune,* September 19, 1996.
51 Rachael Rettner, "Brain's 'Fairness' Spot Found," February 24, 2010, http://www.livescience.com/9847-brain-fairness-spot.html
52 Matthew 20:4, NRSV.
53 Matthew 20:15, NIV.
54 Matthew 27:46, Mark 15:34, NRSV.
55 Genesis 15:1, NRSV.
56 Revelation 1:17, NRSV.
57 Revelation 1:17, NRSV.
58 Revelation 1:17, NRSV.
59 Exodus 3:6, NRSV.
60 Joshua 1:9, 8:1, NRSV.
61 2 Kings 1:15, NRSV.
62 Jeremiah 1:8, NRSV.
63 Daniel 10:12, 19, NRSV.
64 Luke 1:13 NRSV.
65 Luke 1:30 NRSV.
66 Matthew 1:20 NRSV.
67 Matthew 14:27 NRSV.
68 Acts 18:9; Acts 27:24, NRSV.
69 Matthew 6:31,34, ESV.
70 Luke 24:36; John 20:19,21,26, NRSV.
71 Genesis 17:20, NRSV.
72 Isaiah 41:10,13,14, NRSV.

73 Genesis 26:24 and ten other citations, NRSV.
74 Psalm 23:4, KJV.
75 Psalm 23:1, KJV.
76 John 10:11, NRSV.
77 John 10:14, NIV.
78 Psalm 23:4, KJV.
79 Psalm 23:1, KJV.
80 Psalm 23:1, KJV.
81 Matthew 9:22, NIV.
82 Matthew 9:28-30, NIVUK.
83 Matthew 15:28, NIV.
84 Mark 10:52, NIV.
85 Barbara Brown Taylor, Op. Cit., p. 168.
86 Psalm 51:3-4, NRSV.
87 Psalm 51:10, NRSV.
88 Psalm 51:2,7, NRSV.
89 Psalm 51:2, NRSV.
90 Psalm 51:7, NRSV.
91 Psalm 51:14, NRSV.
92 Psalm 51:12, ESV.
93 Psalm 51:6, NRSV.
94 Romans 8:26, *The Message.*
95 Exodus 16:4, NRSV.
96 Psalm 18:24, NRSV.
97 Matthew 6:11, NRSV.
98 Philippians 4:6-7, NRSV.
99 http://www.livestrong.com/article/17388-causes-leiomyosarcoma/
100 1 Corinthians 13:12, NRSV.
101 2 Timothy 4:7, NRSV.
102 Isaiah 55:8, NIV.
103 Matthew 5:45, CEV.
104 1 Corinthians 13:12, NRSV.
105 *Sourcebook of Funerals, Volume 2* (Canton, OH: Communication Resources, Inc., 2001), p. 67.

CPSIA information can be obtained at www.ICGtesting.com
Printed in the USA
BVOW02s1831071014

369846BV00002B/5/P